"More than offering signs of hope in the city, this book insp[...] stories of faithful followers of Jesus with their sleeves rolled up, their eyes and ears attentive to the real people that populate the cities in which these practitioners serve and minister. More than merely inspiring hope, this collection of chapters points to the living hope that emerges out of the urban ministry experiences of a quite unique assembly of writers."

Darrell Jackson
Chair, Lausanne International Researchers' Network
Senior Lecturer in Missiology, Morling College

"A book whose contributors live and write in some of the world's most challenging urban contexts--in places where one does not expect to find Christian hope. The essays are creative without being glib, practical but not simplistic, realistic but by no means hopeless. This book will be encouraging to those who by faith live and minister among "the least of these" in the world's great cities, and gently instructive to those who should and could do more."

Jonathan Bonk
Research Professor of Mission, Center for Global Christianity & Mission, Boston University School of Theology

"My heart sang as I picked up this book! Each chapter took me into a deeper dimensions of the complexity of post-modern glocal metropolises and the infinitely flexible Wind and authoritative Word that engage and transform. I've been looking for a text that defines the challenges of urbanization in the 2020's and here is a goldmine of rabbit trails based on action-reflection from the coalface. Read it and your mind will race to create new responses with the rapidity that being a bearer of the good news demands."

Viv Grigg
International Director, MA in Transformational Urban Leadership, Azusa Pacific Seminar

"By 2050 two thirds of the world's people will live in urban settings, with billions entrenched in poverty. The forward-thinking contributors to *Signs of Hope in the City* expertly contend with these realities. By advocating for increased education, community engagement, and interfaith dialogue, each offers practical wisdom for cultivating the call of all Christians to know and love others, especially the most vulnerable."

Gina A. Zurlo
Assistant Director, Center for the Study of Global Christianity, Gordon-Conwell Theological Seminary

"The growing edge of global population is now urban. This volume goes a long way to help the church around the world navigate complicated issues related to this unprecedented urbanization in ways that demonstrate and proclaim the new realities of God's kingdom. This book is a wonderful blend of thoughtful reflection and experienced action. Informed voices from all over the world collaborate to set this volume apart from much of the urban mission literature available."

Michael Crane
Professor of Urban Missiology in Southeast Asia

"Graham Hill's new book builds on his *Salt, Light and a City* to investigate the meaning of the body of Christ in the cities of the world, as we live in glocal ecclesiastical communities. This delightful collection of essays revitalizes our thinking and re-imagines our engagement in urban ministry as it dynamically explores critical issues of urban ecology, urban churches, and Christian discipleship. This book presents an opportunity to develop an expansive perspective on urban communities that inspire change, renewal, and transformation."

Grace Ji-Sun Kim
Associate Professor of Theology at Earlham School of Religion

"Signs of Hope is evidence God's people are at work in the world for the Kingdom's cause. It is practical, humble, inspiring, and academically rigorous. This is more than a series of opinions on urban mission, it's a handbook for thoughtful mission and neighborliness as we enter into an unprecedented era of urban life. We highly commend these reflections to you as you enact integral mission in your city."

Geoff and Sherry Maddock
Urban Missionaries and Micro-farmers in Lexington, Kentucky

"Urbanization is a growing trend that poses significant challenges for Christianity globally. This book provides hope as it explores the personal, theological, missiological and dialogical issues involved in seeking to reach our cities and some particular people groups within them with the Gospel. Graham Hill has brought together voices that speak from the centre, from the margins, from experience and from the heart; some voices that rarely get heard. Those of us not able to attend the Summit in Kuala Lumpur in 2014 will now be able to reap the benefits of that gathering and rise to the urban challenge."

David Turnbull
Senior Lecturer in Intercultural Studies, Tabor College Adelaide

"Hope is a small word but represents a huge ambition. This wonderful volume connects stories of hope with the kind of action that flows from incisive reflection. Hope needs substance and this volume helps to give structure to the intention for change."

Martin Robinson
CEO of ForMission

Signs of

HOPE

in the

CITY

Renewing Urban Mission,
Embracing Radical Hope

Edited by
Graham Hill

National Library of Australia Cataloguing-in-Publication entry

Title:	Signs of Hope in the City: Renewing Urban Mission, Embracing Radical Hope / Graham Hill, editor.
ISBN:	9780992394110 (paperback)
Subjects:	Church work with the poor.
	City missions.
	City churches.
	Urban poor.

Other Authors/Contributors: Hill, Graham, editor.
International Society for Urban Mission, issuing body

Dewey Number: 261.8325

Editor: Graham Hill
Design: Les Colston

Contents

Foreword

Michael Frost

James Davison Hunter says we change the world when we embrace the simple work of honouring God, of loving our neighbours, of serving the common good, and of pursuing God's restorative purposes over all of life. If we accept that God indeed has such restorative purposes for all dimensions of life, then we must take the necessary steps to bring about holistic transformation in cities.

The United Nations recently predicted that by 2025 over 60% of the world's estimated 8.3 billion people will live in cities. That will mean that just short of five billion souls will be living and working and raising families in urban areas. Other predictions have the urban population of Asia alone hitting 2.5 billion by 2020, having doubled in twenty-five years. If that's true then more than half of the urban areas of the planet will be in Asia and they will contain over one-third of the entire world's population. These population shifts are mind-blowing.

Who could have imagined our world would one day be shaped like this? Who could have anticipated the enormous challenges this poses for humanity? In 1700 less than 2% of the world lived in urban places. Peking and London were the only cities that had populations more than one million. By 1900 the urban population was estimated to be 9% and by 1950 only 27% of the world's population lived in cities. But things started changing dramatically in the latter half of the twentieth century, and by 1996 the majority of the world's population lived in cities. People continue to be drawn off the land, away from rural areas, and into urban centres through migration and immigration.

Today, governments around the world are struggling to address the challenges of urban growth — economic disparity, high costs of living, overcrowded and substandard housing, public transport and traffic challenges, pollution, crime, and violence. In this volume, Jayakumar Christian describes the rise of the cities resulting in (1) obscene economic disparity, (2) the collapse of governance due to corruption, weak governments, and lack of political will, and (3) a complex urban economic system in which the once-skilled rural labourers who migrate to the city become mere tools of production. And still the people come, drawn to the city in the hope of better incomes and better education options for their children.

Christian churches, aid agencies, and urban mission organizations are being forced to explore what the boom in urban centres means for their work. Does God have a purpose in all this? Is this good news for the good-news people? What does the reign of God look like in real terms for the billions of people who now make urban places their home? Tim Keller makes much of the strategic nature of cities as business and finances centres, as well as being hubs of communication, transportation, education, entertainment, and power. He says that to reach the world for Christ we will have to not merely include urban ministry but prioritise it.

The contributors to this book clearly agree but, more than sounding a call for the importance of urban mission, they are presenting the signs of hope that God is indeed already at work in our urban centres. As grass-roots practitioners and world-class scholars in this field, they are well placed to know the ways in which that hope is being enfleshed in cities around the world. Still, the contributors to *Signs of Hope* are not naïve about the enormous challenges they must address — challenges related to recruiting for, equipping, and sustaining urban mission today; challenges related to releasing urban church-planting movements; questions about what principled contextual mission looks like and how the gospel transforms urban communities; concerns about how to embrace the political dimensions of the gospel that include serving and liberating the oppressed, struggling for justice in the city, and helping urban neighbourhoods to develop economically as well as spiritually.

Whatever the solutions to these questions and challenges, I believe they should be rooted in the mission to alert all people everywhere to the universal reign of God in Christ, a reign that includes peace and justice, harmony, prosperity, and welfare, as well as the worship of our king Jesus. This is the redemptive plan of the creator God, established ultimately in Christ, and carried on by his people. And it has untold implications for the burgeoning cities of the world. Indeed, if we cannot figure out what the reign of God looks like in the city then the mission of the church will be significantly impeded.

To explore all this, Graham Hill has brought together contributions by some giants in the field — John Perkins, René Padilla, Viv Grigg, Howard Snyder, and Jayakumar Christian — as well as many lesser known, but no less impressive, practitioners and thinkers. Picking their way through their areas of expertise, these contributors address such diverse issues as urban poverty, interfaith dynamics, human trafficking, environmentalism, asylum seekers and refugees, and the local church's role in urban transformation. This book not only contains signs of hope, but it might help us crack the code in knowing how to pursue God's restorative purposes over all of life *everywhere.*

Michael Frost
Morling College, Sydney

Introduction: Exploring Signs of Hope in the City

Graham Hill

On July 18, 2009, the sounds of helicopters and sirens pierced the tranquillity of our North Epping neighbourhood. Our local newsagent Min Lin, his wife Yun Lin, her sister Irene Lin, and their two sons, Henry and Terry, had been brutally slain in their own home, overnight. The murders were so vicious that police needed to use forensics to identify the family members.

The Lin family was a popular and loved family in our neighbourhood. The boys went to school with my children — Henry was twelve and Terry was nine. Terry was in my daughter Grace's class. Their fifteen-year-old daughter Brenda was on a school trip in New Caledonia at the time of the murders.

The violent murder of this family rocked our neighbourhood to its core. North Epping is a small Sydney suburb of just over four thousand people. It's a quiet, leafy, middle-class, cul-de-sac suburb, with only one street leading in and out. It's surrounded by the spectacular bushland of the Lane Cove National Park. Community and trust and relational connection characterize our suburb. Families see it as a safe and quiet and neighbourly place to raise children. Children and families develop their closest connections within the neighbourhood. All my children's best friends live within a few streets from each other.

As you might imagine from this description, the Lin family murders had a shattering effect on our neighbourhood. This vicious murder of a family in their sleep splintered our suburb's sense of safety and identity.

In the shadow of this horrendous event, something surprising happened. Hope emerged. The neighbourhood began to pull together, in a collective move toward healing and solidarity, and community and hope. Class mates, teachers, neighbours, friends, family, those who regularly visited their news agency, and many others, pulled together to provide support and care to each other and to the Lin's surviving fifteen-year-old daughter, Brenda.

Roger Green, the pastor of the neighbourhood's Anglican church, took the lead in helping the community deal with its shock and grief. The church invited a registered clinical psychologist and a team of counsellors to attend a community night. During the evening, this team addressed what to expect when a tragedy like this occurs, and how to respond as a community. Hundreds of people from our neighbourhood attended this night at the church. The psychologist gave insights into how to best answer children's questions. She guided people on how to reassure children as they try to make sense of what happened. There was opportunity for adults and teenagers to ask questions and grieve together. There was also a chance to make commitments to work together to rebuild a wounded community. The church joined with the psychologists to develop a resource for families to use in talking through the tragedy with children. This church also joined with many other community organizations in holding a memorial service.

Children planted a tree in the school in memory of Henry Lin and Terry Lin. The school also established a counselling service. Our local bank set up a support fund to help Brenda Lin. The bank also created two white "grief boxes" for Henry and Terry, for anyone (especially children) to leave messages and photos for the boys or the family.

Our neighbourhood came together to grieve and heal, and to support each other and Brenda. And the local church was at the centre of this care. My family witnessed "signs of hope" in our little neighbourhood in the city of Sydney. Neighbours connected in fresh and profound ways. They were God's grace to each other. Neighbours became a source of hope and courage, and transformation and community. Our neighbourhood experienced healing and hope.

The church of Jesus Christ can be God's instrument of transformation in neighbourhoods. We need kingdom-oriented approaches to neighbourhood transformation and community building. Our churches must address need, addiction, violence, and racial tension. We need to be agents of change, reconciliation, and transformation. We need to be "urban neighbours of hope" who testify to Christ's hope, notice "signs of hope" in our cities, and serve the person and mission of the God of hope.

By 2025, there will be 3 billion urban poor living in poor neighbourhoods. These urban poor face great challenges and difficulties. But these neighbourhoods are also places of hope and transformation. And the church is called to be "hope enfleshed": seeing signs of hope in the city, and embodying the hope and redemption of Jesus Christ. When this happens, signs of hope spring up in the most unexpected places. For a collection of such hope-filled stories, see Urban Neighbours of Hope's book, *Voices of Hope*. It's a 98-page collection of extraordinary stories of hope and renewal in urban neighbourhoods.[1] Similarly, the Mission Advanced Research and Communications Centre (MARC) has a *Cases in Holistic Ministry* series. It covers inspiring case studies in holistic mission, neighbourhood renewal, community transformation, and radical hope. These stories are from all over Africa, Asia, Latin America, and other parts of the Majority World.[2]

The International Society for Urban Mission (ISUM) held a summit on *Signs of Hope in the City*, in Kuala Lumpur, Malaysia, in 2014. This summit was a partnership between ISUM, Urban Neighbours of Hope (UNOH), the Micah Network, and the World Evangelical Alliance's (WEA) Theological Commission. It involved "interactive, participatory, hands-on, immersion opportunities, keynotes, lectures, and workshops". Participants came from all over the globe. A few hundred Majority World, indigenous, First Nations, and Western thinkers and activists came together for those days. They explored the theology and practices of integral, transformational, and urban mission. And, together, they looked for "signs of hope in the city". They identified places where God is at work bringing hope, healing, reconciliation, life, and transformation.

In Working Groups, participants considered these themes (and got involved in relevant immersion experiences):

- Urban Poverty and Disabilities

- Sensitivities and Confidence in Interfaith Dynamics

- Christian Spirituality and Theology for a New Urban World

- Indigenous Peoples in Urban Places

1   Ashleigh Newnham, ed., Voices of Hope: Stories from Our Neighbours (Dandenong: UNOH, 2013).

2   Tetsunao Yamamori, Kwame Bediako, and Bryant L. Myers, eds., *Serving with the Poor in Africa*, Cases in Holistic Ministry (Monrovia, CA: MARC, 1996); Tetsunao Yamamori, David Conner, and Bryant L. Myers, eds., *Serving with the Poor in Asia*, Cases in Holistic Ministry (Monrovia, CA: MARC, 1995); Tetsunao Yamamori et al., eds., *Serving with the Poor in Latin America*, Cases in Holistic Ministry (Monrovia, CA: MARC, 1997); Tetsunao Yamamori, Kenneth L. Luscombe, and Bryant L. Myers, eds., *Serving with the Urban Poor*, Cases in Holistic Ministry (Monrovia, CA: MARC, 1998).

- Environmental Resiliencies in the City
- Urban Issues of Homelessness, Drug Abuse, and Imprisonment
- Local Churches' Role in Urban Transformation
- Business, Employment, and Labour Rights in a New Urban World
- Migrant Workers, Asylum Seekers, and Refugees
- Action, Advocacy, and Public Engagement
- Trafficking and Exploitation in Urban Communities
- Children and Urban Poverty

The overall theme of the 2014 ISUM Summit and this book is *signs of hope in the city*. Majority World and Western leaders participated in discussion, prayer, integral mission, and the ISUM Working Groups listed above. The goal was to grapple with key issues to do with the theme of *hope*. Where are the "signs of hope" in our cities? How do we become "hope enfleshed"? What does it mean to serve the God of hope and transformation? How do we recruit, equip, and sustain people for hope-filled and hope-enfleshed urban mission today? How do we release church movements among the urban poor? How can we immerse ourselves in and transform urban neighbourhoods? How do we empower urban children and young people? How does the church serve and liberate the oppressed — and others suffering from urban injustice? What needs to happen for poorer urban centres to develop economically, socially, and spiritually? How do we join with the Spirit of Christ where he's working — noticing "signs of hope in the city", cooperating with the Spirit of hope, and embodying the hope of the gospel? Some of the fruit of these discussions is presented in this book.

Jayakumar Christian, in "Rise of the Urban Poor", shows how engagement with the city is crucial if we are to transform our nations. We especially need to engage with the urban poor. Jayakumar Christian writes, "Poverty and oppression in the city have their own human face. It is the face of a child with nimble fingers and shattered dreams. It is the face of a child with a broken home or no home; a sick mother often battered by an alcoholic father. It is that deep sigh of the child when she sees other children walk past her, as if she never existed. The church — the prophetic community — must rediscover itself in its own neighbourhood. The church must locate its mission in the space between the two Jothis — between hope and hopelessness, life and joy, and pain and death. The church is the evidence that our God has not given up on the urban poor. The presence of the church among the urban poor is really an expression of the answer of our Father in heaven to the cry of the poor when they pray, "thy kingdom come on earth as it is in heaven".

In "Shaping Christian Spirituality and Theology for a New Urban World", I unpack how urban theology, spirituality, and mission are connected. Urban missionaries need to cultivate robust expressions of urban theology and spirituality. I show how "we need a spirituality of missional engagement" and a global theology that "shows the many-sided wisdom of God".

Michael D. Crane, in "Dashboard Symbolism: Sensitivities and Confidence in Interfaith Dynamics", reveals, "Christians must learn how to engage with multi-religious communities with sensitivity towards other religions and confidence in our own faith in Christ. In a globalized world where interfaith conflicts abound, Christians have a model in Christ for maintaining a humble and loving presence while maintaining a public witness of the gospel as truth for all of humanity. This calls on all Christians to re-evaluate the ways they engage those from other faith traditions".

Brad Coath, Angela Akamine, Laurie Krepp, Hwa Hui-En, and Andy Sparkes contribute a chapter on refugees and asylum seekers. The article is called "You Took Me In: Seeking Transformation for Migrant Workers, Refugees, and Asylum Seekers". These urban missionaries explore ways in which Christians, organizations, and the church may bring transformation and hope when serving with migrant workers, refugees, and asylum seekers. "Around the globe, there are an estimated 51 million people in need of protection — 10.5 million of them refugees. Of these, only 80,000 will be resettled each year by UNHCR. It doesn't take a degree in mathematics to realize that that's like trying to pour an entire beach worth of sand through an egg timer... While finding a 'solution' to these problems is beyond us, we can find ways to be 'signs' of God's reign and to be part of creating and sustaining ecologies of welcome, inclusion, and justice".

Howard A. Snyder, in "The Ecology of Urban Mission", shows how urban mission needs to be understood ecologically. " Christians without ecological awareness miss key dimensions of mission just as surely as secular ecologists miss key dimensions of the Spirit... The church is an organism that partakes of the mystery of the very body of Jesus Christ and the mystery of the Trinity — and, as such, is called into mission".

René Padilla, in "Global Urbanization and Integral Mission", offers examples of ministries bringing hope to cities and the urban poor. These are "responding from a Christian perspective to the dehumanizing challenges" posed by cities. "For the sake of authenticity in a large urban world, where hundreds of millions of people are unable to cover their basic human needs, the Christian witness cannot and must not be reduced to words — it has to be incarnational, in line with God's justice and compassion. It has to be integral mission".

Viv Grigg contributes a chapter called "Hovering Spirit, Creative Voice, Empowered Transformation: A Retrospective". The Holy Spirit is calling people in cities to commit to economic and human development, and to the transformation of slums. The voice of the Spirit "continues crying out, creating order in the chaotic pain of today's megacities, through individuals and through a new wineskin. And the Voice perhaps calls you to be filled with that Spirit and to become that voice in the world's desperate places".

Kimberly Drage, Pham Thu Huong, Bruce Edwards, and Jacob Bloemberg consider the role of the local church. They do this in the chapter: "The Role of the Local Church in Urban Transformation: Mobilizing Members and Engaging Powers". The church needs to mobilize its members for urban transformation, and engage the powers. The local church "is an integral part of moving toward God's shalom for our cities. Being a part of God's holistic restoration and transformation in our cities is not optional, side-work for the people of God, rather, it is our identity. This is and has always been the calling of the people of God".

Glenn Miles and Jarrett Davis, in "Trafficking and Exploitation in the Urban Context", show how organizations and local churches can offer hope and healing in these contexts. The church cannot ignore issues surrounding trafficking, exploitation, and sexuality. We need to find ways to be a liberating and healing presence.

Jacob Bloemberg, in "Global Nomads: Expats on Mission in a New Urban World", reveals how international churches can strategically engage in urban mission. They have "a wealth of resources, know-how, and well-connected people, and they can have a huge impact within their cities".

Trish Branken, Nigel Branken, Rod Sheard, Paul Lau, and Pebbles Parkes offer a chapter called "The Church's Call to Action, Advocacy, and Public Engagement". This ground-breaking chapter calls us to relinquish our "comfort-seeking, apolitical, and judgmental exclusivity in order to embrace a suffering world and to work towards greater equality and dignity between all people, regardless of gender, race, religion, class, or sexual orientation". It invites us to "re-examine our lives, and the life and teachings of Christ… in order to arrive at a fairer and more loving representation of the heart of God himself towards all of his created image-bearers".

Emil Jonathan Soriano and Rey Lemuel Crizaldo, in "Engaging the Powers in Transforming Community", present a case study that shows how "churches, united and conscious of their distinct role in the community, could be a potent force in transforming [politics]".

John Perkins and Jayakumar Christian served as the two main keynote speakers for the 2014 ISUM Summit *Signs of Hope in the City*. Recordings of keynote sessions are available by going to www.newurbanworld.org and following the links to YouTube. In the final chapters of the book, I've provided transcriptions of their sessions. John Perkins casts a compelling vision of "the whole church on a whole mission to the whole world". Jayakumar Christian redefines perspectives on poverty and transformation. Together, John Perkins and Jayakumar Christian call the church to transformational responses, radical love, and renewed hope.

I want to say thank you to all those who provided editorial support, transcription, and proofreading for this book. And I want to say thanks to the ISUM Summit organizers, hosts, presenters, working group facilitators, volunteers, briefing paper compilers, and chapter writers. This volume, *Signs of Hope in the City: Renewing Urban Mission, Embracing Radical Hope*, has come together because of your passion for urban mission, and because of your willingness to see Spirit-enabled and Christ-honouring signs of hope in your city and beyond.

Graham Hill
Editor

Rise of the Urban Poor

Jayakumar Christian

The Parable of Two Jothis

In our work and relationship with the poor, we often come across paradoxical situations that raise more questions than we have answers for. In fact, it is these situations and experiences that keep us humble and prevent us from playing god in the lives of the vulnerable poor.

One such situation emerges from the story of two young girls whom I met — one in New Delhi and another in Bangalore; strangely both with the same names — Jothi (meaning "light" in Hindi). These encounters raised two completely different sets of questions out of almost similar contexts (the urban poor).

In New Delhi, I met Jothi (at that time probably about 14 years old; today a young lady) in a meeting with children from our program areas. She was brimming with confidence; she was an average student.[1] She was the president of her children's club in a crowded Delhi slum — a visionary leader and proactive. In fact, she had started other children's clubs in adjacent slums. She had clear plans to transform her community. I visited her home and met her proud parents. She narrated how once she had actually confronted her elected representative in a public meeting about the poor state of civic amenities in the community. She proudly mentioned that "the elected representative did not venture to return to the community" after that incident — most such visits were to seek votes whom they claim to "represent".

I walked away very proud of what one Jothi could do in a crowded Delhi slum,

---

1 Today Jothi is close to completing her undergraduate program — Bachelor of Arts. She continues to be active in the community transformation efforts.

bringing hope and pride. I thought to myself, if only we had more Jothis among the 62 million urban poor in India's cities and towns. I was grateful to God for Jothi and the hope she inspired.

In Bangalore, a few months later, I met a young girl living in the middle of a major vegetable market in the heart of the city. Her name was also Jothi. She would have been at that time about 11 years old. She was playing with her friends on the streets that morning. My friends and I stopped to talk to Jothi and her friends. We were told that young Jothi is already married; married to a 16-year-old boy (who was also in the vicinity playing with his friends). A World Vision program was trying its best to mainstream Jothi and her husband into a formal school. Over the next few months, Jothi disappeared into the urban jungle to be another missing child. The system did not have space for Jothi; she was a child bride and a misfit in the system. She would be one more young mother who would give birth to another malnourished baby — adding to the 1.8 million children below five years of age who die every year due to malnutrition — a shame for the nation, but more importantly, a personal humiliation for the malnourished child.

As I reflected on the Jothi from Bangalore, I felt the deep sense of hopelessness that must fill the little hearts of our children. We call them "missing" children; one more child lost. The system neither knows nor cares where they disappeared to and how.

This article seeks to examine the space between the two Jothis — the space between hope and hopelessness. What does "rise of the urban poor" really mean in the lives of our two Jothis? Urban mission often operates between these two Jothis — one inspiring hope and another grappling with death, hopelessness, and decay. Agents of transformation — the church, the government, and the civil society exist in this space between hope and hopelessness, confronting symbols of death and decay on a daily basis. Do these stories offer any cues and clues for us in our response to the urban poor?

Urban Poverty — Three Extremes

Urban poverty is not a mere spillover of rural poverty. It has its own personality. The rise of the urban poor is more complex. Let me explain.

The City — a Vulgar Display of Wealth

Today's poverty is not merely about actual numbers of the poor and the oppressed but about the growing "gap" between the rich and the poor. Government policies and strategies of civil society are usually geared to address the actual poverty and often fail to address the gap. This gap is consequently filled by fundamentalists and militants, such as the Maoists, often feeding on discontent and frustration.

In a strange way, the city brings to the fore in a pronounced manner the gap — the worst of urban poverty. The rich display their wealth as if the poor do not exist in the cities. The malls and neon lights overshadow the dark corners where the poor eke out their living. Shining India happily coexists with abject poverty as though poverty was a mere landscape issue. One wonders if this is a consequence of our religious philosophies and worldview. As we walk through a community of rag pickers in the heart of Delhi, one does not see a spirit of resignation but, on the other hand, a resilient spirit. However, this resilient spirit is rooted in the quest for somehow making a living off the rich in the city. There is a parasitical relationship — not manipulation but helplessness. In the process, the poor and vulnerable children are exploited and oppressed.

The city systems do not even have disaggregated statistics about the urban poor. The ugly reality of urban poverty is camouflaged by the "urban" statistics, which often look rosy and shining. This gap is about the poor being marginalized from the mainstream of the city. It is about fractured relationships — communities deeply divided based on ethnicity and language.

So, what are the implications for the rise of the poor (empowerment) in the city? This process is not merely a socio-economic phenomenon; it is about addressing the vulgarity of the gap. It is about the people of God daring to stand in the gap between hope and hopelessness, and speaking truth in the face of death and decay.

Jothi from New Delhi is surely a symbol of hope speaking truth in the public domain, challenging forces that marginalize. It is about being prophetic — challenging the gap and ensuring that it does not set in concrete. It is about refusing to allow Jothis to simply go missing from the systems.

Collapse of Governance

It is common knowledge in most analyses of poverty that the burden of responsibility lies squarely in the corridors of power in our nations. Governance is fully responsible for the neglect of the poor. The face of this collapse involves corruption, weak governments, lack of political will, and so on. The poor and the common citizenry consequently lose faith in the political system.

However, in the city there is a strange twist. As the city is the seat of power (governance) — the collapse is even more real and palpable. Basic services are very much within the reach of the poor, and yet are so far away. The poor in the city are often forced to pick up the crumbs from the table. In a strange twist of fate, the very political system that ignores the poor cleverly co-opts the poor for their survival. These poor make up the numbers for political rallies and mass protests. The urban poor are politically aware, but acutely powerless — an irony.

What is often touted as a "lack of political will" in our governance and bureaucratic leadership is really an intentional (ideological) effort to crush (never allow) any uprising of the poor and to suppress any emergence of hope. This is about a powerful collective playing god in the lives of the poor and wounding the souls of the poor, reducing them to a state of hopelessness. A casualty of this neglect and deliberate crushing of hope is young Jothi, who disappeared from the system out of shame and pain. The system does not even notice; she is just one more child reported missing.

Economics that "Mars"

Cities are often the political and economic capitals of a region/state. Within this complex urban economic system, rural migrants, once skilled labourers, often become mere tools of production. Today with major investments in infrastructure, cities are attracting large numbers of migrants who do not even know or understand the local languages. For the building up of our infrastructure, we need the poor; once the task is done, though, the poor need to move out to keep the city clean!

The effect of these exploitative economics is not merely low income and unemployment, but the marring of the self-image of the poor. The ripple effect of this marring of self-image is often expressed in a vicious cycle of violence and death-dealing habits such as alcoholism. Urban poverty is characterized by these features. Women and children often bear the brunt of this vicious cycle of poor self-image and the cycle of violence. The city system does not care for these — economies must run, GDP must grow, and the race with the global economy must be won.

The children end up paying the price. In a nation with over 17 million child labourers, one Jothi missing is considered not significant; but for Jothi 100 percent of her life is lost. What politicians and bureaucrats consider as a national shame is really a personal humiliation for the child — she will always be a second-class citizen in her own country. Growth with justice is a myth in a stratified society. The DNA of growth does not somehow promote justice unless there is a definite purposeful intention. The urban poor are left to the mercy of a trickle down. Policy makers are not bothered about the lowest rungs of our society, even though the government vowed to protect them when the economy was opened up. Whatever happened to economics with a human face?

How Then Will the City Rise?

Even as we consider the task of being a prophetic community — standing in the gap between the two Jothis, between hope and death — it is critical for us to consider the following fundamentals. Let me examine three leads.

Beyond Beautifying the Slum

The space between the two Jothis is not a pretty space. It is marked with violence, neglect, stink and decay, pain and death. Often development workers, along with governments, have been content to clean up the slums. The poor did not come into the city to live in squalor. However, in that squalor, they find their identity. If we seek sustainable solutions for urban poverty, we must challenge the squalor and its realities — not simply allow the squalor to define the identity of the urban poor.

The space between the two Jothis is about their dignity. It demands more than cleaning up the gutter. It requires moving them out. A rise of the urban poor requires a prophetic voice in a socio-political and economic system that mars; it requires truth-telling to confront collapsed governance structures.

Triggering a Movement[2]

The urban opportunity for a movement is vast compared to the rural areas. Civil societies thrive on taking advantage of this situation. Highly connected and informed communities allow us to go beyond sporadic, disconnected changes. We can launch movements — ripples of transformation. A classic parallel is the narrative of Jesus' healing of an urban poor person — a man who had been blind from birth (John 9). The disciples thought it was an opportunity to discuss the theology of sin. The religious leaders thought it was an excellent trap by which to capture Jesus. The man's own parents conveniently avoided the awkward questions. The healing of the blind man — the transformation of the urban poor — upset the disciples (their theology), the fearful parents, and the hypocrisy of the religious leaders. The connectedness of the city allows

2   A movement is a purposive, collective, sustained, and expanding (in numbers, time, and social composition) interaction that seeks to challenge and renew (transform) existing values, relationships, and structures. See Tharailath Koshy Oommen, Protest and Change: Studies in Social Movements (New Delhi: SAGE, 1990).

for these ripples of transformation. It is critical that a prophetic community leverages this opportunity. Sporadic examples of excellence will not sustain change. Movements are critical.

A critical component for triggering a movement is to be rooted in the neighbourhood; our feet must be rooted in the neighbourhood. The prophetic community must be incarnated in the neighbourhood; otherwise, its work would be mere activism. Solutions for a transformative movement affecting the nation should be moulded, tested, and shaped in the neighbourhood.

Investing Life

In a strange manner, the most inhumane of situations (poverty) requires the most humane of investments — investment of life. Without investment of life, there is no role model and reference point. Of all the engagements, the most critical of interventions is the life of the staff/agent/practitioner. Let me elaborate.

- Grassroots practitioners must be radically re-equipped for the city. Grassroots practitioners/agents of change must:

- Reflect their "inner being" through their engagement. Poverty and powerlessness are human and relational; therefore, responses to poverty must also be human and relational. This requires investment of life. It cannot be reduced to mere action plans.

- Demonstrate covenant-quality inclusive relationships based on truth — practitioners must allow truth to confront their public and private life.

- Be competent to exegete God's work among the poor — trace the "patterns" in God's movement among the poor in the city.

- Be competent to analyse the worldview of a people and the ideology that drives the economic, political, and other systems that crush the poor.

- Be countercultural in a society that values entitlement over sacrifice.

Rising with the Urban Poor

Engagement with the city is foundational if we are to transform the nation. It has the potential to send out ripples of transformation across the nation. Poverty and oppression in the city have their own human face. It is the face of a child with nimble fingers and shattered dreams. It is the face of a child with a broken home or no home; a sick mother often battered by an alcoholic father. It is that deep sigh of the child when she sees other children walk past her, as if she never existed.

The church — the prophetic community — must rediscover itself in its own neighbourhood. The church must locate its mission in the space between the two Jothis — between hope and hopelessness, life and joy, and pain and death. The church is the evidence that our God has not given up on the urban poor.

The presence of the church among the urban poor is really an expression of the answer of our Father in heaven to the cry of the poor when they pray, "thy kingdom come on earth as it is in heaven".

References

Oommen, Tharailath Koshy. *Protest and Change: Studies in Social Movements.* New Delhi: SAGE, 1990.

Shaping Christian Spirituality and Theology for a New Urban World

Graham Hill

> To take head on oppressive structures like consumerism, technology, militarism, multinational capitalism, international communism, racism, and sexism, we need a spirituality of missional engagement… Mission without spirituality cannot survive any more than combustion without oxygen.
>
> *Orlando E. Costas*

> A xeroxed copy of a theology made in Europe or North America can never satisfy the theological needs of the Church in the Third World. Now that the Church has become a world community, the time has come for it to manifest the universality of the Gospel in terms of a theology that is not bound by a particular culture but shows the many-sided wisdom of God.
>
> *C. René Padilla*

The world is rapidly urbanizing. Urban theology, spirituality, and mission are deeply connected. Urban missionaries need to cultivate robust expressions of urban theology and spirituality. In 2014, an International Society for Urban Mission (ISUM) Summit Working Group on "Spirituality and Theology for a New Urban World" spent a few days considering this issue. There were twenty-six participants in that ISUM Working Group. Our conversations were an expression of *glocalisation*. Local stories and global themes enriched each other. Applying processes of Appreciative Inquiry and World

Café, this ISUM Working Group explored the shape of "spirituality and theology for a new urban world". And we did this through conversations, storytelling, prayer, immersion experiences, meals, tears, and laughter. We also formulated a "call to action" for the broader church. A new urban world demands new forms of urban Christian spirituality and theology.

Glocal Conversations in a New Urban World

Urban theology, spirituality, and mission are deeply connected. Urban missionaries need to cultivate robust expressions of urban theology and spirituality. Orlando E. Costas and C. René Padilla are right. "We need a spirituality of missional engagement." And we need a global theology that "shows the many-sided wisdom of God".

The International Society for Urban Mission held a summit on *Signs of Hope in the City*, in Kuala Lumpur, Malaysia, in 2014. This summit was a partnership among ISUM, Urban Neighbours of Hope (UNOH), the Micah Network, and the World Evangelical Alliance's (WEA) Theological Commission. It involved "interactive, participatory, hands-on, immersion opportunities, keynotes, lecturers, and workshops". Participants came from all over the globe. A few hundred Majority World, indigenous, First Nations, and Western thinkers and activists came together for those days. They explored the theology and practices of integral, transformational, and urban mission. And, together, they looked for "signs of hope in the city". They identified places where God is at work bringing hope, healing, reconciliation, life, and transformation.

Majority World and Western leaders participated in discussion, prayer, integral mission, and ISUM Working Groups. The goal was to grapple with key issues and ask key questions. How do we recruit, equip, and sustain urban mission today? How do we release church movements among the urban poor? How can we immerse ourselves in and transform urban neighbourhoods? How do we empower urban children and young people? How does the church serve and liberate the oppressed — and others suffering from urban injustice? What needs to happen for poorer urban centres to develop economically, socially, and spiritually? How do we join God in the challenges and opportunities of multi-faith cities?

The Summit was a thrilling example of how Majority World, indigenous, First Nations, and Western leaders can cooperate. It was a time to come together in an environment of mutual learning and enrichment; a window into how local contexts and global themes can enrich each other. This emerged from ISUM's commitment to "solidarity, fellowship, and insight between urban Christian leaders in the Western and Majority Worlds".

Majority World, indigenous, and Western leaders, thinkers, and churches can stretch and enrich each other. But they need to be open and attentive to each other. They need learning postures and open hearts and minds. And passion for learning and collaboration, and for Jesus and his kingdom. And their vision and values must align with those of the kingdom of God.

The global church needs global theologies. And it needs local theologies. Local and global theologies are both necessary if we are to shape theological reflections that are adequate for a globalized world.

The church needs theologies that are ready for the emerging shape of Christian spirituality and mission in a new urban world.

Harold A. Netland defines globalized theology this way:

> "Globalizing theology is theological reflection rooted in God's self-revelation in Scripture and informed by the historical legacy of the Christian community through the ages, the current realities in the world, and the diverse perspectives of Christian communities throughout the world, with a view to greater holiness in living and faithfulness in fulfilling God's mission in all the world through the church. Thus, theology is to be an ongoing process in which Christian communities throughout the world participate."[1]

This definition is helpful. The church needs both a globalized and *glocalised* theology. A *glocal* theology happens when local voices engage global conversations. And it's a theology rooted in spirituality and mission.

What do I mean by *glocal*? The local (the local, contextual, homogeneous) and the global (the global, universal, heterogeneous) interconnect. Our globalized world has blurred the boundaries between the local and the global. The local is a dimension of the global. The global shapes the local. The two are interdependent. They enable each other. They form each other, reciprocally. While tensions exist, the global and local are not opposing forces. They connect — deeply and inextricably. "Not only are the global and the local inseparably intertwined; they also determine each other's respective forms. From a sociological perspective, the glocalisation means generally

1   Craig Ott and Harold A. Netland, *Globalizing Theology: Belief and Practice in an Era of World Christianity* (Grand Rapids, MI: Baker Academic, 2006), 30.

the organic and symbiotic relationship between the global and the local."[2]

All local Christian theologies and spiritualities can contribute to *glocal* conversations. We need Western, indigenous, First Nations, and Majority World voices. Local and global conversations must meet and enrich each other in constructive ways. When they do, we end up with worthwhile *glocalised* theologies and practices. I believe that we must develop urban missions through glocal conversations. *Glocalisation* can help us apply urban theology in the concrete practices of urban mission and spirituality. Worthwhile *glocalisation* is about dialogue, learning, and partnership. It is about the courage to listen to others, and venture into the unknown.

This is what the 2014 ISUM Summit in Malaysia was all about. Local and global conversations enriched each other. And this resulted in enriched urban missions, theologies, and spiritualities. Christians from all over the world came together at this Summit. They listened, conversed, and learned from each other. And they formed partnerships in urban mission. What a thrill and a privilege!

René August and I (Graham Hill) had the privilege of co-facilitating an ISUM Working Group at the 2014 ISUM Summit in Kuala Lumpur. The Work Group was on "Spirituality and Theology for a New Urban World". There were twenty-six participants in that ISUM Working Group. Our conversations were an expression of *glocalisation*. Local stories and global themes enriched each other. This happened through prayerful conversation. Working Group participants came from all over the globe. Together, we explored the shape of "spirituality and theology for a new urban world". And we did this through conversations, storytelling, prayer, immersion experiences, meals, tears, and laughter. This paper summarizes our discoveries and learnings.

Processes of Discernment

With the theme, "Christian Spirituality and Theology for a New Urban Context", the twenty-six participants in our ISUM Working Group agreed to discern important themes in urban spirituality and theology through two group processes: (1) Appreciative Inquiry, and (2) World Café. We integrated these two group processes. And we sought to hear what the Spirit was saying to us about urban spirituality and theology in our conversations, ministries, contexts, immersion experiences, and prayers.

---

2   Al Tizon, *Transformation after Lausanne: Radical Evangelical Mission in Global-Local Perspective* (Eugene, OR: Wipf and Stock, 2008), 207.

1. First Discernment Process: Appreciative Inquiry

The first process our ISUM Working Group applied was Appreciative Inquiry. Appreciative Inquiry is a popular method for group discernment and leading organizational change. The Spirit of Christ is at work in almost every setting. This means that we can discern the positive, life-giving, and transformational activity of the Spirit in almost every setting. We only need eyes to see. We need to learn to "appreciate" where God is at work and what he is doing. As we reflect on our ministries, contexts, conversations, and immersion experiences, we appreciate what God is doing and what he is saying to us.

"Appreciative" here means, "to value what is best about a human system… To deliberately notice, anticipate, and heighten the positive potential… To see beyond obstacles, problems, and limitations, and to generate hope in the human capacity to achieve potential…. [Appreciation is] the art of valuing those factors that give life."[3]

Building on the work of Jane Watkins, Bernard Mohr, and others, Mark Lau Branson says that Appreciative Inquiry has five generic processes. (1) Choose the positive as the focus of inquiry. (Affirmative topic choice). (2) Inquire into stories of life-giving forces. (*Discovery* — "appreciate what is"). (3) Locate themes that appear in the stories. Then, select topics for further inquiry. (*Dream* — "imagine what might be"). (4) Create shared images for a preferred future. (*Design* — "determine what should be"). (5) Find innovative ways to create that future. (*Destiny* — "create what will be").[4]

Jane Watkins and Bernard Mohr write the following about these five processes: "The limitations of the written word impose certain constraints on our description of the generic processes. For ease of comprehension, we have listed them above in sequence. But… the generic processes don't begin and end neatly. They overlap and repeat themselves without predictability, which is another reason that you must be grounded in the theory, research, and principles of AI as you begin translating these generic processes into practice."[5]

---

3   Frank J. Barrett, "Organizational Dynamics: Creating Appreciative Learning Cultures," *American Management Association* (1995), 10.

4   Mark Lau Branson, *Memories, Hopes, and Conversations: Appreciative Inquiry and Congregational Change* (Herndon, VA: Alban, 2004), 28–29.

5   Jane Magruder Watkins and Bernard J. Mohr, *Appreciative Inquiry: Change at the Speed of Imagination*, 2nd ed., Practicing Organization Development Series (San Francisco, CA: Pfeiffer, 2011), 40.

Here's the diagram Jane Watkins and Bernard Mohr provide, which describes the five processes. They say: "As can be seen, each process is part of a larger whole and each overlaps with other processes."[6]

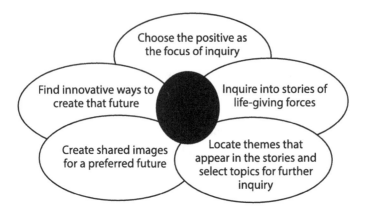

Diana Whitney and Amanda Trosten-Bloom illustrate the five processes in this way:[7]

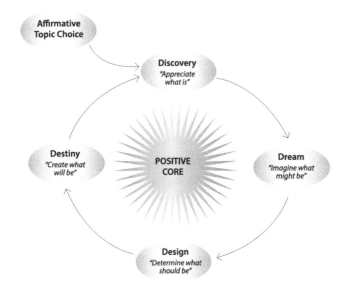

6   Ibid.

7   Diana Kaplin Whitney and Amanda Trosten-Bloom, *The Power of Appreciative Inquiry: A Practical Guide to Positive Change*, 1st ed. (San Francisco, CA: Berrett-Koehler, 2003).

Mark Lau Branson describes the value of Appreciative Inquiry this way: "Leadership… is about creating spaces and environments in which the people of God can discern God's presence and initiatives in their lives, among their neighbours, and in their contexts. This is not the work of experts but rather a way of life among the everyday people in our churches. Keys to this work include how we ask questions, receive and interpret the stories and perspectives we hear, and then shape experiments for next steps… The thesis of Appreciative Inquiry is that an organization, such as a church, can be recreated by its conversations. And if that new creation is to feature the most life-giving forces and forms possible, then the conversations must be shaped by appreciative questions."[8]

2. Second Discernment Process: World Café

The second process our ISUM Working Group applied was World Café. We found World Café a helpful overlay upon Appreciate Inquiry. It enhanced conversations, hospitality, questioning, contribution, cross-pollination, and harvesting collective discoveries. Juanita Brown and David Isaacs describe the seven principles of World Café as:

1. *Set the context.* Clarify the purpose and parameters of the conversation and its place in the larger environment in which it will happen.

2. *Create hospitable space.* Provide a welcoming, safe, life-serving environment.

3. *Explore questions that matter.* Invite collective attention into what's important to the participants.

4. *Encourage everyone's contribution.* Engage meaningful participation by each person, with real respect.

5. *Cross-pollinate and connect diverse perspectives.* Facilitate juicy diversity and equally juicy interconnectedness.

6. *Listen together for patterns, insights, and deeper questions.* Help coherent group insight emerge naturally from the dance of individual perspectives and passions.

7. *Harvest and share collective discoveries.* Make the group's collective intelligence visible to itself.[9]

8   Branson, *Memories, Hopes, and Conversations*, xiii.

9   Juanita Brown and David Isaacs, *The World Café: Shaping Our Futures through Conversations That Matter*, 1st ed. (San Francisco, CA: Berrett-Koehler Publishers, 2005).

3. Integrating Appreciate Inquiry and World Café

Our 2014 ISUM Working Group on "spirituality and theology for a new urban world" sought to integrate the two processes of Appreciative Inquiry and World Café. Combined, Appreciate Inquiry and World Café offered our ISUM Working Group a process for discerning emerging themes in urban spirituality and theology.

Here's the process that unfolded. We followed these steps as an ISUM Working Group:

1. *We identified carriers of hope.* (We recognized stories from our lives, contexts, urban missions, and immersion experiences that show us where God is working to form fresh approaches to urban spirituality and theology. These are stories that give us insight and fill us with hope.);

2. *We identified challenges to hope.* (We detected things that dampen or extinguish such hope.);

3. *We identified questions that emerge.* (We named questions about urban Christian spirituality and theology that emerge from these stories of hope and challenges to hope.);

4. *We celebrated being Christians in an urban and diverse context.* (We asked, "What do we celebrate about doing spirituality and theology in an *urban* context?" And, "What do we celebrate about doing spirituality and theology in a *diverse* context?");

5. *We connected urban theology and urban spirituality.* (We investigated the practical connections between urban theology and urban spirituality, witness, life, and service.);

6. *We identified new practices and habits.* (At the end of the process, we discussed how we might form new practices and habits that enhance urban spirituality and theology. We also considered lifestyle issues and developing resources. We considered the shape of a "call to action". This included recommendations to the broader church).

I describe some of our findings in the rest of this paper.

Carriers of Hope

Many of the twenty-six people in our ISUM Summit Working Group on "Spirituality and Theology for a New Urban World" are serving among the urban poor. So, we began our time together by sharing stories from our lives, contexts, urban missions, and immersion experiences. These stories show us where God is working to form fresh approaches to urban spirituality and theology. These are stories that give us insight and fill us with hope.

ISUM Working Group participants shared stories where Christian urban leaders and teams exemplify these characteristics (i.e., stories of hope):

Care for urban dwellers and groups, and their wellbeing: Many urban missionaries care for the broken, silenced, ignored, wounded, marginalized, and those at the "bottom of the ladder";

Concern for the real needs of communities: Many urban missionaries meet real needs, are present among people, and build meaningful relationships. They care for whole communities and engage in community development;

Connection with urban communities: Many urban missionaries listen, learn, hear concerns, and communicate authentically. They connect with the needs and insights and histories of the slum communities among whom they serve;

Witness to the kingdom of God in urban settings: Many urban missionaries are people of joy, mercy, hope, justice, love, faith, gentleness, encouragement, and liberation;

Compassion for people and their wellbeing: Many urban missionaries are compassionate servants who are passionate about justice, healing, reconciliation, mercy, mission, and community.

The ISUM Working Group also engaged in three "immersion experiences" in Kuala Lumpur. This involved looking for "signs of hope" in the areas of urban theology and spirituality. We joined in these three immersions experiences:

1. City Discipleship Presbyterian Church (CDPC). In obedience to the Great Commission set forth by Jesus, CDPC seeks to help individuals establish good and mature relationships with God and to produce fruitful disciples impacting both their personal life as well as the lives of people around them. Since its establishment in July 2000, CDPC has been collaborating with churches around the Klang Valley to work with the community of Subang Jaya, USJ, and Petaling Jaya. CDPC serves various communities, ranging from university students to children with learning disabilities.

2. KingdomCity. KingdomCity is one church in three cities — Kuala Lumpur in Malaysia, Perth in Western Australia, and Phnom Penh in Cambodia. This church believes everybody deserves to belong. Their heart and vision are to connect, equip, and empower people to bring the reality of God to their world. They're passionate about the miraculous, and about transforming communities. They're committed to relevant Christian mission, theology, and spirituality for Kuala Lumpur. KingdomCity sees its own community as a mission-field, filled with people who need Jesus. They believe that God has called them to go beyond their own community to reach people of the world by sharing the love of Christ.

3. A Theological Seminary in Kuala Lumpur. I have purposely obscured the name of this seminary. This way, I can describe its ministries while protecting its anonymity. Out of the three immersion experiences, I'll focus on this one here. I'll provide a snapshot of the "signs of hope" present in the way it does urban theology and spirituality.

- This theological seminary is committed to equipping pastors, missionaries, and ministry leaders for effective ministry in Asia. The seminary's commitment to holistic training includes equipping leaders to serve among transient urban dwellers in Kuala Lumpur. In this immersion experience, we were able to interview seminary students who have come to Malaysia either as migrant workers or refugees. Ministering in churches of transient urban dwellers poses particular challenges for these young leaders. Training transient urban dwellers for mission and ministry poses other challenges for this theological seminary in Kuala Lumpur.

- This innovative Asian theological seminary is exploring fresh approaches to urban mission, theology, spiritual formation, and ministry training. They are training people in new ways to serve and empower transient urban dwellers (e.g., asylum seekers, migrants, refugees, stateless people, people in refugee-like situations, and others of concern). Kuala Lumpur is a strategic location for this, since it has around 250,000 such people — Myanmarese, Persians, Afghans, Iraqi, Tamils, Indonesians, Somalis, Sri Lankans, Nepalese, and other groups. These arrive in Malaysia and apply for refugee status through the UNHCR (the United Nations refugee agency).

The UNHCR writes the following about Malaysia:

> "Malaysia has not yet signed the 1951 Refugee Convention or its 1967 Protocol and lacks a formal legislative and administrative framework to address refugee matters. With no work rights, refugees, in particular women and children, tend to be at a high risk of exploitation, particularly refugee

children who have no access to government schools. UNHCR works with some partner organizations to support refugee health, education, and community empowerment. However, as the non-governmental sector in Malaysia remains limited, the Office also directly implements activities. The Malaysian Government provides access to public health care at a reduced rate for refugees recognized by UNHCR. The Malaysian Government implements strict policies to deter undocumented migrants from its territory. Since refugees and asylum-seekers are not distinguished from undocumented migrants under Malaysian law, they are vulnerable to the same penalties, including arrest, detention, and deportation."[10]

This seminary is asking important questions as it trains men and women for mission and ministry. It wants to equip them to build spiritualities and theologies adequate for new urban environments. Here's a sample of some of these questions: What does contextual theology and spirituality look like for particular transient and vulnerable populations? (E.g. Myanmarese, Afghan, Iraqi, Tamil, Indonesian, Somali, Sri Lankan, and Nepalese refugees). How do we do contextual theology, given these groups' sense of attachment and non-attachment to their cultures and societies? (Their feelings about their cultures and societies are often mixed). How do particular missiological themes shape our approaches to theological reflection and spiritual formation? Such themes include holism, transformation, comparative religions, cultural studies, and contextualization. How does Christian theology and spirituality change when individuals and Christian communities immerse themselves in the love, service, and fellowship of the poor and marginalized and transient? What does it mean not only to *read* the Scriptures but also to *do* the Scriptures (individually, as churches, and as theological colleges)?

When this seminary was first planted in Kuala Lumpur, its aim was to train middle class Chinese Christian leaders. Of course, there's nothing wrong with that. But, over time, the focus has shifted to training leaders in urban mission. This is especially training for mission among the urban poor, and among vulnerable people groups. This makes the seminary innovative missiologically. But it's also vulnerable to the fates of these transient, marginalized, and persecuted urban dwellers.

Two students of this seminary illustrate the theological, missional, and spiritual concerns of its faculty and students. Our ISUM Working Group had an opportunity to interview both students. The first is a Myanmarese student and the second is from a country in Western Asia (it's better that I don't name the country).

10   http://www.unhcr.org/pages/49e4884c6.html

The Myanmarese student is working with Myanmarese refugee communities in Kuala Lumpur. Many Myanmarese in Malaysia hold a UN card. They are awaiting resettlement in Australia, Europe, or North America. This student holds English language classes and Bible study groups at midnight many nights of the week. (Myanmarese refugees work such long hours that this is the only time they're available for fellowship and training.) People in power "shake down" these refugees regularly (easy money). This makes them fearful, insecure, and uncertain about their incomes and futures. It prevents their children from getting a proper education. This Myanmarese theological student serves among this refugee community. He visits Myanmarese in factories and homes. He provides pastoral support. And he offers theological, biblical, and English language training.

The second student is from a country in Western Asia. Many people from this country arrive legally in Malaysia. They then seek asylum, but are prevented from working. Their families struggle to survive. They can't find opportunities for work and education and social connection. There are few churches in Malaysia that cater for people from this country. So, mission activities and worship gatherings among this group are rare. Asylum seekers from this country are often depressed, financially desperate, and lonely. They are often forced to work illegally, and fear arrest and deportation. They are emotionally affected by persecution and violence (both in their home country and since they left). They often don't trust other refugees and asylum seekers from their country. Their country has spies in Malaysia who monitor refugees and asylum seekers. So, they're fearful of the consequences for them and their families in Malaysia and in Western Asia. Another challenge for mission among this group is the reason for their conversion *from* Islam *to* Christianity. Sometimes conversion is *a protest against Islam*, and not a real conversion. The seminary student from this nationality is serving among this group at great personal risk and cost. But he's passionate about mission. And he's committed to healing and reconciliation among people from his country.

All three immersion experiences offered stories of hope and transformation. And we had the opportunity to share stories from our lives, contexts, urban missions, and experiences. Together, these stories show us where God is forming new and life-giving approaches to urban spirituality and theology. These are hope-filled and hopeful stories.

Challenges to Hope

Our 2014 ISUM Working Group focused on *signs of hope in the city*. We focused on stories that give us insight into emerging urban theology and spirituality, and that fill us with hope. But we also consider challenges to such hope. Challenges for robust urban theology and spirituality are widespread. Here are some of them:

Firstly, the presence of dichotomies in the church. (E.g. evangelism vs. social action, conservative vs. emerging forms of theology, and so forth). These dichotomies are often artificial, divisive, and unhelpful.

Secondly, the scarcity of resources and writings on holistic ministry, theology, and spirituality among and for the urban poor.

Thirdly, the dominance of Western forms of theology and spirituality, and the neglect of voices from the Majority World. As C. René Padilla says, "A xeroxed copy of a theology made in Europe or North America can never satisfy the theological needs of the Church in the Third World. Now that the Church has become a world community, the time has come for it to manifest the universality of the Gospel in terms of a theology that is not bound by a particular culture but shows the many-sided wisdom of God."[11]

Fourthly, superficial attempts at contextualization of theology and spirituality in new urban environments. Again, C. René Padilla writes,

> "The contextualization of the Gospel can never take place apart from the contextualization of the Church... The truly indigenous Church is the one that through death and resurrection with Christ embodies the Gospel within its own culture. It adopts a way of being, thinking, and acting in which its own cultural patterns are transformed and fulfilled by the Gospel. In a sense, it is the cultural embodiment of Christ formed within a given culture. The task of the Church is not the extension of a culture of Christianity throughout the world, but the incarnation of the Gospel in each culture... The contextualization of the Gospel will not consist of an adaptation of an existing theology to a given culture. It will not be merely the result of an intellectual process. It will not be aided by a benevolent missionary paternalism intended to help the young church to select those cultural elements that can be regarded as positive. The contextualization of the Gospel can only be a gift of grace granted by God to a church that is seeking to place the totality of life under the lordship of Christ in its historical situation. More than a wonder of nature, the incarnation is a wonder of grace."[12]

11   C. René Padilla, "The Contextualization of the Gospel," *Journal of Theology for Southern Africa*, no. 24 (1978), 28.

12   Ibid. 28–30.

Fifthly, the Western nature of so much spiritual and mystical theology. Such theology is often written from a Western, middle-class, suburban, rural, or monastic perspective. Such spiritual theologies — and resources in spiritual formation — are inadequate for urban missionaries. Often, they don't help those serving among the urban poor in densely populated cities.

There are many other challenges to Christian spirituality and theology in a new urban and global world. These are not insurmountable. But we must take them seriously.

Questions that Emerge for Urban Spirituality and Theology

The world is rapidly urbanizing. More than 6.5 billion people will live in cities by 2050. Most of these urban dwellers will be in developing countries. Around 80 percent of this burgeoning urban population will live in Africa and Asia. The United Nations claims that the world is unprepared for the challenges this will raise for resources — e.g., the increasing demands for energy, water, and sanitation. The world is unprepared for the challenges urban growth raises for public services, land-use, food scarcity, employment, transportation, education, and health.

The church faces its own challenges as the world rapidly urbanizes, and as the church shifts its centre of gravity to the Majority World. As Philip Jenkins writes,

> "We are currently living through one of the transforming moments in the history of religion worldwide. Over the last five centuries, the story of Christianity has been inextricably bound up with that of Europe and European-derived civilizations overseas, above all in North America. Until recently, the overwhelming majority of Christians have lived in white nations… Over the last century, however, the centre of gravity in the Christian world has shifted inexorably away from Europe, southward, to Africa and Latin America, and eastward, toward Asia. Today, the largest Christian communities on the planet are to be found in those regions."[13]

Urbanization and the shift of the church to the Majority World raise important questions for Christian spirituality and theology. Here are some questions that our ISUM Working Group identified. We didn't seek to answer these questions. But we believe that they are worth further investigation. Our answers to these questions will help us form robust spiritualities and theologies for a new urban world.

---

13   Philip Jenkins, *The Next Christendom: The Coming of Global Christianity*, 3rd ed. (Oxford: Oxford University Press, 2011), 1.

Here are the questions we identified:

When we talk about an "urban world", do we mean the poor, marginalized, and exploited, or do we mean all those living in urban settings? And how does this affect our theology and spirituality? Do theology and spirituality look different for different groups living in urban settings?

What's the point of Christian theologies and spiritualities specific to an urban world? And how do we pursue and practise Christian theologies and spiritualities specific to urban environments?

How do Christians put Christian spirituality and other spiritualities into conversation?

How do Christians lead with the Spirit cross-culturally?

What should be the role of a privileged Western person in a developing community? How can such a person join in the shaping of indigenous Christian spiritualities and theologies?

How can theology be multi-voiced and multi-peopled?

How can we know Jesus more deeply when serving with the urban poor? How can we express this relationship through our spirituality and theology?

How are theology and spirituality enhanced through food, laughter, tears, celebration, rituals, and community development in a new urban world?

What does spiritual formation look like in an urban world and among the urban poor? Much of the literature on spiritual formation suggests a quiet and tranquil setting. But the settings urban missionaries serve in are densely populated. And people have little free time and personal space. What do rest, peace, and spirituality look like in noisy, busy, mega-cities and slum settings?

How do theology and spirituality change in the context of urban mission and service? How do they grow, mature, and deepen?

How do we find rest and stillness in the city (stillness in the midst of cacophony and frenetic activity)?

How does the urban church connect urban theology, urban mission, and urban spirituality?

What does it mean for the urban church to move from invitation (evangelism and social concern) *to* hospitality (discipleship and welcome) *to* embrace (reconciliation and community)?

What processes facilitate the growth of theology and spirituality relevant to particular urban communities?

What is the meaning of the incarnation, the cross, and the resurrection in the context of urban poverty?

What do theology and spirituality look like when they are relevant to specific communities and contexts?

What does spiritual warfare look like in urban settings, slum communities, and among the poor and marginalized?

How do we create a spirituality that sustains and inspires not just "expats" — that is, not just a small, foreign, Christian group living among the poor — but everyone in that context?

How do spirituality and theology connect with the *reason* we do what we do among the urban poor?

What does it mean to be a part of a kingdom of peace and non-violence? And to be witnesses of the now-but-not-yet of the kingdom of God? How does this shape Christian theology and spirituality?

What does it mean to formulate theology and spirituality *in* urban practices?

What aspects of spirituality and theology does our mission within urban settings illuminate?

How can we embody faithful theological practices that deepen our spirituality? And what can we do to make this possible in our communities?

As we live and serve among the urban poor, how can we live between grief and hope, between exhaustion and renewal, between isolation and community, between the present realities and the coming kingdom?

How do we *live out* and *live in* the kingdom of God in a new urban world?

These are just some of the questions that a new urban world raises for Christian spirituality and theology. The church will enrich its theology and spiritual vitality as it explores these questions through local-global conversations.

A Call to Action: Nurturing Spirituality and Theology in an Urban Context

At the end of our few days together, our ISUM Working Group discussed how we might form new practices and habits that enhance urban Christian spirituality and theology. We offer these here as a "call to action". They are recommendations to the broader church. The Christian church — and especially the urban church — needs to do the following over the next decade:

- Explore fresh ways to nurture urban Christian spiritualities and theologies. We need ones that sustain, challenge, and inspire those living and working among the urban poor. These urban missionaries need spiritual and theological resources. They need help to express the kingdom of God in their communities, and draw people into the ways of the kingdom.

- Discover ways in which a lifestyle of peace enhances spirituality, theology, and mission in a new urban world. A peace-filled Christian lifestyle is less frenetic and "blindly active".

- Gather examples of ways those working and living among the urban poor express Christian spiritual practices and disciplines. Learn from these examples. Develop resources and tools that sustain urban mission, urban communities, and urban faith.

- Expand our ideas and practices of prayer in urban contexts. Appreciate how prayer is practised among and with the poorest of the poor, in some of the largest and most densely populated cities of the world.

- Investigate practical and rigorous answers to the questions our ISUM Working Group proposed above. (See "Questions that Emerge for Urban Spirituality and Theology".) Don't just come up with theoretical answers. Pursue local and concrete practices and responses.

- Address the "challenges to hope" identified by our ISUM Working Group. (See the section above on "Challenges to Hope".)

- Support the church to fulfil her urban mission and the missional mandate God has given her in the world. Seek to be a Bride without blemish. Such a church puts faith and love into action. It witnesses to the kingdom of God on earth. And it does this through liberating forms of urban mission, theology, and faith.

- Facilitate Christian spirituality that emerges within built environments — cultures, poverty, buildings, smells, noise, connections, etc. Discern where God is at work there.

- Discover how poverty, difficulties, and challenges provide opportunities for connections, mission, and justice. Trials and troubles often bring people together — the Spirit is present and working.

- Find ways to be agents of peace, justice, hope, and reconciliation in urban settings. Witness to the kingdom of God amidst the brokenness, injustices, and woundedness of cities.

- Understand that love is better than mere theories, theologies, or strategies. Genuine love is better than "best practices". Let this truth permeate the urban church's spirituality, mission, and theology.

- Foster a lifestyle of invitation, hospitality, and embrace (even of enemies and persecutors).

- Cultivate habits of quietness and stillness (internal and external). Do this through personal and communal spirituality. And do this in the midst of the noise, busyness, and chaotic natures of large urban centres.

- Nurture capacities for celebration, lament, liberation, and meaning-making in urban settings. Such practices can enrich both churches and their local communities.

- Explore ways to make Jesus infectious in diverse, pluralistic, and sometimes hostile environments.

- Develop a deeper theology of the kingdom and an associated kingdom-oriented Christian spirituality. Ask, "What does it mean to be a part of a kingdom of peace, hope, reconciliation, justice, love, and non-violence?" And, "How can the urban church witness to the now-but-not-yet of the kingdom of God?"

- Celebrate being in diverse and urban contexts. Form Christian spiritualities and theologies characterized by peace-making, truth-telling, and justice-bringing, but also by celebration. Celebrate a wide range of things, such as those that follow. (1) In slum areas there's hardship, poverty, and suffering. But there's also community, love, and joy. (2) We can celebrate the food, languages, relationships, innovations, and cultures in urban settings. (3) The urban context is often invigorating. It brings energy. And it can make us aware of God, life, humanity, redemption, and personal and communal transformation. (4) We can celebrate how urban and diverse contexts enlarge our faith, spirituality, and theology. If we let them, they can inspire the church to be truly ecumenical, multi-racial, multi-cultural, multi-peopled, and multi-voiced. There are so many things we can celebrate about being in new urban settings. (And we celebrate while striving to be agents of peace, healing, and change where there is sin and brokenness.)

- Develop a theology and spirituality of missional engagement. This sustains urban faith, discipleship, obedience, community, and mission amidst suffering, struggle, liberation, and celebration.

Orlando E. Costas writes,

> "To take head on oppressive structures like consumerism, technology, militarism, multinational capitalism, international communism, racism, and

sexism, we need a *spirituality of missional engagement*: a devotional attitude, a personal ethic, a continuous liturgical experience that flows out of and expresses itself in apostolic obedience. Prayer, Bible study, personal ethics, and worship will not mean withdrawal from the world but *immersion in its suffering and struggles*. Likewise, participation in the struggles of history will not mean an abandonment of piety and contemplation, but an experience of God from the depths of human suffering.

Mission without spirituality cannot survive any more than combustion without oxygen. The nature of the world in which we live and the gospel that we have been committed to communicate therein demand, however, *that it be a spirituality of engagement not of withdrawal.* Such a spirituality can only be cultivated in obedience and discipleship, and not in the isolated comfort of one's inner self. By the same token, it can only be verified in the liberating struggles against the principalities and powers that hold so many millions in bondage."[14]

14   Orlando E. Costas, *Christ outside the Gate: Mission beyond Christendom* (Maryknoll, NY: Orbis, 1982), 171–72. Italics added for emphasis.

References

Barrett, Frank J. "Organizational Dynamics: Creating Appreciative Learning Cultures." *American Management Association* (1995).

Branson, Mark Lau. *Memories, Hopes, and Conversations: Appreciative Inquiry and Congregational Change.* Herndon, VA: Alban, 2004.

Brown, Juanita, and David Isaacs. *The World Café: Shaping Our Futures through Conversations That Matter.* 1st Ed. San Francisco, CA: Berrett-Koehler Publishers, 2005.

Costas, Orlando E. *Christ outside the Gate: Mission beyond Christendom.* Maryknoll, NY: Orbis, 1982.

Jenkins, Philip. *The Next Christendom: The Coming of Global Christianity.* 3rd Ed. Oxford: Oxford University Press, 2011.

Ott, Craig, and Harold A. Netland. *Globalizing Theology: Belief and Practice in an Era of World Christianity.* Grand Rapids, MI: Baker Academic, 2006.

Padilla, C. René. "The Contextualization of the Gospel." *Journal of Theology for Southern Africa,* no. 24 (1978).

Tizon, Al. *Transformation after Lausanne: Radical Evangelical Mission in Global-Local Perspective.* Eugene, OR: Wipf and Stock, 2008.

Watkins, Jane Magruder, and Bernard J. Mohr. *Appreciative Inquiry: Change at the Speed of Imagination.* Practicing Organization Development Series. 2nd Ed. San Francisco, CA: Pfeiffer, 2011.

Whitney, Diana Kaplin, and Amanda Trosten-Bloom. *The Power of Appreciative Inquiry: A Practical Guide to Positive Change.* 1st Ed. San Francisco, CA: Berrett Koehler, 2003.

Dashboard Symbolism: Sensitivities and Confidence in Interfaith Dynamics

Michael D. Crane

Interfaith realities and tensions have been accelerated by rapid globalization and urbanization. Christians must learn how to engage with multi-religious communities with sensitivity towards other religions and confidence in our own faith in Christ. In a globalized world where interfaith conflicts abound, Christians have a model in Christ for maintaining a humble and loving presence while maintaining a public witness of the gospel as truth for all of humanity. This calls on all Christians to re-evaluate the ways they engage those from other faith traditions.

1. Dashboards and Interfaith Dynamics[1]

While sitting in the inevitable traffic of my city, I peered into the windows of cars around me. The dashboard of the taxi next to me was covered with religious symbols and statues. On display was a variety of Hindu gods, representing a complex pantheon of interrelated deities. Dangling from the mirror above these statues was a large, shiny crucifix, calling to mind the sacrifice of Jesus on the cross for the sake of the world. Another car proudly displayed a statue of the Buddha. Just ahead of me a car had a Muslim prayer rug thrown in the back window and a bumper sticker proudly declaring

---

1   This paper was the result of a working group on "Sensitivities and Confidence in Interfaith Dynamics" during the International Society of Urban Mission (ISUM) Summit held in Kuala Lumpur, Malaysia on June 28–July 1, 2014.

to the world their Islamic faith commitment. With no opportunity to interview each of the drivers, I am left to speculate whether each display of religious symbolism demonstrates their genuine devotion or simply publicly aligns them with a religious identity. I am wildly curious how the taxi driver reconciles his devotion to many Hindu gods with the powerful symbol of Jesus' crucifixion, which has universal implications.

Just as each of the vehicles displays a staked-out religious loyalty, we too are reminded of the active presence of different faiths all around us in our cities. We are all sharing in the common experience of sitting in a traffic jam. These symbols in or on our cars suggest that faith is important in our day-to-day living and the image we project to others. We certainly do not live in the highly secularized world once predicted by the academics.[2] There is an edge to these displays, subtle as it may be, that marks space for a particular faith tradition. The car, the home, the roadside altars are not neutral, secular spaces as we suppose them to be. Like the apparent confusion between a crucifix in the same space as Hindu idols, our relationships with those of other faiths can be points of tension, both inwardly and outwardly.

The Twin Engines of Globalization and Urbanization Accelerate Interfaith Interaction

In 2005, a church in rural North Carolina put a message on their kiosk urging the Islamic holy book be flushed down the toilet. It was almost immediately reported on the front pages of newspapers throughout the Muslim world. In today's world, news travels fast which translates into quickly flared emotions.

More recently in 2013 in Myanmar, a city's religious composition changed almost overnight. Buddhist Arakanese began assaulting the Muslim Rohingya population until they were completely expelled from the provincial city of Sittwe. Interfaith conflict forced neighbours to become ex-neighbours. The conflict did not stop there but sparked acts of revenge from Muslims in India, Indonesia, and Malaysia.[3] In our globalized world, a local religious conflict is no longer only local.

Even as the population of the world reaches unprecedented levels, people are more globally connected than ever before. And if you do not believe it, you can find a Facebook app that will show you the global connectivity of your friends. Reports of a rapidly globalizing and urbanizing world are not new news. We have been inundated

2   Harvey Cox, *The Secular City: Secularization and Urbanization in Theological Perspective*, Rev. ed. (New York: Macmillan, 1966).

3   "Fears of a New Religious Strife," *The Economist*, July 27, 2013, http://www.economist.com/news/asia/21582321-fuelled-dangerous-brew-faith-ethnicity-and-politics-tit-tat-conflict-escalating.

with concerns about the economic implications of globalization or seen it as a media phenomenon. Not only are our economics and pop culture affected by globalization, so too are our interfaith dynamics. Interfaith conflict has been around for thousands of years, but now it can rear up from the most unsuspecting corners of the globe and be reported in an equally inaccessible opposite corner of the globe almost immediately.

As a people called into the city to love our neighbours and proclaim a radical reordering of life in Jesus the Messiah, these interfaith dynamics call for deep reflection and a response from the church. It seems the natural defaults are collision-course interfaith conflict or having a faith that is emptied of its truth claims and transformative living. This paper seeks to find a middle path for Christians serving in interfaith communities.

Immersion Experiences: Short Descriptions

A key component to the ISUM Summit working groups was to participate in immersion research experiences. Our working group went to three different locations, each with a stake in interfaith dynamics. In each case, working group participants were treated to the hospitality of another group and given the opportunity for extended observation and interviews. The three locations were as follows: Projek Dialog; the Buddhist Missionary Society; and a Sikh *Guruwara* (place of worship).

Projek Dialog (Project Dialogue) was birthed in the midst of multi-ethnic, multi-religious Malaysia as the brainchild of Ahmad Fuad Rahmat, a professor, radio show host, and public intellectual.[4] The purpose behind Projek Dialog is to create spaces and paths for interfaith dialogue. In Fuad Rahmat's experience, conducting big, highly publicized interfaith dialogues does little to advance understanding of other faiths. He also recognizes that different groups tend to take in their news through trusted sources in their preferred languages. Projek Dialog attempts to put news in the hands of Muslim Malays with the intention of exposing readers to alternative perspectives. The organization also seeks to create small venues for interfaith exchange that is not open to the public. The goal is to foster greater understanding despite barriers between religious groups. When an interfaith gathering is publicized and open to the public, it is more often thought of as an opportunity to amplify one's own religious message rather than hear from others. In contrast, it is clear Projek Dialog organizers are working diligently for a society where people of all creeds are free to practise and propagate their faith without fear and to create an atmosphere of understanding that

4   "Projek Dialog," accessed October 1, 2014, http://www.projekdialog.com/.

allows for an exchange of ideas.

The Buddhist Missionary Society is located in the centre of the teeming Brickfields community of Kuala Lumpur, Malaysia. With temples, churches, and mosques in every direction, the mere location of this temple-society complex viscerally communicated the need to reflect on interfaith dynamics in our cities. Our group was welcomed into a conference room to engage in an extended interview and discussion with the chairman of the board of directors and a Sinhalese monk.[5] The society is a story of international migration, adaptation, and religious propagation. It began as a temple started in 1884 by Sinhalese immigrants and became a hub for the Sri Lankan enclave. A Buddhist missionary challenged them to look outward in order to spread the faith. In response, they switched their medium of communication from Sinhala to English and began a literature outreach program that went all over the world. In their own words, "we share the truth". They offer three services each day and have a Sunday school with over seven hundred children attending. Their goal is to embed habits and rituals of the Buddhist tradition that will become normative for all of life and to encourage the use of their temple complex 24/7. Although they eschew a conversion-type process, they believe in the necessity of meditation and self-purification in order to save themselves.

The team visited the Guruwara (place of worship for Sikhs) located on the north side of Kuala Lumpur.[6] The Guruwara runs a primary school with 220 students and provides religious classes for some 600 members of the Sikh community in the area. Central to the Sikh faith is the concept of seva or service to the community. In the Guruwara we visited, this was expressed by a common kitchen, i.e., food will be cooked each morning by volunteers and served for free to anyone and everyone who visits Guruwara, irrespective of background or faith tradition. This seeks to uphold the principle of equality of all people, a concept developed in contradiction to the caste-based practices where Sikhism originated. The Guruwara also has a welfare society that looks to the needs, firstly of the needy Sikhs in their community, as well as for others in their society. They engage in other aspects of seva like serving food to street dwellers and homeless people one evening a week, organizing blood donations, health screening, and supplying a hearse and related services to poor Sikhs.

One feature that was quite impressive was that they have a minimum of staff and

5   The Sinhalese are the largest ethnic group of Sri Lanka.

6   The description of the Guruwara was contributed by working group member, Ajit Hazra. He serves as Director for Faith and Development with World Vision International, South Asia and Pacific Region.

all their activities are primarily run by volunteers. Regarding interfaith collaboration, they indicated that this has not been a focus, although they are in contact with other faith groups in their community. They expressed the reason for their caution in interfaith collaboration as primarily fear of being proselytized, especially by Christians. They also noted that interfaith marriages can be divisive and they discourage it in their community.

2. Signs of Hope: Confidence

A shoe cobbler from England named William Carey sparked the modern missions movement by moving with his family to India, a country wracked by interfaith tensions. Among Carey's incredible works was starting a college that would be open to every "caste, colour, or country". He was committed to allowing Hinduism, Islam, and Christianity to be taught at the new college because "Carey was committed to pluralism… to the idea that the state should not support one religious belief over another".[7] Carey's confidence in the truth of the gospel was such that it would shine even while other religions were being explained.

There is a common narrative that predicts increased globalization and urbanization will bring us into a worldview clash.[8] In reaction to this tension, many have proposed a path of tolerance and/or secularization as the way forward. We are left to think that our only choices are interfaith conflict or a secularization in which faith is relativized and privatized. There is a third choice which emerges from the Scriptures and which has been modelled by faithful Christians throughout history. We are called to a persevering faith in the one God who is good and great, and to live a life of service and witness that attests to God's character.

We cannot build our own faith in God by tearing down the religious traditions of others. Our faith in God should be based on who God has revealed himself to be throughout the Bible and ultimately in Jesus Christ. We acknowledge God's greatness as both Creator and Redeemer. The goodness of God is seen broadly in his common grace and more specifically in God's saving grace through the finished work of Christ on the cross.

The Bible consistently enjoins us to serve all people as if they are our own family.

---

7   Vishal Mangalwadi, *The Legacy of William Carey: A Model for the Transformation of a Culture*, 1st US ed. (Wheaton, IL: Crossway Books, 1999), 85.

8   Samuel P. Huntington, *The Clash of Civilizations and the Remaking of World Order* (New York: Simon & Schuster, 1998).

Leviticus 19:33–44 clearly indicates that we are called to love others indiscriminately. We do not love in order to gain something from the relationship; we love because God loves (1 John 4:7). Gavin D'Costa crystallizes this point: "If we are to avoid the danger of allowing love of neighbour to turn into various forms of power, manipulation, and coercion over our neighbour, then we require the pattern and practice of suffering self-giving love".[9] Our love for those who hold different religious convictions is never conditional on their agreement with our beliefs or on their reciprocated love. God loved us at a point when we were best thought of as enemies of the kingdom (Romans 5:8), and now as God's children we are to love with that kind of unflinching love.

In our interactions with people of other faiths, we also bear testimony to who God is and what he did through Jesus. Acts 1:8 calls on Jesus' disciples to be witnesses in Jerusalem, Samaria, and to the farthest reaches of the globe. Even as Jesus' disciples enter Samaria, they enter a context of conflicting faith convictions. One challenge we have is that faith is always clothed in cultural and ethnic identity. When Jesus was himself bearing witness in Samaria, he separated faith in God from ethnic identity with the implication that faith in Jesus is life-giving for *all* people (John 4:21–24). Our faith is not tied to a particular culture or ethnicity; in fact, ethnic distinctions diminish in the faith family (Gal. 3:28). Our faith is not guaranteed by our works or successes; it is guaranteed by faith in Christ (Eph. 2:5).

The Christian should find confidence here. As we enter interfaith situations with confidence in our faith, we are less prone to react out of insecurity or territorialism. We are called to serve and bear witness. We entrust our actions and words to the work of the Holy Spirit in the lives of others. Thus, we do not have to feel responsible or defensive about the results.

3. Challenges to Hope: Sensitivities

If news media are to be believed at all, interfaith conflict is the norm throughout the world. Exclusion based on creed, religious persecution, and even some wars stem from an inability of the people of different faiths to coexist peacefully. There are some factors that provoke conflict. While no effort is being made to offer a comprehensive list of provoking factors, we will offer those factors that surfaced in our research and discussions.

9   Gavin D'Costa, "Christ, the Trinity, and Religious Plurality," in *Christian Uniqueness Reconsidered: The Myth of a Pluralistic Theology of Religions*, ed. Gavin D'Costa (Maryknoll, NY: Orbis Books, 1992), 21.

Language and Attitude

The childhood adage "Sticks and stones may break my bones, but words will never hurt me" is not true. Words have a way of searing our soul like few other things. When Christians use language of exclusion and derision it harms interfaith dynamics. It seems obvious, but it still needs to be repeated. This does not mean we avoid giving witness to the hope that is in Jesus for all people, but we must be vigilant in doing so respectfully and gently (1 Peter 3:15). It also means we speak of other religions in ways that strike a balance between respect and honesty.

Internet and Social Media

There is a common perception that the Internet has created greater exposure to different beliefs, which fosters open minds and liberalization. However, contrary to common perception, Fuad stated that the Internet and social media have not necessarily led to liberalization or more open minds. The anonymity actually allows for angry online interactions that can mimic a mob mentality. Fuad said, "There is a parallel world online where religious controversy grows". Our group was told of a highly publicized case in Malaysia where Buddhists used an Islamic prayer room for their own religious ceremony. The local community was working through the issue amicably until it grew into a social media firestorm by Muslims from other parts of the country. In other words, social media has the dangerous potential to ignite religious controversy.

Power Plays and Political Involvement

Power is seductive, even for those with altruistic beginnings. Religious organizations want to have a say in the ways a society is structured, and when different religious groups are present, it can increase attention to political influence. There is a desire to legislate religiously influenced moral standards.[10] This becomes particularly troubling when a religious creed includes political dominance, much like a now antiquated Christendom model of Christian existence or Islam as it is practised in many nations.[11]

Religious tensions are further aggravated when religion is tied to ethnic

---

10   Two examples of religiously influenced legislation demonstrate the point. The Christians were a vocal influence during the prohibition era in the United States. In countries with Islamic majorities there has been heated debate about Islamic (shari'a) law and whether it extends to non-Muslims.

11   Irving Hexham, "Evangelical Illusions: Postmodern Christianity and the Growth of Muslim Communities in Europe and North America," in *No Other Gods Before Me?* ed. John G. Stackhouse Jr (Grand Rapids: Baker Academic, 2001), 155.

identity. Such tensions have flared up all over the world.[12] These tensions will likely continue because there is no way for religious communities to be entirely apolitical. Nevertheless, there is a need for each religious community to learn how to continue their faith practices while allowing for other religious communities to thrive.

Competitive Evangelism

There was a clear perception from those of the other religious communities we interviewed that Christianity was among the more aggressive in seeking to make converts of people from their communities. When asked about their own pursuits of converts, they used different terms to describe their own practice as opposed to the practice of Christians. They described their own efforts as "welcoming" others into their community. This is in contrast to a perception that Christians use pressure and coercion in order to "win" them. When we examine ourselves honestly, we do not have to look far to see examples of questionable evangelistic tactics. Of course, Christians are not alone in using questionable tactics in order to gain converts or adherents. Each religion brings with it an analysis of the human condition and offers a unique solution. When there is a strong conviction that their solution is indeed true, it is an act of concern for fellow humanity to offer the solution to others. As a consequence, every person becomes a contested soul, which then raises the temperature on interfaith dynamics.

Challenges do come to us as opportunities to improve. Some challenges have clear solutions. Christians must avoid language that disparages people of other faiths as well as limit terms that connote violence.[13] Other challenges lack clean solutions. They are natural repercussions of a world condensed by globalization and urbanization. For instance, we cannot stop the spread of news through the Internet or misinformed reactions on a social media website. But we must learn to live with the knowledge that our every word and deed can be reported around the world.

4. Ways Forward for the Church

12   The links between ethnicity and religion can be formal, as it is in Malaysia, or informal, as it is in France. In a country like Malaysia, where ethnicity is linked to religion by law, political debate becomes intertwined with religious debate. In France, the immigrant community has been associated with Islam, which has resulted in anti-immigrant discrimination aimed at the Muslim community. For more on immigrant faith and religion see Phillip Connor, *Immigrant Faith: Patterns of Immigrant Religion in the United States, Canada, and Western Europe* (New York: NYU Press, 2014), 12.

13   It can be argued that the issue goes deeper than mere language; deeper worldview issues are involved that need to be addressed. Hostile language is an outward sign of inward attitudes.

Sensitivity amidst Confidence in Athens

The New Testament church took root in cities rife with diverse and vibrant religious communities. Rodney Stark notes the pluralistic nature of the Roman cities: "To say that the Greco-Roman world was polytheistic is a gross understatement."[14] We can see how the early church navigated the need for sensitivity as well as confidence in the midst of faith communities competing for the hearts of Roman citizens in Acts 17:16–34. Paul was waiting for his teammates, Timothy and Silas, to join him in the city of Athens. Athens was past its prime as a political city, but still retained its reputation as the gathering place of intellectuals. What struck Paul, however, was the overwhelming presence of idols. With tens of thousands of statues of gods all around the city, idols may have outnumbered citizens.[15]

We are told in verse 16 that Paul is "greatly distressed" when he sees that the city is full of idols. "Instead of being impressed by Athenian architecture and learning," notes Dean Flemming, "Paul is 'deeply distressed' over the pervasive idolatry and religious pluralism he observes there".[16] We do not get the impression from the text that Paul is being religiously arrogant or intolerant. Rather, his confidence is so deeply placed in the universal God (v. 24) that it is destabilizing for him to see so much devotion given to these idols.

Though upset, Paul chose not to speak angrily or condescendingly to the Athenians. Instead, in verse 22, Paul compliments the people of Athens for their religious fervency. He is not acquiescing to the truthfulness of their religious beliefs. Paul is unequivocal in asserting the God in whom he has faith has overcome a universal human problem (v. 30) by appointing Jesus as the solution for all of humankind (v. 31). Paul's tone and language remain respectful and congenial, yet his message provocatively invites Athenians to believe in God's solution through Jesus.

5. Statement from the Working Group

As our working group came together to discuss the topic and reflect on our field research, a few common themes emerged. From these common themes, we formulated

14   Rodney Stark, *Cities of God: The Real Story of How Christianity Became an Urban Movement and Conquered Rome* (San Francisco: HarperSanFrancisco, 2006), 32.

15   Eckhard J. Schnabel, *Acts: Exegetical Commentary on the New Testament* (Grand Rapids: Zondervan, 2012), 722; John B. Polhill, *Paul and His Letters* (Nashville: B&H Academic, 1999), 208.

16   Dean Flemming, "Contextualizing the Gospel in Athens: Paul's Areopagus Address as a Paradigm for Missionary Communication," *Missiology: An International Review* XXX, no. 2 (April 2002): 200.

a statement that represented our conclusions. The statement:

> "We believe in God the Creator, Redeemer, and the Sustainer who calls us to
> work amongst all peoples in the cities. Our hope lies in the birth, death, and
> resurrection of our Lord Jesus Christ.
>
> Our aim in relating with different faith traditions is to develop deep relationships
> of trust and openness so that we can work together on projects of mutual
> concern and interest, and experience life in its fullness as God intended it. In
> such encounters, our confidence is strengthened when we come in love and with
> integrity, with no hidden agendas, engaging in mutual listening and recognising
> that God has been working and continues to work in both our communities.
>
> Our confidence is also strengthened as we seek to understand each other's faith
> traditions, identify key commonalities that allow us to work together, note key
> differences that may be obstacles in relating to each other, and reaffirm our
> understanding and personal commitment to our faith in Christ."

Comments on the Statement

The statement consolidates the key points from the ISUM working group. Some further
thoughts here might benefit from further commentary.

Humble Learning Posture

Christian confidence must not be confused with Christian arrogance. Our message to
others is understandably rejected when we show no interest in listening while making
assumptions about their beliefs. We must learn how to listen honestly to those from
other faiths. Our confidence in the gospel does not warrant a one-way conversation
directed at the non-Christian. An important element of loving others should always
include listening and humility. No matter the beliefs of a person, they are indisputably
made in the image of God (Gen. 1:27).

There is also the question of where truth can be found. All of humanity has access
to generally revealed truths about God (Romans 1:20). At the risk of oversimplifying
the theological landscape, evangelicals have tended to fall into two categories.[17] There
are some evangelicals who believe there are unique theological truths that Christians

---

17   Paul J. Griffiths, "An Evangelical Theology of Religions?" in *No Other Gods Before Me?*, ed. John G.
Stackhouse Jr (Grand Rapids: Baker Academic, 2001), 166–167.

can learn from other religions.[18] Others who acknowledge that theological truths can be found may not believe those truths add to theological truths found through God's Word.[19] Views on this topic depend on theological positions on revelation, the work of the Spirit, and epistemology. There remains a general agreement in the unique and finished work of Christ as the only sufficient solution for salvation for all nations.[20]

Christians have benefitted from philosophers who have influenced our theology. Paul Griffiths draws on the examples of Augustine and Aquinas to say: "The greatest advances in Christian thinking have come when serious Christian thinkers have paid close attention to alien particularity."[21] Can the same be said of other religious perspectives? It can certainly be acknowledged that other religions may offer further insight into human nature and the human condition. It is more difficult to acknowledge that truths about God can be discovered in other religions. In the final analysis, however, God's Word still stands as the final arbiter of competing truth claims. If another religion holds up an understanding of God that is impersonal and unknowable, it conflicts with our knowledge of God as not only personal and knowable but also actively pursuing us. We know God through his personal revelation and relate to God because he brought reconciliation through Jesus.

More Work Needed on Theology of Religions

The previous discussion on what truths can be known in other religions highlights the need for more reflection and conversation around the topic of a theology of religions. Evangelicals have tended to zero in on the salvation of the unevangelized, but there is a need for more writing on a theology of religions.[22] In secular societies there is pressure to conflate distinct religious beliefs into a "harmonious" amalgamation. Too often, we have been content to reduce this complex topic to bumper sticker platitudes. Catholic scholar, Gavin D'Costa, poignantly observes what happens when we try to put

18   Amos Yong, *Beyond the Impasse: Beyond a Pneumatological Theology of Religions* (Carlisle, Cumbria, UK ; Grand Rapids, Mich: Baker Academic, 2003); Gerald McDermott, *Can Evangelicals Learn from World Religions: Jesus, Revelation and Religious Traditions* (Downers Grove Ill.: InterVarsity Press, 2000).

19   Lesslie Newbigin, *The Gospel in a Pluralist Society* (Grand Rapids; Geneva: W.B. Eerdmans; WCC Publications, 1989); Vinoth Ramachandra, *The Recovery of Mission: Beyond the Pluralist Paradigm* (Grand Rapids: W.B. Eerdmans, 1996).

20   Veli-Matti Kärkkäinen, *An Introduction to the Theology of Religions: Biblical, Historical and Contemporary Perspectives* (Downers Grove Ill.: InterVarsity Press, 2003), 148.

21   Griffiths, "An Evangelical Theology of Religions?" 167.

22   Kärkkäinen, *An Introduction to the Theology of Religions*, 21.

all religions on equal standing: "The Enlightenment, in granting a type of equality to all religions, ended up denying public truth to any and all of them."[23] In others words, to assume all religions are basically the same, is not fair to any of the religions. We need thinking and writing that is not content with reductionist adages.

Religions can be dangerous and manipulative. Religions have been used to oppress and tyrannize in terrible and imaginative ways. Religious adherence has been the cause of wars, schisms, suicide bombings, and exploitive empire building. We even see the people of God use religion to oppress others (cf. Ezek. 22; Isa. 58). The church has perpetuated injustices from the pulpit.[24] A theology of religions is needed that aids in our discernment of religions both in their positive attributes as well as their shadow side.

More reflection is needed regarding sources and critical assessment of other religions. Some have made the case that the operation of the Holy Spirit in those of other religions calls us to acknowledge their spiritual development as guided by the Spirit.[25] While we do not dispute the work of the Spirit we must also acknowledge the potential for other revelatory sources to deceive and distort any truths claimed by those other faiths. As evangelicals, we acknowledge human frailty extends to the mind and the activity of the spirit world. The human mind is prone to believe deceptions when it is advantageous to do so. This frailty can lead to religious views built on untruths rather than truths. And the spirit world can be a source of religious knowledge that has the potential to be damaging rather than a source for hope. Even though in the West we may not readily acknowledge the presence and activity of spirits, all would quickly agree (I hope) that the person who hears a voice calling for mass human sacrifice is deceived.[26] Religions cannot simply be dismissed as devoid of all truth nor can different religious beliefs be placed on the same pedestal.

There are other aspects of interfaith dynamics needing more reflection that will directly impact our urban ministries. For example, is there room for collaboration across religious lines in working with the poor when our respective theological beliefs about poverty differ? Or, how do interfaith dynamics work in cities upheld

---

23   Gavin D'Costa, *The Meeting of Religions and the Trinity* (Maryknoll, NY: Orbis Books, 2000), 1–2.

24   Just as one example, the church in the South of the United States continued prejudice in churches and public statements long after slaves were emancipated in 1871. Alan Cross, *When Heaven and Earth Collide: Racism, Southern Evangelicals, and the Better Way of Jesus* (Montgomery, AL: NewSouth Books, 2014).

25   D'Costa, "Christ, the Trinity, and Religious Plurality."

26   Amos Yong has done the most toward discerning between demonic inspiration and divine inspiration. Yong, *Beyond the Impasse*, 137–161.

as sacred in one faith and not others? There is a need for a more open and frank discussion at times when religious communities contribute to an ongoing injustice due to a theological conviction. These issues and many more need biblical reflection and continued discussion.

Confidence in Witness

In order to develop a pattern of listening and learning from others, we need spaces for dialogue, but we cannot let go of our witness. Dialogue across religious lines can be invaluable in many ways. It helps us in learning about others. Open conversations can reduce natural build-up of mistrust and prejudice between religious communities. Dialogue can even help us crystallize our own beliefs and restore confidence in our faith in the triune God. But "...dialogue is neither a substitute nor a subterfuge for mission".[27] Dialogue cannot stand in for our witness.

When Jesus was teaching his disciples in anticipation of his ascension in Acts 1, his primary mandate for the church was to be his witnesses in every corner of the world. This is not intended as a privatized, "Jesus was great for me", kind of witness. The late missionary statesman Lesslie Newbigin contended that the good news of Jesus Christ's incarnation, ministry, death, and resurrection is public truth for all of humanity. "If these things are really true, they have to be told."[28] This is public news that does not discriminate based on status, language, gender, age, or religion. We can and must minister with the confidence that this truth of the gospel is liberating to those of every creed.

Unconditional Love and Respect

As we can confidently attest to the truth of the gospel, our lives mirror this truth. When we live more deeply in the story of the gospel, then we witness to the truest demonstration of sacrificial love in Jesus. But witness entails cost. Jesus predicts those who are his disciples will suffer for his name (John 15:18–27). Persecution and suffering are normative for the Christian life.

Jesus' disciple Peter wrote to the church undergoing persecution. Peter's plea to the church was that it persist in personal holiness and public good works even in the

27   David Bosch, *Transforming Mission: Paradigm Shifts in Theology of Mission* (Maryknoll, NY: Orbis Books, 1991), 487.

28   Lesslie Newbigin, *A Word in Season: Perspectives on Christian World Missions* (Grand Rapids, Mich.: W.B. Eerdmans Pub. Co., 1994), 151.

midst of being reviled by the multi-faith public (1 Peter 2:11–20).[29] When interfaith dynamics become hostile, the church is not to fall into interreligious competition. The model is always that of Christ, who suffered and died in order that we might be declared righteous. We are to love and respect others no matter their response to us. We bring honour to Christ by our witness and our lives.

6. Conclusion

Multi-religious life is our reality. We, as Christians, have a long way to go in learning how to live and speak with greater sensitivity. But we are not to become so sensitive that we lose our confidence in the public truth of the cross of Christ. Newbigin asserts the word "confidence" as the best one to describe our interfaith engagement:

> "The world into which the first Christians carried the gospel was a religiously plural world and — as the letters of Paul show — in that world of many lords and many gods, Christians had to work out what it means that in fact Jesus alone is Lord. The first three centuries of church history were a time of intense life-and-death struggle against the seductive power of syncretism. But if the issue of religious pluralism is not entirely new, it certainly meets our generation in a new way. We must meet it in the terms of our own time."[30]

As faith symbols displayed on car dashboards assert religious allegiances, Christians will need to learn afresh how to meet this religiously plural urban world. We must do so with the humility of Christ to serve and love, while never forsaking the call to upend the status quo with good news of the Saviour.

---

29   For a thorough treatment of 1 Peter 2 see Bruce W. Winter, *Seek the Welfare of the City: Christians as Benefactors and Citizens* (Grand Rapids: Wm. B. Eerdmans Publishing Company, 1994).

30   Newbigin, *The Gospel in a Pluralist Society*, 157.

References

Bosch, David. *Transforming Mission: Paradigm Shifts in Theology of Mission*. Maryknoll, NY: Orbis Books, 1991.

Connor, Phillip. *Immigrant Faith: Patterns of Immigrant Religion in the United States, Canada, and Western Europe*. New York: NYU Press, 2014.

Cox, Harvey. *The Secular City: Secularization and Urbanization in Theological Perspective*. Rev. Ed. New York: Macmillan, 1966.

Cross, Alan. *When Heaven and Earth Collide: Racism, Southern Evangelicals, and the Better Way of Jesus*. Montgomery, AL: NewSouth Books, 2014.

D'Costa, Gavin. "Christ, the Trinity, and Religious Plurality." In *Christian Uniqueness Reconsidered: The Myth of a Pluralistic Theology of Religions*, edited by Gavin D'Costa, 16–29. Maryknoll, NY: Orbis Books, 1992.

———. *The Meeting of Religions and the Trinity*. Maryknoll, NY: Orbis Books, 2000.

"Fears of a New Religious Strife." *The Economist*, July 27, 2013. http://www.economist.com/news/asia/21582321-fuelled-dangerous-brew-faith-ethnicity-and-politics-tit-tat-conflict-escalating.

Flemming, Dean. "Contextualizing the Gospel in Athens: Paul's Areopagus Address as a Paradigm for Missionary Communication." *Missiology: An International Review* XXX, no. 2 (April 2002): 199–214.

Griffiths, Paul J. "An Evangelical Theology of Religions?" In *No Other Gods Before Me?* edited by John G. Stackhouse Jr, 163–69. Grand Rapids: Baker Academic, 2001.

Hexham, Irving. "Evangelical Illusions: Postmodern Christianity and the Growth of Muslim Communities in Europe and North America." In *No Other Gods Before Me?* edited by John G. Stackhouse Jr, 137–60. Grand Rapids: Baker Academic, 2001.

Huntington, Samuel P. *The Clash of Civilizations and the Remaking of World Order*. New York: Simon & Schuster, 1998.

Kärkkäinen, Veli-Matti. *An Introduction to the Theology of Religions: Biblical, Historical, and Contemporary Perspectives*. Downers Grove Ill.: InterVarsity Press, 2003.

Mangalwadi, Vishal. *The Legacy of William Carey: A Model for the Transformation of a Culture*. 1st US ed. Wheaton, IL: Crossway Books, 1999.

McDermott, Gerald. *Can Evangelicals Learn from World Religions: Jesus, Revelation, and Religious Traditions*. Downers Grove Ill.: InterVarsity Press, 2000.

Newbigin, Lesslie. *A Word in Season: Perspectives on Christian World Missions*. Grand Rapids Mich.: W.B. Eerdmans Pub. Co., 1994.

———. *The Gospel in a Pluralist Society*. Grand Rapids; Geneva: W.B. Eerdmans; WCC Publications, 1989.

Polhill, John B. *Paul and His Letters.* Nashville: B&H Academic, 1999.

"Projek Dialog." Accessed October 1, 2014. http://www.projekdialog.com/.

Ramachandra, Vinoth. *The Recovery of Mission: Beyond the Pluralist Paradigm.* Grand Rapids: W.B. Eerdmans, 1996.

Schnabel, Eckhard J. *Acts: Exegetical Commentary on the New Testament.* Grand Rapids: Zondervan, 2012.

Stark, Rodney. *Cities of God: The Real Story of How Christianity Became an Urban Movement and Conquered Rome.* San Francisco: HarperSanFrancisco, 2006.

Winter, Bruce W. *Seek the Welfare of the City: Christians as Benefactors and Citizens.* Grand Rapids: Wm. B. Eerdmans Publishing Company, 1994.

Yong, Amos. *Beyond the Impasse: Beyond a Pneumatological Theology of Religions.* Carlisle, Cumbria, UK : Grand Rapids, MI: Baker Academic, 2003.

"You Took Me In": Seeking Transformation for Migrant Workers, Refugees, and Asylum Seekers

Brad Coath with Angela Akamine, Laurie Krepp, Hwa Hui-En, and Andy Sparkes

This chapter explores ways in which Christians, organizations, and the church may bring transformation in regard to the world's migrant workers, refugees, and asylum seekers. While finding a "solution" to these problems is beyond us, we can find ways to be "signs" of God's reign and to be part of creating and sustaining ecologies of welcome, inclusion, and justice. This paper will look at signs of hope, challenges to hope, and ways toward transformation.

Introduction

Having gathered to discuss the challenges facing migrant workers, refugees, and asylum seekers across the globe at the 2014 ISUM Summit in Kuala Lumpur, participants in our working group very quickly realized that it is a task of enormous proportions, with multiple causes and symptoms, and certainly no easy answers. Indeed, the task of a small group of committed practitioners gathering to imagine solutions to such problems seems in the realm of the absurd.

Around the globe, there are an estimated 51 million people in need of protection — 10.5 million of them refugees. Of these, only 80,000 will be resettled each year by

UNHCR. It doesn't take a degree in mathematics to realize that that's like trying to pour an entire beach worth of sand through an egg timer. The challenges are deeply systemic and of global magnitude. They are the results of wars, ethnic conflicts, exploitative economic systems, food insecurity, and increasingly, of environmental degradation.[1] The challenges are also profoundly personal. Each number represents a name and a face, a family member, someone with dignity, hopes, and dreams. And each number represents a life created in the image of God, whose reign is most certainly not expressed through their suffering, displacement, and poverty.

Our ISUM working group recognized that developing solutions to such problems is well beyond us, but that nevertheless we must explore ways to bring transformation for migrant workers, asylum seekers, and refugees. The magnitude of the numbers, as well as the lives of those known personally to members of the working group across three different continents, means that this task is an urgent one. To paraphrase Jean Vanier, we may not be a solution, but we must be a sign.[2]

The task that our working group undertook, therefore, was not to come up with a "solution" to the problems faced by migrant workers, refugees, and asylum seekers. Rather, it was to explore ways of being "signs", or perhaps to ask, "What might the in-breaking of God's reign look like in regard to migrant workers, refugees, and asylum seekers?" This paper, then, will look at this question, and explore how followers of Jesus and the church might better practise and understand mission in relation to migrant workers, refugees, and asylum seekers.

The focus of our ISUM working group — migrant workers, refugees, and asylum seekers — is incredibly broad. It encompasses people in many situations, with many contributing factors. The following definitions, then, will seek to give clarity, while acknowledging that there is still overlap and ambiguity.

The term "migrant worker" refers to people who have crossed a border and are working in the new country. While some migrant workers can move to some countries to work with legitimate visas, this paper will use the term to refer to those who have, typically because of persecution, danger, or extreme poverty, crossed a border in a way normally considered illegal, and therefore who are particularly vulnerable in the new country. They may have applied for, received, or intend to apply for refugee status and are awaiting resettlement, or they may not have applied for refugee status, intending to stay in the transit country or go back to their country of origin.

1   Susanna Snyder, *Asylum Seeking, Migration and Church* (Surrey: Ashgate, 2012), Kindle Location 1344.

2   Ashley Barker, *Risky Compassion* (Birmingham: Springdale Collage, 2014), Kindle Location 2418.

A "refugee" is, under the definition of the United Nations Refugee Convention, "someone who is unable or unwilling to return to their country of origin owing to a well-founded fear of being persecuted for reasons of race, religion, nationality, membership of a particular social group, or political opinion".[3]

An "asylum seeker", then, is someone who is outside the country of his or her origin, and has made a claim to be a refugee. While that claim is in the process of being verified, they are an asylum seeker.

What is common, generally speaking, to migrant workers, refugees, and asylum seekers is that they are outside of their home country, for reasons not of their own choosing, and they find themselves on the political, social, and economic underside of their new environment. In essence, they are forced migrants. Though this is an imprecise term, I will, when referring to all three categories, use this term.

Two other terms are in need of clarification: "transit" and "resettlement countries". I will use the term "transit country" to refer to a country that is not a person's country of origin but is one in which a migrant worker, refugee, or asylum seeker finds themself but is not able to legitimately settle there. Countries such as Malaysia and Indonesia are typical transit countries because they are not signatories to the UN Refugee Convention, but are places that many people in the region flee to. The term is a loose one because, while "transit" implies being in a location for a short period, many migrant workers and refugees find themselves in transit countries for decades. It is also loose because many migrant workers who not have applied for refugee status may intend neither to do so nor return home.

"Resettlement countries", on the other hand, are countries forced migrants can legitimately settle in; typically they are signatories to the UN Refugee Convention, and are countries that refugees, having gained refugee status in a transit country, may be resettled to.

We are not beginning a new work. Already, God is active in responding to the cries of the poor and the foreigner. At ISUM, we saw and talked about a number of "signs of hope" emerging in difficult situations. We will firstly look at some of these. We will then begin to articulate some of the challenges to hope that are faced in both transit and resettlement countries, before exploring ways that Christians and the church can join in God's work of moving toward a transformed world in regard to migrant workers, refugees, and asylum seekers.

---

3   *UNHCR Convention and Protocol Relating to the Status of Refugees*, http://www.unhcr.org/3b66c2aa10.html.

1. Signs of Hope

Hope in Transit Countries

In transit countries, there are many ways that churches, NGOs, and individuals are responding to migrant workers, refugees, and asylum seekers with welcome and caring. Organizations such as Migrant Ministry Klang are working with UNHCR to provide schooling for refugee children. Others, like Malaysian Care, are equipping churches to work with migrant workers, refugees, and asylum seekers. Organizations such as Ruth Education Centre (REC) are training students who are themselves refugees to teach other children in their own communities and those in other ethnic groups. In Malaysia, various Pakistani communities are coming together to form service centres for refugees. Collaboration is happening amongst other groups, such the Alliance of Chin Refugees, which comprises about 43,000 refugees and is run by refugees for refugees, with the support of Transform Aid International, an Australian Baptist aid agency. Churches in Malaysia and other countries are welcoming migrant groups to worship and meet on their premises.

During the ISUM Summit, participants took part in immersion experiences and witnessed first-hand some of the signs of hope for forced migrants. One participant, Jill Birt, from Perth, Australia, wrote of the experience:

> *"The group spent an afternoon with students from the Ruth Education Centre, a community-based residential school for 26 Burmese teenagers from seven different people groups.*
>
> *During the Saturday afternoon visit, the visitors sat on the tiled floor of the main teaching room on the second floor of a shop house in Kuala Lumpur's southern suburbs, talking with small groups of students.*
>
> *They generously shared their stories with the visitors — stories of rapid change from their rhythmic village life in Myanmar to the manic intensity of life in Kuala Lumpur — a life where fear destroys peace, where opportunities are limited, where uncertainty pervades.*
>
> *But hope keeps breaking through.*
>
> *Sixteen-year-old Bosco, who has been in Kuala Lumpur for three years, talked about the music program at REC. He said he was learning to write songs, something he had never dreamed of doing.*

I gently asked if he would sing his song for us. And he did. He sang from his heart, confidently looking into our faces. He sang his song called "Life". I asked why he wrote this song.

'I wrote this song to encourage my people to live', Bosco said.

An amazing sign of hope in the city."[4]

Hope in Resettlement Countries

In resettlement countries, again, there are signs of hope. In the UK, there are many faith-based responses to asylum seekers and refugees, such as taking part in grassroots service, political advocacy, and supporting worship opportunities and spaces for theological dialogue.[5] In the US churches are also increasingly speaking out on behalf of working migrants from Central and South America.[6] Straddling the Mexican border, church services, or *"Posada sin Fronteras"*, are held each Advent with American and Mexican participants on both sides of the wall engaging in public liturgy that re-enacts the journey of Mary and Joseph seeking shelter.[7]

In Australia, we are also seeing churches and organizations assisting refugees and asylum seekers in many ways. A number of Baptist churches, for instance, have been actively supporting Burmese refugees in Malaysia. One such church, Westgate Baptist Community, has sought to assist those seeking resettlement through regular group visits to Malaysia, helping to provide education, and helping with resettlement applications. As refugees gain admission to Australia the church has supported their adjustment to life in Australia, helping them find housing, schools, churches, and employment.

The church in Australia is also becoming increasingly vocal in advocating for refugees and asylum seekers. Examples of this include the Australian Churches Refugee Taskforce (ACRT),[8] a body made up of representatives from a cross-section of Christian denominations working together to speak out and lobby government

4   Jill Birt, "Signs of Hope in the City", In *The Advocate* (Baptist Churches in Western Australia, August, 2014), 9.

5   For a detailed summary of these responses, see Snyder, *Asylum Seeking*, chapter 3.

6   Daniel Carrol, *Christians at the Border: Immigration, the Church and the Bible*. 2nd ed. (Grand Rapids: Brazos, 2013), 40–41.

7   Ched Myers, and Matthew Colwell, *Our God Is Undocumented: Biblical Faith and Immigrant Justice* (Maryknoll: Orbis, 2012), 170–172.

8   Australian Churches Refugee Taskforce, http://www.australianchurchesrefugeetaskforce.com.au

for policy change; and the "Love Makes a Way" movement, which has seen Christian leaders across the country engage in nonviolent direct action to ask for the release of children from detention.[9]

2. Challenges to Hope

Of course, while having eyes to see signs of hope is vital to us maintaining a healthy perspective, challenges to hope abound. Here, we will look at some of the challenges faced by forced migrants in transit countries and resettlement countries respectively. We will then look at some of the challenges faced by organizations and churches who are serving forced migrants in both transit and resettlement countries, since there is much overlap and an individual treatment is beyond our current scope.

Challenges in Transit Countries

For forced migrants in transit countries, many challenges await as they step outside their own borders. The following two stories highlight some of these challenges.

> As Rina[10] sat and listened to the doctor's voice, she felt her fragile world being shattered, all over again. Rina had been in Malaysia for two years now, after fleeing from Myanmar in 2012 with her husband, Ahmad. They were Rohingya refugees. Rina usually spent long hours at home while Ahmad worked at the factory, but this week he hadn't worked, forfeiting his pay. When Rina's pain and vomiting started, he tried to get doctors to see her, eventually being sent to the General Hospital, but they were totally unprepared for the news. She was pregnant, she had cancer, and the hospital wouldn't treat her because they deemed that Rina and Ahmad would be unable to pay the costly foreigner rates. They were discharged without treatment.

> Over the next few months, Rina and Ahmad battled desperately against the odds. UNHCR would not help them as they were not yet registered, and when they did register, the hospital still refused them treatment, telling them that the oncology department doesn't treat foreigners. When their caseworker pressed the hospital, they were told there would be no treatment as Rina's cancer was terminal.

9   See, for example, "Religious Leaders Arrested for Protesting" in *The Age*, October 13, 2014. http://www.theage.com.au/victoria/religious-leaders-arrested-for-protesting-inside-shadow-immigration-ministers-geelong-offices-20141014-115kaj.html accessed 17 October 2014.

10   All names have been changed to protect identities.

Not speaking Malay or English, it was difficult to know exactly what was going on or what to do. Already in financial difficulties as they had been without income for many weeks, and with Rina experiencing much pain, Ahmad borrowed money from friends to pay for Rina to undergo treatment at a private hospital despite her late stage of cancer and pregnancy. Eventually, Rina gave birth to a healthy baby, though Ahmed was becoming increasingly worried about how he would care for the baby as well as pay back his large debt. Hope was becoming all too hard.

Ling fled the brutality of the Burmese soldiers in southern Chin State with his wife and two-year-old daughter in 2007. Making the dangerous journey through Thailand, they arrived in Malaysia where they settled at a jungle camp about an hour from Kuala Lumpur.

As an asylum seeker with no papers, working was illegal. However, like hundreds of others, he obtained work on a construction site several miles from the camp. Early one morning, as he and others were about to leave for work, several hundred law enforcement officers surrounded the camp, arresting as many of the refugees as they could catch. They then burnt and destroyed the camp.

Ling was among those arrested, who were handcuffed and taken to a detention centre in the back of lorries. Seven months later he was released due to the intervention of the UNHCR. Ling doesn't speak of his treatment in the prison, but upon his release he was in need of serious medical attention. Access to government hospitals, though, was barred for someone in Ling's situation, and he could not afford treatment at a private hospital. Even if he had the money, he would most likely have been reported and arrested.

When he finally rejoined his wife and daughter, they lived precariously in Kuala Lumpur, and Ling worked long hours in Chinese restaurants to survive, awaiting resettlement that would take years. Yet the fear of what might happen to him and his family if he were arrested again was always close at hand.

These stories highlight challenges faced by forced migrants in transit countries.

One challenge is the lack of work rights and the illegitimate status that forced migrants have outside of their own countries. For most, this means living in fear of harassment by authorities, which is commonplace and linked with corruption. Even those who have refugee status are not immune — in Kuala Lumpur we heard many stories of people having their refugee cards confiscated until they handed over cash or their mobile phones.

A second challenge is the time it can take for resettlement. Resettlement can take anywhere from a few years to well over a decade. One woman, with whom one of our group spoke, and whose story is surely not uncommon, was told she would be resettled after fifteen years of waiting. The huge numbers of refugees and limited places for resettlement offered by third countries mean that the process is very slow and uncertain. There are 10.5 million refugees worldwide and only about 80,000 get resettled each year.

A third challenge is the difficulty in accessing medical care. For forced migrants, this can mean that problems which would otherwise be easily treated can become life-threatening.

A fourth challenge is education. In Kuala Lumpur alone, there are 31,916 children below the age of eighteen,[11] who are not permitted to enrol in Malaysian schools. Only about 5,000 children are participating in an educational setting, 1,000 of whom attend UNHCR schools. The remaining 4,000 attend schools run by refugee communities, schools which are overcrowded and under resourced. Only 3% of thirteen- to eighteen- year olds attend school, due to a lack of facilities and the need to engage in low paid work to enable their families to survive.

A lack of legitimacy and work rights, the constant threat of harassment and jail, long waits for resettlement, and inadequate access to medical care and education are factors which too often combine to keep people in a quagmire of poverty, stripping people of the dignity to live meaningfully.

Challenges in Resettlement Countries

In resettlement countries, refugees and asylum seekers will face different sets of challenges, depending on their circumstances. Those who are entering as refugees in resettlement programs will be confronted with all of the difficulties inherent in finding oneself newly arrived in a foreign place, while still likely carrying the pain of past trauma and separation from home and loved ones. Asylum seekers, though, with their lack of legitimacy and the often hostile reception they will face, perhaps face the greater difficulty.[12] The following story will explore some of these challenges.

---

11   UNHCRhttp://www.unhcr.org.my/About_Us-@-Figures_At_A_Glance.aspx accessed 9 October 2014.

12   Migrant workers too will face many challenges which we don't have the space to deal with here. For a more in-depth look at migrant workers in a US context, see Carroll, *Christians at the Border.*

"Ganu"[13] *came to Australia by boat from Sri Lanka in June, 2013, with his wife and two of his children. His hometown of Trincomalee, on the island nation's north-east coast, had suffered much during the civil war that ended in 2009, and for many, the terror had never stopped. Having endured imprisonment and torture under government-sponsored para-military groups, and having had two of his brothers "disappeared", the terror of not knowing who would be next, or when the white van would stop out the front of his home, became too great to bear.*[14] *With the help of an uncle, Ganu and his cousin, who was also fleeing threats from the police, contacted an agent to arrange for passage to Australia. The agent told them he could have Ganu's family on a boat the next week, but they would only be able to take one child per adult, meaning they would have to make the impossible decision to leave one of their children in the care of grandparents. Believing they would soon be able to re-unite in Australia, they paid their money and made plans to leave Sri Lanka. Ganu's cousin, his wife and five-year-old son left Sri Lanka a month later.*

On arrival on the Australian territory of Cocos Island, Ganu and his family were picked up by a navy customs boat and taken to Christmas Island. There they would spend the next five weeks, before being transferred to a detention centre on the Australian mainland. After four months in detention in Australia, Ganu's family was released into community detention. There, they would be subject to the Australian government's "no advantage" policies, designed to deter others who might try to come to Australia by boat to claim asylum. They would receive a minimal payment leaving them barely able to live day-to-day, and they would not be allowed to work. They were told that they would never be given a permanent visa, even if their claims for asylum, which had been put on hold, eventually proved genuine. Most devastatingly, not being able to gain permanent residency, they would have no avenue of family reunification, meaning they now had no way of bringing their son to Australia.

Over the next few months, with the memories of torture and trauma back home still lingering, the guilt of leaving their son, the boredom of not being able to work, and the anxiety of uncertainty of the future, the mental health of Ganu and his wife suffered greatly.

13 To protect identities, the following story is composed of a number of real-life situations known to the author and reported by documented sources.

14 For more information on ongoing persecution of Tamils in Sri Lanka, see Amnesty International: *Sri Lanka's Assault on Dissent* (2013)

> *Meanwhile, because of a change in government policy on July 19, 2013, Ganu's cousin and his family were faring even worse. Having arrived on Cocos Island, they were taken to Christmas Island, and after medical checks hastily conducted in under two days, were sent to detention on Nauru. There, they would languish indefinitely in conditions the UNHCR would describe as unsafe and inhumane conditions.*[15]

The above story highlights a number of challenges faced by asylum seekers in Australia including prolonged periods of detention in harsh conditions; lack of work rights; no access to family reunification; prolonged time frames for assessment of claims; and lack of certainty about the future. These challenges often combine to produce anxiety and other mental health issues, particularly when compounded by the effects of past trauma.

For people being held in detention, the challenges are more severe. Added to the anxiety and uncertainty surrounding their future and the effects of trauma from past experiences, the lack of freedom, inadequate access to education and healthcare, harsh conditions, and the indefinite nature of their detention can be especially debilitating.

A further significant challenge faced by forced migrants in resettlement countries is, as mentioned above, the frequently hostile reception that they receive from the host population, often borne out through the media and in political debate. Carroll, writing from the US context, names "nativism" and economic concerns as key factors in negative attitudes toward forced migrants.[16] Snyder, writing from a UK context, adds to this list security fears.[17] These three factors combine in many contexts, including my own Australian one, and have been seized upon by politicians trying to secure the popular vote, and heightened through mainstream media, combining to create what Snyder calls an "ecology of fear".[18] It is this very ecology of fear which has driven immigration policy in many countries to increasingly closed and deterrence-based stances toward forced migrants, cutting off hope for countless people.

---

15   *UNHCR Monitoring Visit to the Republic of Nauru*, http://unhcr.org.au/unhcr/images/2013-11-26%20Report%20of%20UNHCR%20Visit%20to%20Nauru%20of%207-9%20October%202013.pdf. Accessed 17 October 2014.

16   Carroll, *Christians at the Border*, 6.

17   Snyder, *Asylum Seeking*, Kindle Location 2342.

18   Snyder, *Asylum Seeking*, Kindle Location 2709.

Challenges for Organizations and Churches

Organizations and churches serving forced migrants in both transit and resettlement countries naturally face huge challenges. While it would be too big a task to give a comprehensive treatment here, some of the challenges named by practitioners in the ISUM working group are as follows.[19] First, the ever-changing demographics of forced migrants means that needs are always evolving. Because of this, approaches and methods also need to evolve and new ones need to be developed. Secondly, language barriers often make communication difficult. Thirdly, government restrictions and sensitivities can be difficult, for example, for Christian groups working with Muslim migrants in Malaysia. A fourth challenge is tensions between communities, or within communities. Participants noted, for example, the difficulties in setting up services to serve Pakistani refugees, a group that comprises both Muslims and Christians. A final challenge is mobilizing the church. While many responses to problems faced by forced migrants are from churches and Christian organizations, it is certainly small in terms of both the responses needed and the potential that the church has in terms of raising up workers and resources. The lack of theological underpinnings to respond to migrant workers, refugees, and asylum seekers was seen as a prime factor.

3. Working towards Transformation

As long as there is violence and inequality in the world — or until God's reign comes in its fullness — we will always have people who are forced from their homes in the desperate search for safety and security. How then might we become signs of God's reign, and move toward transformation for forced migrants?

Here we will look at ways to move toward transformation in both transit countries and settlement countries, outlining some practical suggestions which were articulated in our ISUM working group. These suggestions are by no means exhaustive — they are perhaps better seen as examples of ways that we might respond as individuals and churches. Indeed, more creative responses are imperative.

Transformation is not only practical. We recognize that practical responses must come from a deeper understanding of the gospel and mission in relation to forced migrants. With this in mind, I will outline some important theological starting points with which to move further toward transformation for forced migrants.

---

19   For a more comprehensive treatment, see Snyder, *Asylum Seeking*.

Transformation in Transit Countries

In moving toward transformation for forced migrants in transit countries, firstly, we need to *develop greater partnerships among organizations* working with forced migrants. As the issues facing migrant workers are infinitely broad, it is imperative that organizations work together to meet their diverse needs.[20] Effective service to migrants will mean integration between NGOs, international aid organizations, and government agencies, as well as Christian organizations and churches. Each organization's effectiveness is multiplied when it is able to partner with others serving the same population, but perhaps through a slightly different focus.

Secondly, *community mapping and networking* are needed to increase awareness of the opportunities to serve and services available to meet needs. This might mean, for example, a church mapping out what services are available within a five kilometre radius of their location. With this information, people willing to serve might more easily find appropriate volunteer opportunities, and organizations will be able to avoid "reinventing the wheel".

Thirdly, it was identified that churches may need to *work more closely with and draw on the knowledge of refugee communities* in order to work more sensitively and in more empowering ways with these communities. Serving vulnerable communities in ways which are culturally inappropriate to them, or ways which deny the skills and abilities within the communities to bring about change for themselves can be most unhelpful, and in the long term do more harm than good.[21]

Fourthly, we need to *partner more effectively with the expatriate community.* Many transit countries such as Malaysia find themselves home to large expatriate communities, and many people are wanting to find ways to make a difference. Expatriates can bring, among other things, expertise, resources, and avenues of sponsorship, and may be willing to volunteer their time and energies.

Fifthly and finally, churches can help to *create spaces for meeting and living* which will help forced migrants feel a sense of connectedness and community. Examples of ways this might be done include providing a safe place for migrants who are separated

20   Needs include meeting basic on-going and acute medical needs, providing temporary housing, organizing a food bank and/or food deliveries, educating migrant children, assisting with paperwork and registration with international bodies, providing legal assistance, including jail visits, developing cottage industries and other income sources, particularly for migrants awaiting asylum status or resettlement, and reaching out to meet spiritual needs through pastoring.

21   For an excellent resource on working with vulnerable people in empowering ways, see Steve Corbett and Brian Fikkert, *When Helping Hurts: How to Alleviate Poverty without Hurting the Poor...and Yourself.* (Chicago: Moody, 2009).

from family members to communicate with their families via Skype, language groups, second-hand shops and toy libraries, sporting groups, and avenues to serve in church ministry. These spaces should grow from listening well to refugee communities, and may well be initiated and run by those in the communities themselves. Such ministry may well represent a risk to churches, but the opportunities for growth and blessing are immense.

Transformation in Settlement Countries

In seeking transformation in settlement countries, we must recognize that governments will rarely change until public opinion does. And public opinion begins with people. In beginning to counter the "ecology of fear" and starting to create an ecology of welcome, we need to engage personally, publicly, and politically.

Engaging *personally* is a first step. Face-to-face encounters are invaluable in helping residents of settlement countries understand the difficulties faced by forced migrants, as well as the strengths and richness that they bring to their new community. Volunteering with organizations or church groups who work with refugees and asylum seekers can be an ideal way to begin engaging, and can help make people form connections in their own neighbourhoods. Through activities such as teaching English, offering appropriate material assistance,[22] or visiting people in detention, often friendships are formed and lives are changed.

Resettlement countries' responses to forced migrants, for better or worse, have largely hinged on public opinion. Engaging *publicly*, then, is a second way that Christians and churches in these countries can help create an ecology of welcome. Public views are often based on perception rather than facts, perceptions which can be manipulated by politicians and media. Churches can play important roles in helping build better understanding in the community. A number of churches around my home in Melbourne have held conversation and information nights on the topic of asylum seekers. These have been, for some, eye-opening times and opportunities to hear from those with first-hand experience of seeking asylum.

Engaging *politically* is a third important area where Christians and churches can create an ecology of welcome. The examples of the ACRT and Love Makes a Way, as mentioned above, show what this may look like. Imagination, creativity, and a refusal to dehumanize political leaders, even as the policies they create may dehumanize

---

22   See Corbett and Fikkert, *When Helping Hurts* for an excellent discussion of when giving material assistance is appropriate.

asylum seekers, are much needed. Christians must both bring critique of the unjust actions of leaders and systems created by those in power, and help them to imagine a new way. They must "on one hand… show that the dominant consciousness… will indeed end and that it has no final claim upon us [and o]n the other hand, present an alternative consciousness that can energize the community to fresh forms of faithfulness and vitality".[23]

Challenges for Christians and Churches

Why should the church see responding to forced migrants as integral to its call to mission? In beginning to answer these questions I will briefly explore three themes which weave their way through the biblical tradition and find their culmination in the Gospels. Though we can only touch on them here, I believe that as we follow them through we may find that responding to forced migrants is not an "add-on" to living out the way of Christ, but central to the good news that Jesus proclaimed.

The first of these themes is *legitimation of the poor*. In the world in which the Gospels were written, the plight of the poor and oppressed was seen as somewhat deserved. They were that way, it was thought, because they were in some way a "sinner". It was in this world that Matthew's Jesus proclaimed that the poor, the hungry, the meek, and those who were on the underside of justice were in fact those whom God looks on favourably (Mt 5:1-11).

One of the stories where this legitimation of those on the underside can be seen is the story of the healing of the paralyzed man (Mt 9:2-8). In this story, we often miss the reason the teachers of the law are so incensed: "[t]heir complaint that none but God can remit debt… is not a defense of the sovereignty of Yahweh, but of their own social power".[24] It is their job to reckon who is living according to the law and who is not, and therefore to declare who is a "sinner". The good news for the paralytic is that how the teachers of the law see him is not how God sees him.

It is this view of forced migrants as "illegitimate" — be it illegal workers in Kuala Lumpur or those trying to reach Australian shores by boat — that the Gospels challenge. The common view of such people as illegitimate is underpinned by the assumption that they have, like the man who was paralyzed, done something wrong to be in that situation, and the tragic outplay of this view is that, because

---

23   Walter Brueggemann, *The Prophetic Imagination,* 2nd ed. (Minneapolis: Fortress, 2001), 59.

24   Ched Myers, *Binding the Strongman: A Political Reading of Mark's Story of Jesus.* (Maryknoll: Orbis, 2008), 155.

they are illegitimate, at best, they don't deserve help. At worst, it opens the way for mistreatment. The Gospels call us to refuse to de-legitimate forced migrants, and instead to take seriously Jesus' command to "do to others whatever you would like them to do to you" (Matt 7:12).

The second theme is *hospitality*. One of the distinctive features of the Torah in comparison to other ancient Near Eastern law codes is its concern for the sojourner.[25] The provisions in, for example, Exodus 23, require Israelites to "not oppress foreigners" for "[y]ou know what it's like to be a foreigner" (Ex 23:9).

In the gospel of Luke, hospitality is, according to Brendan Byrne, a central theme.[26] Many times we find Jesus sharing table fellowship with others, coming as a guest to be welcomed, and those who receive him "find that he brings them into a much wider sphere of hospitality: the 'hospitality of God'".[27]

This theme is perhaps most clearly seen in Luke 14:15–24, where Jesus paints a picture of radical hospitality extended to those with whom a Jew of good standing should definitely *not* have been eating.[28] Drawing on the vision of Isaiah 25, those on the margins, and even those *outside* the people of Israel, are invited to the banquet. It is a vision of hospitality which is inclusive and even subversive.

Matthew's parable of the sheep and the goats (Matt 25:31–46) is even more pointed. A defining mark of our practice as God's people is the way we welcome the stranger. The stance, if not the precise actions, that this calls God's people to in regard to forced migrants is one of hospitality that is radical in its inclusion and welcoming of those in need. "Hospitality", says Christine Pohl, "is central to the meaning of the gospel… [it] is a lens through which we can understand much of the gospel, and a practice by which we can welcome Jesus himself".[29]

A third theme that calls us to respond to forced migrants is *prophetic justice.* Jesus not only re-legitimated those on the underside of his world and practised radical hospitality amongst them, he also confronted the powers which kept them marginalized and mistreated.

25 Carroll, *Christians at the Border*, 88.

26 Brendan Byrne, *The Hospitality of God: A Reading of Luke's Gospel* (Collegeville: Liturgical Press: 2000), 4.

27 Byrne, *Hospitality of God*, 4.

28 Bruce Malina, and Richard Rohrbough, *A Social Science Commentary on the Synoptic Gospels* (Minneapolis: Fortress, 1992), Kindle Location 2247.

29 Christine D. Pohl, *Making Room: Recovering Hospitality as a Christian Tradition* (Grand Rapids: Eerdmans, 1999), 8.

In the episode of the temple cleansing, Jesus confronted a system which was exploiting the poor, forcing people further into indebtedness and poverty. The temple was not only the religious centre of Israel, but also the political and economic centre. Loans were made to the poor with the predictable outcome that the poor fell into debt and lost their land.[30] Many, in the face of destitution, turned to social banditry — the very thing that Jesus accuses the temple elite of (Matt 21:13). The chief priests, he says, are "the real social bandits[!]"[31]

Jesus' confrontation of systemic injustice stands in the tradition of the prophets who called out the injustice of Israel's kings, even it cost them their lives, and it is a call that followers of Jesus must take on. "[M]ission among the poor", says Jayakumar Christian, "is a prophetic kingdom-based presence that critiques the world's understanding of power that keeps the poor powerless".[32] This is no more relevant than to migrant workers, refugees, and asylum seekers.

Toward Conclusions

This paper has not sought to find a solution to the massive problem of the world's migrant workers, refugees, and asylum seekers. Rather, to use Vanier's term, we have looked at signs — signs that God is already at work bringing hope where it is desperately needed. But we have also seen signs that the world is not as it should be — there are still huge challenges which face forced migrants and those who minister to them, both in transit countries and in places of resettlement.

We have looked, then, at ways in which we can move toward transformation in transit and resettlement countries, exploring ways in which organizations, individuals, and churches can be part of creating an ecology of welcome in which systemic change might more readily take place.

Finally, we began to explore why the church must seek to bring transformation for migrant workers, refugees, and asylum seekers. In re-legitimating the de-legitimated, sharing hospitality with the stranger, and practising prophetic justice in the face of systemic injustice, we not only help create change for some of the world's most vulnerable, but we also live out the good news of Jesus.

---

30   William R. II Herzog, *Jesus, Justice and the Reign of God: A Ministry of Liberation* (Louisville: Westminster John Knox, 2000), 137.

31   Herzog, *Jesus, Justice and the Reign of God*, 140.

32   Jayakumar Christian, *God of the Empty-Handed: Poverty, Power and the Kingdom of God*, Rev. ed. (Brunswick East: Acorn, 2011), 231.

References

Barker, Ashley. *Risky Compassion.* (Birmingham: Springdale College, 2014), Kindle Location 2418.

Birt, Jill. "Signs of Hope in the City." In *The Advocate* (Baptist Churches in Western Australia, August, 2014), 9.

Brueggemann, Walter. *The Prophetic Imagination* 2nd ed. (Minneapolis: Fortress, 2001).

Byrne, Brendan. *The Hospitality of God: A Reading of Luke's Gospel.* (Collegeville: Liturgical Press: 2000).

Carrol, Daniel. *Christians at the Border: Immigration, the Church and the Bible.* 2nd ed. (Grand Rapids: Brazos, 2013).

Christian, Jayakumar. *God of the Empty-Handed: Poverty, Power and the Kingdom of God.* Rev. ed. (Brunswick East: Acorn, 2011).

Herzog, William R. II. *Jesus, Justice and the Reign of God: A Ministry of Liberation.* (Louisville: Westminster John Knox, 2000).

Malina, Bruce, and Richard Rohrbough. *A Social Science Commentary on the Synoptic Gospels.* (Minneapolis: Fortress, 1992).

Myers, Ched, and Matthew Colwell. *Our God Is Undocumented: Biblical Faith and Immigrant Justice.* (Maryknoll: Orbis, 2012).

Myers, Ched. *Binding the Strongman: A Political Reading of Mark's Story of Jesus.* (Maryknoll: Orbis, 2008).

Pohl, Christine D. *Making Room: Recovering Hospitality as a Christian Tradition.* (Grand Rapids: Eerdmans, 1999).

Snyder, Susanna. *Asylum Seeking, Migration and Church.* (Surrey: Ashgate, 2012)..

The Ecology of Urban Mission

Howard A. Snyder

A chill winter's night has fallen as we walk out of the Hauptbahnhof, Cologne's central rail station along the Rhine. Entering the wintry plaza, we are awestruck by the massive, looming spires of Cologne Cathedral — black, white, grey, illuminated by hidden lights high on the spires.

The vision dominates everything. We and the crowds filling the square seem little crawling things.

I think of Jacques Ellul's words: "The city is man's greatest work" — the pinnacle of human technical achievement.

Technic city. In the case of Cologne Cathedral, the technology dates back to the 1200s. The technical breakthroughs — pointed arch, ribbed vaulting, flying buttress — birthed Gothic architecture. The technology was religious, theological: a monument to glorify God.

But of course the cathedral was also commercial (think relics, pilgrimages, fundraising), as well as political, social, and cultural.

In other words, there is an *ecology* to it all — the cathedral, the city. A river; people; birds and animals; pigeons and rats; air, food, plague, and pollution. All part of the story — and *best grasped ecologically.*

Cologne, one of Europe's oldest cities, became a Roman colony in the days of the first apostles. From early on the town had a Christian community. After the bones of the three wise men came to Cologne as relics, the town attracted thousands of pilgrims. Building a cathedral made increasing economic, ecclesiastical, and political sense.

My wife and I visited Cologne shortly before Christmas. We were fascinated by the cathedral, the Christmas markets, and the crowds. Then incidentally we discovered that the huge building next to our hotel was Gestapo headquarters from 1935 to 1945; it is now a museum. Displays on the rise of Nazism and basement cellblocks alerted me to other realities of urban ecology through space and time.

Urban Ecology

Ecology is in fact a concept in space and time. Ecosystems thrive in particular places and localities; they emerge and change constantly with time. This is true of the ecology of the city and also of urban mission. We can best grasp the challenges of urban mission, in fact, if we view it ecologically.

There is such a thing as an urban ecosystem. Like all ecosystems, it involves inputs, throughputs, and outputs, with complex interrelationships, and feedback loops.

This is true in a city's every dimension. It is true physically: material goods, fuel, food, waste, and the networks linking them. It is true socially, with the complex of urban social systems of all sorts. It is true economically, politically, technologically, culturally.

I learned this in the 1980s when I pastored and worked at Olive Branch Mission in Chicago. Teaching urban intern students from mostly non-urban campuses, I stressed three key points: (1) Chicago is a city of neighbourhoods; (2) each neighbourhood is unique; yet (3) each neighbourhood is enmeshed in a complex web of urban systems. You won't understand urban mission if you don't understand neighbourhoods, diverse as they are. And you won't understand neighbourhoods if you don't look *ecologically*, examining the complex interactions of people and systems, of physical and material things (water, roads, electricity, garbage); the whole range of life from microorganisms to dogs and cats to the flora and fauna of parklands.

Must then the urban missioner really understand all these things, be an expert in everything? No. That is impossible. It means this: effective urban mission requires an ecological mind-set, an ecological sensitivity, and, at a practical working level, ecological knowledge.

An Ecological Approach to Urban Mission

Every city is an ecosystem intimately linked with a vast array of larger and smaller ecosystems. And Christians know the key, essential secret: the urban ecosystem can truthfully be understood only spiritually, in light of the revealed gospel of Jesus Christ. What then is an ecological concept of urban mission? It is an approach to urban mission that makes the concept of ecology central to its every dimension so that mission can be as comprehensive as is the Christian gospel.

Formally, *ecology* is defined as the branch of science that deals with the relations of living things to one another and to their physical surroundings. This includes the study of human interaction with the environment in all its complexity. As a character in Barbara Kingsolver's novel *Flight Behaviour* comments, ecology means studying "biological communities. How populations interact. It does not mean recycling aluminium cans."[1]

Christians know that our human environment is more than just the physical world, or even the social-physical world. It includes all God has made — all things, visible and invisible, on earth and in heaven, as the Apostle Paul emphasizes (Col 1:16 and Eph 1:10, for example). The important biblical phrase "all things" opens a window into the ecological character of the biblical worldview and hence of all Christian mission.

What I mean, therefore, is that we must define Christian mission as comprehensively as the breadth and depth of the Christian gospel, and as deeply and broadly as the actual nature of the urban environment in all its dimensions — in its "all-things-ness". This is my key point.

Unless we thus think ecologically, we will forever be battling half-truths, lop-sidedness, and over-emphasis in some areas, and under-emphasis in others.

An ecological concept of urban mission has five key elements:

1. *Ecological sensitivity and awareness in considering every aspect and dimension of urban mission.* Ecology is a mind-set, a sensitivity — almost like an awareness of music. It's a lens — a way of seeing, as much caught as taught.

Ecological alertness means seeing *every aspect* of urban mission (no exceptions) through an ecological lens. One is forever asking: How does *this* relate to *that*? How does this action affect that situation, or those people, or that piece of urban landscape? It means knowing that every effect has multiple causes, and every cause births multiple effects — not all perceived or understood — and also multiple feedback loops.Effective urban mission requires thinking, planning, and acting ecologically.

1   Barbara Kingsolver, *Flight Behaviour* (New York, NY: HarperCollins, 2012), 324.

2. An ecological concept of urban mission means *recognizing the essential, critical role of spiritual realities in every urban ecosystem.* This is the sworn enemy of dualisms and compartmentalization. Nothing in the city is *not* spiritual, one way or another. Probably at some deep level every urbanite senses this, if not during the day, at least in wakeful night-time hours. The spirituality of the city stirs musicians and artists and poets.

Here enters the uniquely Christian contribution. Christians recognize not only the reality of the spirit; they know how to name the spirits. They know that the key reality is Jesus Christ made real to people by the Holy Spirit. Centred in this reality they know, or can learn, how to pull all other spiritual strands into proper perspective and relation to each other.

In other words, Christians are Christians. They dwell in the city not just with human resources, but with divine revelation. They proclaim and seek boldly to embody Jesus Christ in the city. Since they understand this revelation ecologically, they present not a one-dimensional gospel or church or mission, nor certainly a "spiritual" gospel that denies the reality and legitimate priorities of the "physical". They embody an ecological gospel that is as multidimensional and multidimensionally relevant, as is the living Jesus Christ, present now in the power of the Spirit.

Effective urban mission means Christians serving as channels of "the one thing needful", the reality of spiritual life and illumination that comes uniquely through Jesus Christ.

3. *An ecological approach to urban mission means recognizing the importance of physical, social, economic, and cultural dimensions in urban mission.*

Again, no dualisms. If Christians insist on the reality and priority of things spiritual, they also insist on the reality and proper role of things physical. This of course means things cultural in all dimensions, for culture begins with physical things — food, weather, water, the materials from which we build our homes, literature, and social spaces.

The unique Christian contribution involves the recognition of the constant flow between things spiritual and things material. An ecological concept of urban mission opens missional space to talk about and mess with politics, economics, poetry, technology, healthcare, water quality, building codes, orchestras, poverty, education, family life, gender relationships, and everything else. It is constantly saying: "This, and also that."

Effective urban mission means connecting the spirit to everything that is (or appears to be) non-spirit and recognizing the reality and priority of every physical dimension of God's good creation.

4. An ecological conception of urban mission means recognizing the essential role of face-to-face community.

Ecology is all about relationships. Ecosystems of living things are social communities. What then is human community? It is a kind of ecosystem embedded in other ecosystems. Human communities are biological communities. They are of course much more than this, so we resist reductionism. Any human community — family, neighbourhood, city, church — is much more than a biological community, but it is *not less than this.*

Human community exists at many levels. The ancient Greeks understood this; witness their various terms based on *oikos* (family or household), from *oikonomos* (household steward), to *oikonomia* (economy or plan of a household or city), to *oikomene* (the inhabited earth); hence our terms *economy* and *ecology.*

Christians stress face-to-face community for both sociological and theological reasons: sociologically because we recognize the social power of face-to-face community, and theologically because we believe humans are created uniquely in the image of God and profoundly reflect trinitarian truth. At heart these two reasons are one, for the very sociology of human beings is theologically based: our creation in the image of Holy Trinity.

An ecological concept of urban mission means recognizing the priority of face-to-face community because that's the way we are created and how we function: in community. Life in community may often be dysfunctional, but life without community becomes suicidal. We are social beings.

Effective urban mission requires attention to all kinds of community, but especially to face-to-face community, for this is most basic, and it is where identity is formed or malformed. This bears constant emphasis as the Internet and various forms of virtual community become ever present.

In an ecological conception of urban ministry, four forms of face-to-face community are most essential: family, neighbourhood, church, and small-scale communities such as clubs and civic organizations. These form the infrastructure of society and are key to its health or its dysfunction. Simply put, they are key to urban ecology, so they necessarily play a large role in effective urban mission.

Redemptive urban mission will engage a whole range of issues, no doubt, from the micro to the macro level — not only neighbourhoods but also systems and macrostructures. If not grounded in face-to-face community, however, mission will ultimately be ineffective and will burn out from lack of oxygen.

Face-to-face community is, humanly speaking, the life-source of effective urban mission.

5. An ecological conception of urban mission will be *based in a functional, biblical ecclesiology*. It will teach and embody expressions of the body of Christ that reflect New Testament teaching.

There are big debates about "biblical ecclesiology", of course. What I mean is fairly simple: a focus on the church as the visible community of Jesus followers in particular places. Despite variations reflecting different traditions, I find much consensus across the spectrum of Christianity as to the essentials of (at least) local Christian community.

My own take on this focuses on the three key elements of *worship, community,* and *witness* as the ecology of congregational life.[2]

Whatever the tradition, effective urban mission today will be grounded in local, living communities of *koinonia*, worship, and varieties of witness. Its shared life will be more organic than institutional; more relational than programmatic. But it will also find forms and structures that effectively build the church and help it engage the surrounding urban context.

Key here is a focus on the priesthood of believers, the gifts of the Spirit, and (accordingly) equipping believers for ministry, as taught especially in Ephesians 4:1–16. In my experience, without fail, urban churches that redemptively engage their world have figured out how to practise spiritual gifts and the ministry of all believers; how to practise the "one-another" teachings of the New Testament and to equip all believers for ministry even as they grow in grace.

Effective urban mission must be grounded in visible, redemptive Christian community.

How to embody the powerful gospel of Jesus Christ transformingly in cities today? The answer: Urban mission marked by (1) an ecological mind-set; (2) focus on spiritual realities; (3) attention also to physical and cultural realities; (4) face-to-face relationships; and (5) visible Christian community that resembles in its essence the body of Christ as pictured in the New Testament. Together, these five components

2   Howard A. Snyder, *The Community of the King*, Rev. ed. (Downers Grove, IL: IVP, 2004).

constitute the ecology of redemptive urban mission. These elements all function in ecological interconnection, with constant feedback loops.

Three Big Objections

This ecological approach to urban mission raises a raft of questions. Here are three:

1. *This is all too overwhelming.* If ecology necessarily involves *everything*, we drown in the totality of it all. It's too big to be practical. Don't we risk losing sharp focus by looking at everything? How do we keep balance, establish priorities, and keep fresh the gospel's transforming, redemptive edge?

Answer: We must see the big picture, and this is in fact the big picture. Theologically we can interpret it through biblical teachings, models, and metaphors. Particularly crucial are passages such as John 1, Ephesians 1, Colossians 1, and Hebrews 1. We start where those books start: with the big picture viewed in light of the large economy and ecology of God.

From the big picture, constantly reiterated, we move to the actual practice of Christian community. This is what Paul does in his letters. We take our cue from Ephesians 4:4–7:

> "*There is one body and one Spirit, just as you were called to the one hope of your calling, one Lord, one faith, one baptism, one God and Father of all, who is above all and through all and in all. [The big picture.] But each of us was given grace according to the measure of Christ's gift. [The particularization and application.]*"

This is how the ecology of urban mission works. It is what Paul does all the time. In Romans he begins with "the gospel of God, which he promised beforehand" (Rom 1:1–2) and ends with Priscilla and Aquila and their house church (Rom 16:3–4). We best find the particular and specific within the ecology of the big picture.

This is what Jesus did, showing the big picture (the kingdom of God) and bringing this home to specific people and needs and building community.

In the actual practice of Christian community, working with the fruit and gifts of the Spirit in local contexts and neighbourhoods, we learn how to strategize and determine priorities. The Spirit leads, joining the big picture to specific times, places, and persons. This is why I stress ecclesiology.

An ecological perspective helps us here. We find ourselves involved in a complex ecology of grace where we neither fully understand nor control everything. So we strive to be faithful and trust the Spirit to weave the particular into the larger ecology of his redemptive purposes within the complex ecology of our world.

2. *This approach requires major professional expertise.* Where can we find specialists in urban ecology in all its complexity? The necessary skills and knowledge are way beyond most churches, especially small or poor ones.

There are two answers to this objection, one which involves clarification and the other *networking*.

Clarification: An ecological concept of urban ministry does not mean people have to be academically trained in ecology. Ordinary people can develop practical, ecological sense. We learn, and learn to feel, that everything is tied to everything else both by immersing ourselves in Scripture and by paying attention to what we're increasingly learning about the world around us.

Networking: We need each other. Every church needs other churches, and may need specialized ministries that provide resources for particular challenges. Most cities, as well, are full of resources of various sorts. The key is networking on the basis of and out of the strength of local, living Christian community.

3. *Isn't this ecological approach pressing an analogy way too far?* Is it legitimate actually to take a concept from science and apply it to urban mission? Isn't this a mismatch of categories?

No. This approach makes sense for three reasons. First, the ecological sensitivity we learn from studying living systems helpfully illuminates urban life and ministry, both by way of analogy and in *actual fact*, since urban mission exists within and is part of the real ecology of cities.

Second, the Bible itself radiates an ecological sensitivity based in the very nature of creation and gospel. Modern ecological science actually appropriates realities already embedded in the biblical revelation. The Bible is ecological.

Third, bringing this biblical ecological sensitivity into conversation with today's ecological science births new insights. Ecology as applied to the church and ministry is more than metaphor. It illuminates realities long overlooked.

The smallest microorganisms and micro-ecosystems reveal dynamics that function on much larger scales. Ecological principles run all through God's magnificent creation.

To repeat: The city and urban mission are much more than ecological phenomena, but they are not less. We will understand both city and mission better, at more profound levels, as we view them ecologically.

The Ecology of the City

The city is an ecosystem interacting with multiple other ecosystems. This is the reality that underlies an ecological view of urban mission.

The City as Ecosystem. The city is an ecosystem physically, socially, culturally. But Christians know, as Jacques Ellul discerned, that the city is also a spiritual reality. Better: It is a spiritual ecosystem. It is the locus of principalities and powers of all sorts. Its dynamics are affected by prayer, by worship, by Christian community, and by multiple forms of Christian witness. Its life is shaped as much by spiritual things as by physical things — probably more.

This is fact, not theory. The city is a complex interplay between its physicality and its spirituality. This is what makes the church of Jesus Christ unique. As the body of Christ, the church knows the secret. "We wrestle" in multiple dimensions. And the church's impact — redemptively or not — flows in all these directions, follows all these paths and byways. The church's impact is both physical and spiritual, with the two in constant interaction — as we know personally, with our own body-spirit struggles. So urban mission necessarily touches everything, including how we do or do not care for creation.

The city, in other words, is inescapably and necessarily part of the non-urban environment. City and non-city depend upon each other for their very existence. You can't have Chicago without downstate Illinois and Lake Michigan, or Singapore without oceans. They are all part of one ecology. The literal, watery connection between Lake Michigan and earth's oceans reminds us that every urban ecosystem is connected with the global ecosystem.

The City and the Land. Today much of the world is rapidly urbanizing. Usually urbanization is treated, however, as though it were only a matter of cities.

But urbanization is always only half the story. The other story, of equal ultimate importance, concerns the land — the land that remains and does not move to the city. People move to cities and leave the land behind, but they do not leave their dependence upon the land. Yet, as people move to cities, they lose ancient wisdom about the land.

Urban ecology therefore must include the land and its wisdom. Therefore, urban mission, viewed ecologically, will include the land in its scope.

Our grandparents or great-grandparents understood much about the land. Most knew how to farm, of course. But, equally important, they knew about birds, plants, animals, the flow of rivers, the changing of seasons, the stars, and the cycles of nature. They knew about medicinal plants. They knew how to grow food, and the fresh tang of fruits and vegetables straight from the garden rather than those manufactured in factories.

This is no longer the case for city dwellers the world over. Yet we know — both theologically and increasingly scientifically — that human flourishing requires living in contact with the land, with nature, with the created order. It's built into us as part of God's plan.

Without this bond with the land and its creatures we suffer what Richard Louv calls "nature-deficit disorder". Human development, and especially childhood development, is hampered by lack of unstructured interface with the world of nature.[3]

If we speak of urbanization we must speak also of the land, and what has been lost in the move to the cities. In the study and practice of urban mission, we must heed the land as well as the city. We learn that our cities depend for their very existence on land — both the land they occupy and often pollute, and the land that supplies their food and water.

This doesn't mean Christians should move out of cities and into rural areas. What must happen rather is the recovery of ancient wisdom about the land, and thus the recovery of a harmony between land and people. We must come to understand the real, actual ecology of our relationship with the beautiful but vulnerable created order (urban and non-urban) that God has given us.

This has big meanings for urban mission. No person, and no church, is healthy without healthy interaction with the land. No mission is holistic if it does not include the biblical, covenantal relationship with the land and all God's creatures (Gen 9). No city can be healthy and sustainable over time if it does not learn to live in sustainable harmony with the land.

Here is a call for creativity. It raises issues of urban farming, co-operatives, community markets, trees and flowers, artwork, and poetry. It presents the challenge of getting city people out to the country from time to time and country people into the cities.

"Center Church": The Gospel in New York

New York City has been the scene of much effective urban mission over centuries.

---

3   Richard Louv, *Last Child in the Woods: Saving Our Children from Nature-Deficit Disorder* (North Carolina: Algonquin, 2008).

Some of America's earliest and most creative city ministries began there. In its great complexity, New York to this day offers varied examples of redemptive urban mission, ranging from creative church multiplication to specialized ministries of many sorts.

One of the most creative and comprehensive is Redeemer Presbyterian Church in Manhattan, led by senior pastor Timothy Keller. Founded in 1989 without a building, the Redeemer Church has grown rapidly. Today it attracts some 5,000 people to multiple services at three different sites, though much of its emphasis is on discipleship and church multiplication. Its conception of discipleship is serious but broad, for the church aims "to renew the city socially, spiritually, and culturally". Redeemer has helped plant over a hundred other congregations throughout the metropolitan area.

In his book *Center Church: Doing Balanced, Gospel-Centered Ministry in Your City*, Keller sets out a strategy for reaching cities multidimensionally, using ecological models. Keller outlines a vision embodying three core commitments: gospel-centred, city-centred, and movement-centred. He understands this vision ecologically.

Keller argues that cities can be transformed when a tipping point is reached — "when the number of gospel-shaped Christians in a city becomes so large that Christian influence on the civic and social life of the city — and on the very culture — is recognizable and acknowledged". Keller writes,

> There is no scientific way to precisely determine a city's tipping point — the point at which the gospel begins to have a visible impact on the city life and culture. In New York City, we pray for and work toward the time when 10 percent of the centre city population is involved in a gospel-centered church. In Manhattan, this would amount to about 100,000 people.[4]

Keller's proposals breathe the spirit of gospel optimism — based not on human ingenuity, but in the power of God working through Christians who are savvy both about the gospel and about urban dynamics.

There is nothing unrealistic or outlandish about this vision. The gospel is powerful enough. Where sin abounds, grace can visibly abound yet more.

Keller's vision and proposals are worth considering, particularly in light of Redeemer Church's impact and given Keller's sensitivity to the dynamic of movements and of ecological realities. The book is a good resource in developing an ecological conception of urban mission.

Keller's approach is limited in some respects: people from other theological

4   Timothy J. Keller, *Center Church: Doing Balanced, Gospel-Centered Ministry in Your City* (Grand Rapids, MI: Zondervan, 2012), 376.

traditions may not be comfortable with aspects of the church's conservative Reformed perspective. Keller's emphasis on the ecology of church, city, and movements, however, acknowledges the complexity of urban mission and the fact that God works through various church forms and traditions.

I celebrate Keller's ecological approach, but would press it further. Keller uses the concept of ecology only analogically. "Likening a gospel city movement to a biological ecosystem is an analogy", he writes. The church and gospel ministry are different from "a biological ecosystem". Yet he notes that "the image of the ecosystem conveys how different organisms are interdependent, how the flourishing of one group helps the other groups flourish".[5]

True, but we can push the ecological paradigm further, beyond analogy. Effective urban mission requires that we break through to a real ecological awareness of church, city, and mission.

Much of the dynamic of Viv Grigg's prophetic ministry among the world's urban poor, highlighted in his article "Hovering Spirit, Creative Voice, Empowered Transformation: A Retrospective", in the first issue of the *New Urban World* journal, springs from his large-scale ecological sensitivity and models. Though Grigg does not generally use the term *ecology* in the sense I mean here, his ministry in its comprehensiveness can best be understood by viewing it through an ecological lens.

Conclusion: Ecology of the Church in Mission

Urban mission is more comprehensive and effective the more it's viewed ecologically. Just as the city is an ecosystem so in another sense the church (the body of Christ) is an ecosystem — globally and locally. How the two interact defines the shape of mission.

Christians without ecological awareness miss key dimensions of mission just as surely as secular ecologists miss key dimensions of the spirit. As ecology is more than metaphor, so the body of Christ is more than metaphor. The church is an organism that partakes of the mystery of the very body of Jesus Christ and the mystery of the Trinity — and as such, is called into mission.

5   Ibid., 378.

References

Keller, Timothy J. *Center Church: Doing Balanced, Gospel-Centered Ministry in Your City*. Grand Rapids, MI: Zondervan, 2012.

Kingsolver, Barbara. *Flight Behaviour*. New York, NY: HarperCollins, 2012.

Louv, Richard. *Last Child in the Woods: Saving Our Children from Nature-Deficit Disorder*. North Carolina: Algonquin, 2008.

Snyder, Howard A. *The Community of the King*. Rev. ed. Downers Grove, IL: IVP, 2004.

Global Urbanization and Integral Mission

René Padilla

The astonishing growth of cities all over the world is a contemporary fact that does not need to be proved. Megacities, especially in the Majority World, are multiplying at an amazing rate, quite often without an adequate infrastructure to satisfy the basic human needs of the growing population, such as clean water, food, housing, healthcare, education, and work. According to experts on this subject, most of the world's population a century ago lived in rural areas, while at present more than half live in overcrowded cities. At the beginning of the nineteenth century, there was no city with more than one million inhabitants; in 1945 there were already 30; in 1955 there were 60; and in 2005 there were 336.

No attempt can here be made to explain the reasons for this phenomenon. There is no doubt, however, that one of the main contributing factors for rural people to feel attracted to the city is their hope that the urban setting will enable them to improve their standard of living. Some of them will make it, but sadly, a large percentage of them will sooner or later find out that their dream has turned into a nightmare. My attempt in this chapter is, in the first place, to explore the reasons for this disappointing experience of a growing number of city immigrants and, in the second place, to reflect on the challenge that their situation poses to the church and the Christian response to it.

The City as Institutionalized Apartheid

One of the most memorable conversations I have ever had with peasants was one I had a few years ago in Yalalag, State of Oaxaca, Mexico. Most of them were middle-aged and had children who had migrated first to Mexico City and then to the United States looking for work. The parents were left behind with the idea that they would join their children as soon as work was secured. When I asked them what was going on, they told me their sad story — no longer could they make a living in the rural area because big agribusinesses from the United States were importing into Mexico thousands of tons of corn produced with state subsidy and sold at a much lower price than the price of the corn locally produced. As a result, the peasants were losing their lands, and not only their land, but also the young people who would have inherited it.

The dumping of subsidized corn from the United States into Mexico (a country that lives mainly on corn!) is only one of the many factors that force peasants to leave their homeland and to migrate to the cities where they will most likely become slum dwellers. Another important factor is that technology has displaced thousands of workers from the fields by making them redundant in regards to sowing and harvesting. A small percentage of the peasants migrating to the cities may be able to find a regular job as employees or become agents of an informal economy outside the slum. Many of them, however, in order to survive, will see no other option than to set their eyes on migrating to the United States, or join a gang involved in the trafficking of persons or drugs, in prostitution or delinquency. Conditions in the slums are hardly liveable. And yet, out of a population of over 115 million in Mexico, about 60 percent living in the metropolitan areas dwell in slums, while only 30 percent live in middleclass residential areas and the remaining 10 percent are members of the wealthy minority class whose lifestyle fully reflects the consumer society.

Mexico is a paradigm of today's urban world — a world of institutionalized apartheid with masses of slum dwellers who can barely cover their basic needs, on the one hand, and a small elite minority who enjoy the deceptive benefits that globalization offers to the transnational class, on the other hand.

The Challenge of the City, to the Church, and the Christian Response

If there is one place where the power of the gospel is put to the test today, that place is the city. To be sure, the reality of sin can be perceived everywhere in the world —

in the rural areas as well as in the cities; in the deserts like Sahara or Patagonia as well as in the great metropolises like Buenos Aires, Tokyo, New York, or Bombay. The fact remains, however, that at least in the modern world the city is the most vivid expression of both human inventiveness and idolatry. The urbanization of the world is not merely a question of the demographic expansion of cities all over the world. It is also a question of a mind-set that dominates the modern world and that may be described as the "consumer mentality" — the mind-set of the consumer society marked by the predominant role given to money, sex, and power.

The mass media is used to condition people to a lifestyle in which they work to (1) make money, (2) make money to buy things, and (3) buy things to find value for themselves.

The powerful industry of advertising is controlled by people whose interests are aligned with a constant increase in production, and production in turn depends upon a level of consumption made possible only in a society that believes that to live is to possess. All of life is therefore organized as a function of production and consumption. The city gradually presses people into a materialistic mould, a mould that gives absolute value to things as status symbols and leaves no time for them to reflect on questions regarding the importance of interpersonal relationships, the meaning of work, or the purpose of life. Sad to say, the consumer mentality is not restricted to people who have the financial resources to constantly update the gadgets that industry offers them, but all too often it blindfolds the eyes of the poor to such an extent that they may get into debt to buy a television set instead of using their scarce resources to provide proper nourishment to their children.

The consumer society is the shape that the world, dominated by the powers of destruction, has taken today. This is the world hostile to God and enslaved to the powers of darkness. Nowhere else than in the city under the dominion of consumerism can one see so clearly that "the whole world is under the control of the evil one" (1 John 5:19).

If the power of the gospel is to be manifest in the city today, it has to be proclaimed by a church that does not only speak about but also lives out God's love in Jesus Christ. A large number of Christians have totally misunderstood the gospel. They have assumed that all that God requires from them is that they leave time in their busy schedule to give their dues to him and to secure for themselves inner peace in the present and life beyond death in the future. Much of the practice of Christianity that we see around us is a Christianity that has been accommodated to the consumer society. In a market of "free consumers" of religion, in which the church has no possibility of holding a monopoly on religion, this Christianity has resorted to making it attractive by reducing its message to a minimum in order to make people *want* to become Christians. The gospel thus becomes a type of merchandise, the acquisition of which guarantees to the consumer the highest values — success in life and personal happiness now and forever. The cross has lost its offense: it simply points to Jesus Christ's death as a sacrifice for our sin but it does not present his call to whole-life discipleship. This kind of gospel has nothing to say to people imprisoned by the consumer society and even less to people who suffer the injustices of an economic system characterized by institutionalized apartheid that keeps the well-to-do people separated from the poor.

Churches with this kind of gospel need not take the inner city and the slums seriously — they may as well take flight into the middle- and high-class suburbs, where they can cater to the private religious needs of their members. In a world that is increasingly urbanized, we Christians cannot avoid asking ourselves what it is that God demands from us as urban followers of Jesus Christ, who cried over the city of Jerusalem. We all must seriously consider the possibility that God may be calling us to serve him in the inner city or even in a slum. We cannot take for granted that we can simply be satisfied with giving the Lord a few hours a week and one-tenth of our salary, and then feel free to choose the location for our home and our job according to our own convenience. The greatest challenge that the city poses to the church of Jesus Christ today is the challenge to live out the gospel of the kingdom of life, peace, and justice as a witness to people who are living in a situation of injustice, poverty, and oppression. And there is no proper response to that challenge apart from Christians who are willing to take up their cross and follow Jesus Christ by identifying themselves with the victims of the institutionalized apartheid that prevails in the cities.

According to the Gospels, when Jesus called prospective disciples like Peter, James, and John to follow him, he did not call them to a life of ease and economic security. On the contrary, in unmistakable terms he laid down the conditions for the kind of discipleship he expected from his followers: "Whoever comes to me and does not hate[1] father and mother, wife and children, brothers and sisters, yes, and even life itself, cannot be my disciple. Whoever does not carry the cross and follow me cannot be my disciple... none of you can become my disciple if you do not give up all your

1   The hyperbolic use of hate here is a Semitic way of forcefully expressing that the love for Jesus he expects from his followers is far superior to the family love that was commonly expected in contemporary Jewish society.

possessions" (Luke 14:26–27, 33). By no means does Jesus' call imply that God expects every Christian today to literally give up all his or her possessions and live among the poor. According to New Testament teaching, there is room in the Christian community for "those who in the present age are rich", who are called "not to be haughty, or to set their hope on the uncertainties of riches, but rather on God who richly provides us with everything for our enjoyment. They are to do good, they are to be rich in good works, generous, and ready to share, thus storing up for themselves the treasure of a good foundation for the future, so that they take hold of the life that really is life" (1 Tim 6:17–19).

There are, however, at least two reasons why no person who takes Christian discipleship seriously should simply assume that he or she is exempt from Jesus' call to renounce all earthly possessions in a literal way for the sake of the gospel. The first reason is that Christians are people who know "the generous act of our Lord Jesus Christ, who though he was rich, yet for [their] sakes he became poor, so that by his poverty [they] might become rich" (2 Cor 8:9). Jesus' generous act sets the pattern for the communication of the gospel throughout the history of the church and in today's world, deeply affected by poverty. The second reason is that the most effective way to communicate the gospel to the poor is the incarnational way — integral mission, which includes living it, acting it, and saying it.

The last few decades provide wonderful illustrations of the Christian response to the challenge that the city poses to the church in an urban setting. Let me give you three outstanding examples.

Viv Grigg

One cannot deal with this subject without recognizing the decisive influence that Viv Grigg from New Zealand and Servants Among the Poor have had in the formation of the Urban Leadership Foundation, a global network of missions and religious orders — the Encarnação Alliance — focused on the urban poor.[2] By living in the slums of Manila, he found a new understanding of Jesus' basic motivation and passion for knowing God, and that understanding led him to write the first draft of *The Lifestyle and Values*, which defines the core values of the missions in the network, whose *first and central purpose* is following Christ in terms of sacrifice and service in the slums of the great cities of the world. This involves the closest possible identification with the poor in their lifestyle, language, and culture through non-destitute poverty, recognizing the

2   On Viv Grigg's pilgrimage, see Viv Grigg, *Cry of the Urban Poor* (Georgia: Authentic Media, 2005).

need of housing, food, clothing, tools, and so on, but with an attitude of freedom from possessions, and a willingness to share what one owns with others; inner simplicity expressed in a simple lifestyle based on the renunciation of earthly possessions.

God did not allow Grigg to stay in the slums of Manila, however. God had "a broader vision" than his, and that vision included the writing of *Companion to the Poor,* with the purpose of articulating an evangelical theology on living and working incarnationally among the poor and mobilizing the church in New Zealand for that purpose.[3] The result was the formation of *Servants to Asia's Urban Poor.*

After the first purpose of following Christ came *the second purpose: knowing Christ through loving the poor,* according to the Franciscan perspective, and *recognizing that righteousness implies social justice,* according to the Old Testament perspective. The result was lifestyle commitments and spiritual disciplines for the sake of knowing Christ, such as the following: obedience and devotion; simplicity of possessions and renunciation of wealth (Lk 14:33); incarnation and service among the poor of the slums (Matt 25:34–40); preaching the gospel to the poor (Luke 4:18); seeking justice for the poor (Jer 22:16); and commitment to community.

The third purpose was establishing multiplying indigenous fellowships with shared emphases: evangelism and disciple-making; service to the urban poor; the power of the Holy Spirit; and peace-making, justice, and development.

Grigg claims that God kept speaking to him through visions, moving him to walk through other cities and to intercede for them. God's call was changed from reaching the poor to transforming the cities, including not only the poor but also those causing their poverty. He began walking the streets of other cities and decided to write *Cry of the Urban Poor.* He now saw Jesus as loving the whole world and dedicated himself to developing a broader mission, beyond New Zealand, through the formation of teams that follow *The Lifestyle and Values* and practise participatory decision-making and fellowship of commitment. Recognizing that there are people who love the poor but for some reason are not able to live among the poor, he accepted the Franciscan model of a dual-level missionary order and structured Servants Among the Poor as a religious order with vows of non-destitute poverty that would send North Americans.

The aim for each country is to walk with Jesus and speak his Word, and eventually, as the Word produces life, to form a board and appoint a leader. The setting up of new missions, however, is not sufficient. The effort is therefore made to encourage

---

3   Viv Grigg, *Companion to the Poor* (Monrovia, CA: MARC, 1990). The first edition of this book was published in 1984 in Australia by Albatross Books and in Britain by Lion Publishing. The Spanish translation was published in 1994 in Buenos Aires by Nueva Creacion under the title Siervos entre los pobres.

mission leaders to organize alternative orders within their missions for the work among the poor. Several missions have accepted the challenge. According to Grigg, however, the main focus for accomplishing the missionary task among the poor must not be on Western missions but on Majority World missions serving as the catalysts of indigenous ministries. Urban Leadership Foundation is therefore committed to building and mobilizing networks among existing missions and churches for the sake of the witness to the gospel among the poor.

John Perkins

Another example of integral mission among the poor is the ministry of Black American John Perkins, which he started with his wife Vera Mae as early as 1960 with *The Voice of Calvary* in Mendenhall, Mississippi. He has extended to many places, especially in the United States, through the John M. Perkins Foundation and the Christian Community Development Association (CCDA, formed in 1989). At a time when the large majority of evangelical Christians assumed that the mission of the church could be defined exclusively in terms of evangelism as the oral communication of the gospel and the planting of churches, John's ground-breaking writings were of great encouragement and inspiration to Christians (including me) who were looking for a more holistic and biblical view of the Christian mission.[4] He synthesizes his missionary strategy for the church to respond to urban poverty in three words, "the three Rs", as he calls them: relocation, reconciliation, and redistribution.

Relocation: Faithfulness to the gospel implies the same kind of special concern for the poor that characterized Jesus Christ's ministry. He is our model, and his followers are called to reproduce his incarnation by identifying themselves with the weak, the afflicted, and the oppressed. Only by doing that — from within the situation of the poor — will they be able to feel the needs of the poor, understand the true causes of poverty, and find ways to help.

Reconciliation: Poverty is oftentimes closely related to racism and ethnocentrism. As a black man he suffered mistreatment and violence on the part of white

4   On John Perkins's background as a boy who grew up in utter poverty, and his own story of how he initiated and, under God, was able to develop *The Voice of Calvary*, see John Perkins, *With Justice for All* (Venture, CA: Regal, 1982). This book provides the author's strategy to implement his missiology previously presented in John Perkins, *Let Justice Roll Down* (Venture, CA: Regal, 2006). Translated into Spanish and published in Buenos Aires by Nueva Creacion in 1988, *Justicia para todos* has been very useful in planting the seed of integral mission all over Latin America.

people, including the police. That is the price that black people have to pay to live in a southern state of the United States. As a human being, he was inclined to respond to hate with hate, but God dealt with him and he understood that the whites are victims of their own racism and that both black and white need to be liberated from racial hatred through the gospel of reconciliation. The gospel of reconciliation became an integral part of *The Voice of Calvary*.

Redistribution: There is plenty of food in the world for every person to be properly fed, and yet there are hundreds of millions of hungry people around the world. The root problem is not lack of food but inequity in the distribution of it. This lack of equity affects not only the distribution of food but all aspects of social life. What is urgently needed, therefore, is a redistribution of resources based on the recognition, on the part of the rich, that what they have does not belong to them — that they are called to be stewards responsible before God, who is a God of justice, to share their resources, not just their goods but also their knowledge, skills, and technology with the poor. Furthermore, they need to recognize that the poor are imprisoned by the oppressive economic system that originally caused their poverty, and that the way to break the oppression is by creating free enterprises organized as cooperatives, not for the enrichment of a few but for the common good.

Christian and Christine Schneider

A much more recent example of the Christian response to the challenge posed by the city is the ministry that Christian Schneider, a primary school teacher from Basel, Switzerland, started in the slums of Manila in 1988, a few years before he married Christine, a nurse, also from Basel.[5] An outstanding feature of their account of their ministry is the openness with which they describe their reactions to what they see or experience. To illustrate this point, here is a quotable snapshot:

> "The North American missionary group was an impressive discovery. Most of the 40 foreign colleagues lived in complete American luxury in the heavily guarded areas of the city. The work in the streets, in the prisons, and the nursing homes was performed by 160 Filipinos.... The Filipino helpers were poverty stricken although educated, which one could recognize by their

5   Cf. Christian and Christine Schneider, *Rubble and Redemption: Finding Life in the Slums of Manila* (Carlisle: Coimbrta, 2002).

English language skills. They took me with them in their visits to the prisons, to the youthful gangs and street children, and to the red-light districts, where they ran a tea room at night. What I experienced there shocked me to my depths. Need existed in Basel and London too, but Manila was in a different league. Children and entire families literally lived in the streets, in the dirt. For the first time I encountered people who were forced to suffer real hunger and humiliation, who were ignored by society, or who were maltreated as underpaid workers and were forced to fight for their right to life on a daily basis. I saw child labour, beggars, and prostitution. Earlier, I seemed to have suppressed that there were people who actually physically suffered from hunger. That didn't fit in my theology. This encounter with the poor almost cost me my belief in a merciful God."[6]

During their time living with the poor, the Schneiders make themselves available to fill the gap whenever and wherever a gap appears and they are able to fill it, be it by building a therapeutic community for the rehabilitation of drug addicts, or for street children, or for prostitutes. By doing so they show that God is love and that he has a special concern for the poor.

One of the values of the Schneiders' presentation is its emphasis on the personal relationships that they maintain with a wide variety of poor people that they know by name and that they learn to love and respect. Not all the people that they try to help are able to break away from the vicious circle of poverty that they find themselves in, oftentimes without having anyone else to blame other than themselves. By the time the Schneiders return to their home country after over nine years in Manila, however, they can rejoice that the seeds they planted continue to bear fruit. Back in Switzerland, they continue to support Onésimo, the service organization that they formed and that is now under local leadership.

Conclusion

The brief review of ministries that are responding from a Christian perspective to the dehumanizing challenge that the city poses to the church shows the importance of taking as a starting point a full recognition of God's special concern for the poor, in the first place, and of allowing that recognition to be expressed in terms of a lifestyle that reflects the same concern, in the second place. For the sake of authenticity in a large urban world where hundreds of millions of people are unable to cover their

6   Ibid., 16.

basic human needs, the Christian witness cannot and must not be reduced to words — it has to be incarnational, in line with God's justice and compassion. It has to be integral mission.

References

Grigg, Viv. *Companion to the Poor*. Monrovia, CA: MARC, 1990.

———. *Cry of the Urban Poor*. Georgia: Authentic Media, 2005.

Perkins, John. *With Justice for All*. Venture, CA: Regal, 1982.

———. *Let Justice Roll Down*. Venture, CA: Regal, 2006.

Schneider, Christian and Christine. *Rubble and Redemption: Finding Life in the Slums of Manila*. Carlisle: Coimbrta, 2002.

Hovering Spirit, Creative Voice, Empowered Transformation: A Retrospective[1]

Viv Grigg

> Now the earth was formless and empty, darkness was over the surface of the deep, and the Spirit of
> God was hovering over the surface of the waters… and God said… and it was so.
> — *The first transformation, Genesis 1:2–3, 7.*

Over 35 years ago, as an emaciated university graduate-cum-missionary, I recall the breath of God's Spirit infiltrating a slum, then slums, then cities of slums, and bringing transformation. In those carefree days of youth, through a few of us, the breath began as the preached word. People were changed in Spirit-filled worship. I remember the days of healing and the deaconesses roaming and serving. I recall God's life-giving breath through young graduate professionals learning about economic development and transforming the slums. I remember friends who were defending the oppressed and the first churches that were forming in Manila's slums in the late 1970s.

That Voice and Spirit of creation continues crying out, creating order in the chaotic pain of today's megacities, through individuals, and through a new wineskin. And the Voice perhaps calls you to be filled with that Spirit and to become that voice in the world's desperate places.

1   This chapter was first published in Scott A. Bessenecker (ed.). *Living Mission: The Vision and Voices of New Friars*. Downers Grove, IL: IVP, 2010. It is republished here by permission from IVP.

A great chaos has embraced the earth as the wealthy have legalized rights to the earth's lands. They have excluded a few billion to be landless and to migrate into that chaotic in-between known as *slums* — a reality between the orderliness of peasant and tribal community and the order of the urban corporate existence. It is a state of uncertain dispossession. In the last decade, one billion people, many with chickens under their feet, have careened in overloaded buses from the rural areas to the new megacities. They are setting up illegal shacks wherever they can find space. China alone is creating one thousand new cities this decade because of this migration. This rapid urbanization has progressed much faster than industrialization; thus, most of the migrant slum dwellers live without civic infrastructure and remain underemployed or unemployed. This has created an environment of disorganization and moral and cultural disintegration.

Over time, these new urban poor find footholds in the city, and gradually these slums regularize into thriving communities — if governments find a way of legalizing them, that is. Mostly they continue as places of ongoing alcoholism, violence, and crime. Twenty-five years after their formation come waves of street children, and behind them waves of gangs, and HIV/AIDS-infected individuals.

It is for these responsive, dispossessed, and oppressed poor that Jesus came to preach the good news. It is among them that he lived. It seems we should follow his command and do the same. He calls us to *mission*: wherever the gospel mission goes, people are set free from sin, and poverty begins to change as new economic communities form. When missional churches among the poor grow, injustices are addressed and communities are transformed. The good news brings justice.[2]

The Voice Calling, Birthing: The 1980s

One day in 1980, when I was in my little slum house in Tatalon, Manila, the same Voice of mission called, as clearly as the voice of a child: "Go up the river and preach". And like Philip, I went wandering, preaching, casting out demons — I had never done that before! — and caring for a drug addict. I went, seeing what God would do next.

And again one day, a Voice over coffee as I looked out my squatter window at the higgledy-piggledy panoply of galvanized iron beneath: "Go, disciple the elites at the University of the Philippines. They will change the poverty". I refused at first, for I was called to the poor, you see. But eventually I went, and invited the elites to enjoy the hospitality of the poor. Years later, I have seen hundreds of works transforming poverty,

2   Isa 42:1–4.

transforming structures — many from the hands of these highly educated disciples.

Yet again, in the quiet of a squatter hut during the hours of siesta prayer, I heard the Voice; this time from reading the history of missions, for God's Voice is heard in history. I could see pictures of bands of men and women, wandering Franciscan preachers. The pictures became the basis of a document for an order, *The Lifestyle and Values of Servants*, and within it, a priority for proclamation and mobility to evangelize among the poor.

As the sun beat its 100-degree heat onto the iron roof of that squatter home in 1980, I meditated on the life of St Francis Xavier, apostle to the poor of India, and the life of St Francis of Assisi. It was then that the Spirit revealed to me the centrality of incarnation, communal decision-making, apostolic mobility, and suffering with the poor.

Devastated by sickness and failure to combat demonic attacks, I waited on God in a forest back in New Zealand. The quiet Voice spoke to call the church to the poor, to write the vision down. As I wandered on a 125cc motorbike, I found a church in national revival, waiting to obey. *Companion to the Poor*, prayed into being by seventy intercessors as I wrote, touched many. Servants to Asia's Urban Poor exploded into life as a network of communities living in the slums and catalysing indigenous church movements. Other missions followed in the United States and then Brazil, each through hearing God's subtle nudges.

History's Echoing Voice

I was surprised by the sound of a confirming Voice a few years later in 1985, as I sat under Paul Pierson's teaching at Fuller Seminary when he taught on the history of the Celtic and Catholic orders. From this experience I wrote two seminal papers that Pierson used with other students. Around that time the creative artist John Hayes was also captivated by the scholarship of Paul Pierson, and he pioneered InnerCHANGE. Movements begin with creative women and men like John, who hear the Voice and, with foolish abandonment, seek to translate word into action. They are followed by dedicated fanatics who figure out how to turn the new vision and new wineskin into reality. Capable administrators then harmonize and standardize the vision and the wineskin.

An order is a network of committed communities with common values, direction, and accountability between leaders. An apostolic order clearly sees the mandate Jesus gave to the apostles to go and preach. Ralph Winter was right in his 1976 analysis of structural similarities between the mobile Protestant missions and the mobile Catholic orders. But as I mused upon the question of why Protestants were not in the slums, I realized Winter had missed some central elements. At their core, the Catholic orders are distinctly different from Protestant missions. People enter Catholic communities to find God through engagement with the poor, intercession, proclamation, community, and the pursuit of spiritual wisdom. It is from these that their work springs. Mother Teresa's sisters pray six hours and work five hours. Protestants, by contrast, enter mission "teams", not communities, and then they "work" or found "works" as if they were starting a business.

While living in the slums and wondering why Protestants had failed among the poor, I realized that we must first establish caring communities, not work teams, for the human costs are high. And we must primarily become seekers of God instead of founders of works, for work will not sustain us through the traumas of incarnation. We formed Servants as a movement with aims of seeking God through rapid proclamation among the poor and multiplication of indigenous movements of churches based on a lifestyle of incarnation, community, simplicity, suffering, and sacrifice.

The Voice, Intercession and Indigenous Urban Poor Missions: The 1990s

In response to prayer in 1988, while I was living in a *favela* in Brazil, God touched a gracious apostolic leader, Pastor Waldemar Carvalho, and Kairos was formed. Kairos is a Brazilian mission community, multiplying works and denominations in a dozen cities. There was little talk about values and orders but Kairos closely matched the narrowly focused nature of the early Wesleyan circuit preachers, who emulated the early Franciscan preachers, who in turn had learned from the preaching Lollards.

We dreamed together of Latin Americans in the slums of Kolkata. I believe Kairos was the first truly indigenous Brazilian mission community, and it is now one of the biggest, calling people from the slums to the slums and not dependent on the West. Each worker lives on about three hundred dollars per month, in community houses so they can pool their money. They suffer greatly as they pioneer slum churches. Kairos established a denomination with a Bible school in Lima, Peru, then in Mexico, and then in Africa and China. They started a new denomination in Bangladesh and established soccer clubs (what else would Brazilians do?) for street kids in Kolkata.

The apostolic workers of Kairos come from both Pentecostal and mainline churches, balancing the power of the Spirit and of intellectualism, as middle-class people and poor people serving together. In the West we would call them communities, but to

Brazilians this is just normal extended family dynamics. "What is all this talk about community as a value?" Brazilians ask; for them, it is simply how one does life.

For ten years I sojourned in and out of Kolkata with my new Brazilian wife, spending three or six months at a time preparing the ground for the coming of Kairos there. Our workers experienced a struggle so grotesque that few of those who have become part of the vision can talk of it. It is a city in which only intercessors survive, in which every worker is damaged by the evil one. It is a story in which workers lost their hearing and their emotional health, in which demonic attacks were so devious that they beg for a description, and in which only intense prayer moved officials to place a stamp in a passport. The struggle over those years resulted in the first church in the Kolkata slums, and then fifteen cell groups. These were planted through the work of a simple Bengali disciple and his wife, a healer.

I share some of these instances of pain and hardship to say that our call, in these next decades before the King returns, must be to these most difficult cities. And transformation will not come without intercessory communities entering these cities first. The preaching orders of the twelfth to sixteenth centuries were often partners with an intercessory order of women. We need to see equivalent twenty-first-century orders of intercessors connected to these workers among the poor; in Kolkata we urged every worker to garner seven hundred intercessors just to survive spiritually.

I began to multiply storytelling consultations of slum pastors in cities. I knew from my teen years reading missions history that real apostolic speed is not going to happen predominantly with Western workers, although without them/us, many who are needed to catalyse movements to the poor would be missing. Apostolic speed will happen with indigenous leaders, many of them born and raised in the slums and leading bands of men and women into other slums.

Roy, for instance, was from Nagaland, a state of India that had experienced revival but that for decades has been brutalized by the Indian army. He was a pastor of a three-thousand member church. Touched by this call to live among the poor, he left his position to pursue life among the poor and discovered migrant workers living in a quarry. Roy began a small church, then five churches. Within a year, he had begun training 20 missionaries from Nagaland for the slums of India, forming a new mission for justice. Incarnation, or living with the people we serve, is a critical sign. Evangelizing and establishing churches is a critical focus. Working together with our poor friends to find solutions to the economic and social needs is an essential aspect of pastoral care. Roy devoted himself to these things.

Some of his workers joined a couple in Kolkata to learn how to train women in tailoring. This couple did not preach but, in a most beautiful way, kept on loving and helping until the women asked them about their Lord. Soon the whole group of women tailors from the slums was starting every day with worship and Bible study. When they graduated from training in dressmaking, they set up their own businesses that employed others. Thus economic discipleship continued to multiply hand-in-hand with spiritual transformation. This is inherent in true spirituality.

In the 25 years since writing about socio-economic-spiritual discipleship in *Companion to the Poor*, I have walked with hundreds of slum pastor friends as we have kept expanding ways of implementing these kingdom economic principles. Discipleship is our response to the King and his kingdom. Economic discipleship involves those parts of our lives related to the material world, our living out of what we have come to teach as ten economic discipleship principles: human dignity; creativity; productivity; cooperative economics; work and rest; detachment and simplicity; redistribution for equality; management, savings, and debt; celebration and land ownership.

Some of the missional practices that indigenous workers develop are markedly different from those of minority-world apostolic orders moving into the slums (who are mostly wealthy, middle-class, educated people). The emergent, majority-world missions that rise from among the poor don't, for instance, like the word *order*, and they would never use the word *friar*. My task of bringing unity has often involved bridging incarnational works like Kairos, which are being stirred up from among the poor, with those incarnational works emerging from the West.

Generally, churches come first, becoming economic communities. Sometimes kingdom economics comes first and then leads to gospel proclamation and to church planting. This is illustrated in the work of a dynamic business professor in Manila, who started five thousand microenterprise projects among the poor. One day, when challenged that her ministry was not holistic because the gospel was not being presented, she shifted and set out to establish five thousand Bible studies, out of which have come three hundred churches. The kingdom is spiritual and economic, and in the eyes of our majority-world brothers and sisters living and working among the poor, the kingdom cannot come without the multiplication of churches. Western incarnational workers tend to talk more of mission as justice, because poverty immediately forces us to deal with our wealth. Wealthy people talk of programs and projects, which require money.

Postmodern Learning Networks: Multiplying Voice in the Millennial Decade

In the early 2000s we gathered leaders of both Western and non-Western incarnational movements and orders into the *Encarnação Alliance of Urban Poor Movement Leaders*. At our gathering in Bangkok in 2004, God spoke through a prophet of the need for 50,000 workers from the slums to the slums. All said "Amen!" So this became a goal that we would strive for, with God's help. As part of this we developed training modules on CDs and have been multiplying this curriculum city by city through "city learning networks". This has resulted in many hundreds of new churches.

One day after the Bangkok gathering, I prayed and heard the Voice again: "Go to Africa", it said. "I will provide. Go, find a cluster of pastors in the slums and train them." I asked God to show me someone under the radar. Then, while searching online for references to revival, I noticed an obscure website about a slum pastor's library. As I read the words on the site, I was overwhelmed by the presence of the Spirit. Here was a pastor in the slums, seeking to train others with a library! What days of sweet fellowship I was soon enjoying with slum pastors of Uganda. How intense the debate between them as to whether kingdom economics was from God. From that time together, a network of missional Ugandan slum pastors emerged. They have formed three new denominations in three countries. AIDS victims have been cared for, and small microenterprise projects have begun.

Recently, when I was back in my home country of New Zealand, the Voice spoke again. This time it said: "Go train in India. I will provide." An email from India came the next day, asking for training. Out of that venture one hundred pastors were trained, and God has indeed provided, multiplying that first training experience ten times over. Slum pastors are now being trained in ten different Indian cities (and as I write, another series in another city is happening). Many new churches have been planted, lepers have been reached, widows have been cared for, gypsies and orphans have been loved, and women have been trained in sewing.

"He will guide you into all truth."[3] That guidance can take decades to bring to fruition. In 1975, while meeting with my first community in a park in Manila, I saw, as clearly as one sees a cloud in a still sky, that movements among the poor would not eventuate without the training of movement leaders at a master's degree level. It wasn't until 30 years later that the *Encarnação Training Commission* has shared a wonderful sense of unity around this vision of master's level training. As a result, an MA in

3   John 16:13.

Transformational Urban Leadership has been developed and is being delivered in five schools. Eight others are exploring it. Colin Smith moved a whole Bible school into the slums of Nairobi, for instance, and developed a similar bachelor's level training program.

The Millennial Future: Empowerment of the Cross and Resurrection

So here is the call: to ferment movements of the Spirit created through four phases of empowerment. First there is the *dunamis* of the preached word of God (which is the power of the gospel according to Romans 1:16); then the liberating life of the Spirit, which comes through conversion; then the growth of God-communities of faith expressed in social, spiritual, economic, political, and environmental discipleship. These three lead to a fourth phase of broader cultural engagement and transformation: derivative works, such as community organizations, development projects, urban planning, and health programs, which are all initiated by and infused with the Holy Spirit. Many more people are needed to walk alongside slum leaders — first to learn and then to facilitate, according to one's gifts, the various aspects of these four empowerments.

Lest you put on rose-tinted glasses, remember that along with these great blessings, we must be prepared to live with great pain, daily carrying in our bodies the real cost of the cross. There is daily sickness. There can be hidden costs for children of workers among the poor who are always on the move; at times they become traumatized teenagers. There are unknown costs to some of our spouses as well, who may complain very little but inwardly struggle with the immense pressures of homelessness, chaos, and deep loneliness. There is grief at the loss of workers — a brother pulls back from a critical work when his health fails; a demonic attack proves too much for another; and all of us are tripped up by hidden sins. It would be more graphic to tell you the actual stories, but I can't, since some of these involve living people.

The Spirit, Humility, and Greater Works

Preaching friars? Apostolic orders? These are my reflections on more than 35 years of Spirit-freedom, apostolic mobility, and transformation. Despite our frailties and through many failures, as bands of brothers and sisters among the poor, we have now seen these orders multiply to hundreds of workers, and indigenous movements multiply to many thousands. The daughter works are reaching hundreds of thousands.

Whatever God does endures forever; nothing can be added to it or taken from it.[4] God is the source, and God will determine the ending point of a given new mission or a new wineskin. God alone is to be praised!

I invite you to come and catch the wind! *Come: dance* and run with us as we speed the message of the cross. You may not be perfect, you may not be brilliantly gifted, you may not know what God would do through you, but his voice will lead you, his presence will be with you, and the joy of your children walking in truth will sustain you. *Come, walk* with us as we follow Jesus, the Voice.

4   Eccl 3:14.

The Role of the Local Church in Urban Transformation: Mobilizing Members and Engaging Powers

Kimberly Drage, Pham Thu Huong, Bruce Edwards, and Jacob Bloemberg

How This Chapter Came into Being

This chapter is a combined effort to collect and synthesize the thoughts and reflections of the 2014 International Society for Urban Mission Summit working group: The Role of the Local Church in Urban Transformation. During our time together as a working group, we reflected on questions such as: What is urban transformation? What biblical and theological themes should inform our view of urban transformation and the role of the local church in it? When and where have we experienced the role of local churches at their best working in urban transformation? In addition, our group was able to participate in four different exposure trips to see ways in which the local church in Kuala Lumpur is engaging urban transformation. On our last day, each of us wrote down 3–5 key ideas that stood out to us from our experiences and discussion, and started categorizing them as a group. These key ideas became the core content of this chapter.

We could feel the enthusiasm of our working group grow throughout the time we shared. We grew in hopefulness and in seeing possibilities for our own places of worship and cities as we explored this topic together. It is our prayer that you will be similarly encouraged as you read this chapter.

Introduction

What would our cities look like, if we started praying for them like this?

> *Father, hallowed be your name.*
>
> *Your kingdom come.*
>
> *Give us each day our daily bread.*
>
> *And forgive us our sins for we ourselves forgive everyone indebted to us.*
>
> *And do not bring us to the time of trial.*
>
> *Luke 11:2–4*

Father, be glorified, HERE in this city. Father, your kingdom come, HERE in this city. Father, provide for us, all of us, HERE in this city. Father, empower us to be reconcilers, all of us, HERE in this city. Father, protect us, all of us, HERE in this city… And, who will pray this, but the church, HERE in this city?

1. Defining Urban Transformation

The things we imagine as we pray the Lord's Prayer for our cities are a good starting place for thinking about urban transformation. We see a city under the rule and reign of God, a city where all people's basic needs are met, a city where people are living in peace with each other, a city where people are safe. This is a big vision, yet it is not a new vision.

Throughout the biblical narrative, we encounter the Hebrew concept of *shalom*, God's holistic peace. This concept of peace is not limited to an absence of conflict, but the "opportunity for human flourishing".[1] As the prophet Zechariah writes:

> *A Message from God-of-the-Angel-Armies: "Old men and old women will come back to Jerusalem, sit on benches on the streets and spin tales, move around*

---

1   H. Spees, "Christ Centered Civic Renewal: A 21st Century Movement for Spiritual and Social Renewal of Cities," in *Conference Paper Presented at 2014 ISUM Conference, Signs of Hope in the City* (Kuala Lumpur: International Society for Urban Mission, 2014).

safely with their canes — a good city to grow old in. And boys and girls will fill
the public parks, laughing and playing — a good city to grow up in.[2]

In God's vision for Jerusalem, the two most vulnerable groups in the community, the elderly and the children, could grow up and grow old in freedom and safety.

Shalom means healthy families, affordable housing, and work that dignifies. Shalom means sustainable use of the earth's resources and cultivating God's good provision for all. Shalom reaches beyond building up incomes to building up people, cultivating respect, and restoring the identities of all of us as beloved children of God, with special care for those on the margins. Shalom in the city is "when the whole city works for everybody, all the time, and nobody is left out".[3] Urban transformation is seeking God's shalom for our cities.

2. Defining Local Church

This vision of urban transformation is a gift from God. The hope of resurrection, bringing life where death once reigned, is a gift from God. It is the work of the people of God to partner with God in bringing these gifts to the places they live.

The prophet Jeremiah urges the people of God in exile to "seek the peace [shalom] of the city" (Jeremiah 29). If the city flourishes, so will they. If the city flourishes, they will see the fulfilment of their calling. God's people have always been blessed to be a blessing to the nations (Genesis 12). The same is true for the church today. The blessings of God to the church empower us to be agents of transformation here on the earth.

Before we begin exploring the role of the local church in urban transformation, it is important to define what we mean by local church. Is our definition based on geography? Is it based on nationality? Do expat Christians in a certain location play a role? For the purposes of our discussion, we concluded that two expressions of the local church help us think about the role of the church: 1) The congregation and 2) The body of Christ in the city. These distinct expressions of the local church have different strengths as we look to God and seek how we can be a part of transforming our cities.

2   Zechariah 8:4–5, *The Message.*

3   Spees, "Christ Centered Civic Renewal: A 21st Century Movement for Spiritual and Social Renewal of Cities."

The Congregation

When we think of a local church, we often think first of individual congregations. These are communities of Christians gathered for worship, discipleship, and shared life in Christ. Individual congregations are essential to urban transformation. It is here that God's people bow before God together, seeking him, his will, and his vision as his people in community. It is in this context that the people of God are "blessed". It is here that the people of God are built up in what it means to live under the rule and reign of God. It is here that the people of God are built up in what it means to be God's children. It is here that the people of God are compelled, by God's love, to go out and love the people and engage the brokenness around them.

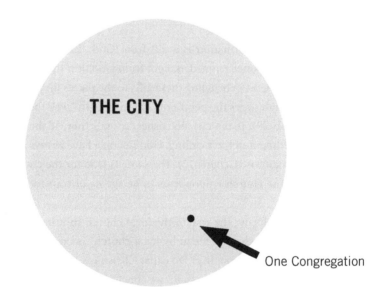

THE CITY

One Congregation

The Body of Christ in the City

At the same time, when we think about urban transformation, we are challenged to think about the local church more broadly. In the book *To Transform a City*, Eric Swanson and Sam Williams challenge the whole church to take the whole gospel to the whole city. From this vantage point, we see the local church as the body of Christ in the city and suddenly, bringing transformation to the entire city seems more possible. We need each other to walk out the calling God has given us.

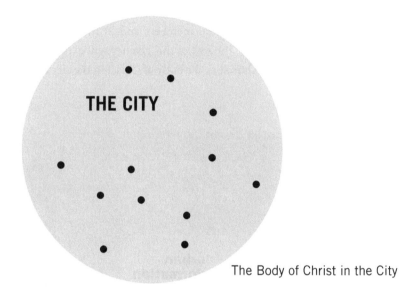

The Body of Christ in the City

Pursuing urban transformation as the body of Christ is not just about broader influence and increased manpower (people-power), it is also about momentum. One woman in our group shared how seeing herself as a part of the body of Christ in her city changed her response to a challenging situation:

> "As I was walking up to a grocery store, I witnessed a man hitting a three-year-old boy with a newspaper. I was on my way to meet a friend for coffee, but something stopped me. I thought of the movement of believers in my city for urban transformation and I was empowered to say to myself, 'this is our city and the responsibility for that little boy in this moment is ours'. So, I stepped in. Jesus entrusted the body of Christ in Hanoi with that moment and we took it."

3. Mobilizing Members and Engaging Powers

Clearly, the church has a key role to play in urban transformation. We are God's people, blessed to be a blessing, called to hope, to pray, and to act on behalf of our cities. So, where do we begin?

Throughout our discussions, our group identified two main ways the church could act: 1) through mobilizing individual members and 2) by engaging powers both within and outside the church. The rest of this chapter will explore how individual congregations and the local church as the body of Christ in the city can do these two things.

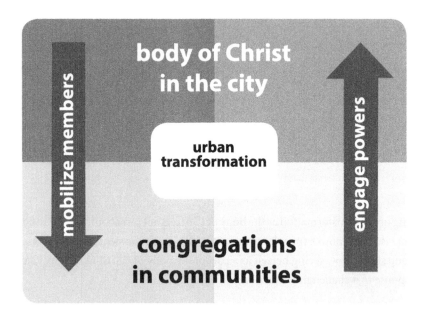

Section 1: Mobilizing Members

John Perkins reminded us during the Summit: "God was in Christ, reconciling the world to himself". God wants to bring transformation, to individual lives, yes, but not only that. Transformation of communities is an integral part of the transformation God makes possible through Christ, and he invites his church to partner with him in this redemptive work.

This is an incredible privilege, yet so many do not take up the invitation. In fact, often, Christians are the ones missing in action. Sheryl Haw of Micah Challenge shared with the Working Group about extending an invitation for those who wanted to be part of city transformation to gather. Forty people showed up. All were all non-believers!

So how do we engage and mobilize members of local congregations, and the body of Christ in the city to be agents of urban transformation?

1. The Congregation Mobilizing Its Members

One key place is in our local congregations — those who gather week in and week out to worship in community. How a congregation relates to its city and how a congregation understands and pursues urban transformation will have a tremendous impact on mobilizing its members for urban transformation.

Mobilizing Leaders with a Vision for Urban Transformation

Leaders with a vision for urban transformation are key. Not all will follow the leaders, but even fewer will embrace their calling if Christian leaders are not actively setting the way.

[Note: Often, experimental activity, started with the hope of bringing transformation, begins at the margins of the church. A small group of believers with vision for change organizes themselves and begins taking action. These grass-roots movements are a form of leadership. When those appointed and/or recognized as leaders fail to lead, God will raise up people to "lead from below". There is need for more recognition of this kind of leadership.]

When appointed leaders in local congregations own the calling to partner with God in his redemptive work of transforming their communities, the potential to generate momentum and mobilize members across the church to participate is increased.

It is therefore critical that we nurture the development of local church leaders through training which shapes a missionally integrated understanding of life and faith. There is a need for investment by those responsible for both formal, institutional theological training, and informal "on-the-job" Christian leadership training (e.g., workshops, mentoring) in reviewing and reframing such training. Whether it is seminaries or seminars, a vital shift must take place, reflecting deeper understanding of the whole scope of the gospel and its implications for the church and its leaders.

Mobilizing Leaders with Leadership Models that Empower

Part of this shift involves moving from holding and managing power to releasing authority to members of the congregation. Pastoral leadership that lacks trust in the congregation, and does not want to share power, or is not ready to empower members is a challenge facing the church in many places. Reclaiming "the priesthood of all believers" (1 Peter 2:5) includes both re-engaging "lay" people who may have abdicated their responsibility to the "professional clergy", and helping those leaders, who perhaps enjoy the prestige and power which has evolved with their position, to relinquish worldly perspectives on power and authority, and embrace the way of Christ.

Jayakumar Christian spoke extensively about power according to God's rule and reign and we recommend further reading of his material, and accessing his summit sessions, as there is not space to do justice to his significant reflections here.

Leaders must also model what they are inviting their congregations to join them in. If we, the redeemed ones, are not, in our own lives, families, and churches, living in a way that reflects the restoration Christ makes possible, we cannot be agents of transformation in our cities. Leaders bear particular responsibility for modelling this in ways congregation members can follow.

Mobilizing Members of the Congregation through Healed Theology/Identity

Like their leaders, congregation members are often deeply entrenched in an understanding of mission and transformation that emphasizes personal salvation, for the afterlife, through belief in an established set of propositional truths about God. The task of proclaiming those truths in a way that is convincing to the unsaved is seen as the responsibility of evangelists. This often results in people contributing money (or not!), and perhaps attending prayer meetings before designated outreach events; yet failing to see themselves as people God wants to use to bring new life and hope to their community.

The way we frame Christian discipleship therefore needs to include a journey toward a healed theology; a "street theology" in which all followers of Jesus come to recognize that everyone is a missionary, with leaders as facilitators. Such reframing also needs to challenge the notion that doing good works is an optional extra for gaining more "brownie points" or even earning the way into the kingdom.

These types of messages are not shared simply by telling congregation members that this is the case. Members need to be taken on a journey of discovery, facilitated by leaders already on it. Teaching from the pulpit, small group Bible studies, simple, accessible immersion opportunities, testimonies, and even new songs can play a part in shifting people's thinking to an understanding of Christian mission which integrates "proclamation" and "demonstration" of a gospel which is truly good news to the world.

The Arts have a valuable role to play in communicating the theological truths that need to be reclaimed and lived out anew in the church. Our working group spoke particularly about the songs we sing, and the way many of them reinforce dualistic thinking.

Too often, we have separated spirituality out and given it its own box, but Jayakumar Christian noted that: "The spiritual undergirds all; it is not a category of its own". When congregation members understand that it is not just our "faith" that is spiritual, and that "faithfulness" is a lived-out expression of that truth, they can be inspired to move beyond "volunteering" to understanding themselves as "a people called" to reflect the good news across every aspect of life.

This also reframes the way we think about and practise prayer. Rather than being a separate activity, it becomes an integral part of the way we, as individual believers and congregations, partner with God in seeking the shalom of the city.

Congregations are made up of busy individuals with many commitments. The diagram above, which helps individual congregations realize they are not alone, also fits for individual believers, helping them to see that when we are in it together, we do not have to do it all. Coming to understand integrated mission as part of an integrated life also helps people discover that many of the things they already do (e.g., sharing meals with friends, helping neighbours with chores, coaching your kid's sports team) simply need to be seen through different eyes and engaged with a sense of kingdom purpose — rather than feeling like they have to sign up for extra activities in order to fulfil their calling.

A Vision for Local Congregations Mobilizing Members

Case Story: Kuala Lumpur, Malaysia

The Opportunity

Student volunteers from [a church] started helping with an underground school for refugee children. Refugees in this area must hide away because they are illegal and, if they are discovered, they may be put in jail. As these students began helping, they realized these kids had needs much greater than just academic education.

The Solution

These student volunteers were given support through AYA, Asian Youth in Action, to begin their own student-led NGO called Refuge for the Refugees (RFTR). Through their efforts RFTR, partnering with AYA, was able to reach out and show the children at this refugee school that there is a God who loves them and cares for their every need. AYA and RFTR mobilized members primarily from this church to start coming to help at the refugee school. Every Saturday morning, church members run personal development programs through faith-based activities such as worship, games, Bible study, arts and crafts, as well as providing food.

The Result

The church, in cooperation with AYA, has raised up two young committed Christian leaders and empowered them to start and maintain an NGO serving this community of refugee children and families. Not only have these two students been mobilized, but they are working to continue mobilizing others from their church to get involved. As far as the kids go, there have been many improvements for them. They are no longer shy and timid but rather, they are affectionate, outspoken, and confident. They have also made significant improvement in their grades and their ability to focus at school.

Case Story: Kuala Lumpur, Malaysia

The Opportunity

In one neighbourhood in Kuala Lumpur, a local church has taken on the rising challenge of young men and boys of Indian descent being drawn into the murky underworld of extortion and stand-over gangsterism.

It began when the pastor of the church and his son Nathanael, one of the ISUM Summit attendees, were waiting to be served in a local Chinese business. A slightly built boy of about 16 came into the shop and demanded of the shopkeeper: "Where's this month's money?"

They recognized a protection racket being played out. It was almost laughable, someone little more than a child issuing the threatening demand — but the menacing and dangerous reality was that there were several older and much more dangerous characters behind the threat.

The pastor stepped in and sent the youth on his way with a threat to call the police. The young man left issuing threats of his own.

Boredom after school. lack of activities, limited options in terms of employment, parents who don't just hand out ready cash for the latest phone or runners, and the promise of easy money, make the young men easy prey for the gangs to lure into their web.

Acts of violence — one local woman had her fingers severed just to get hold of her jewellery — are worn as badges of pride, with no sense of guilt or remorse.

The Action

Nathanael and his father were in two minds. With family connections to several of the youth getting caught up in gangs they wanted to do something constructive to counter the growing and destructive menace; but they knew very well the dangers of engaging and challenging the powers of darkness at work in the community also.

With prayer, courage, and the support of the congregation in which they minister, they began to provide after school activities including *futsal*, badminton, and occasional outings. Plans are also underway for the development of a media centre/cyber-café as a safe place to hang out.

At the same time, they began visiting families of at-risk youth and local businesses, hoping to connect young men to real employment opportunities.

The Result

It is slow going, but one local youth has been connected with a job, and is excited about the future. There is more that could be done, lessons are still being learned; but the hope of a real alternative — new life — is being held out in the name of Christ to lost young men in this community in an encouraging example of one local church recognizing a need and responding; a local church embracing its calling to community transformation, and getting on with it.

2. The Body of Christ in the City Mobilizing Its Members

Just as we recognize that our action toward urban transformation is a part of something bigger than ourselves that started with the resurrection, we recognize, too, that it is bigger than the local congregation. So, how can the church of the city mobilize its members? What is written above applies by extension here; however, there are also additional realities to address.

Mobilizing Members by Walking Together in Our Calling as the Body of Christ

Building trust and respect among members of the body of Christ for a shared and compelling purpose is key. Denominational and theological differences need to be identified and acknowledged. Again leadership is key in helping people develop a broader perspective and larger vision for the body of Christ, and in helping bring ordinary people together with a sense that they can make a difference as a part of a movement to bring God's kingdom to the city.

Local church leaders learning to put ego, and micro-kingdom mentalities, aside and coming together to build citywide networks; meeting together regularly for prayer and mutual encouragement; learning and growing together; sharing findings and ideas; and casting vision together will all shape and nurture the vision they seek to bring and keep alive in their local churches.

A united network of Christian leaders, recognized as genuinely seeking the shalom of the city, can develop a relationship of mutual respect with local civic and business leaders, enabling them to influence decision-making in these areas for the benefit of all. This is reflected on further below in the "Engaging the Powers" section.

Mobilizing Members through Christian NGOs

In some places, due to political and religious resistance to Christian faith, it is difficult for a local church to engage directly in community transformation work under its own name. The body of Christ in the city can, however, foster an integrated response among church members through the development of an umbrella NGO. Such organizations can provide vision, raise awareness, access resources, train and equip church members, and provide legitimate oversight for the church to be the expression of the holistic mission of Jesus.

A Vision for the Body of Christ Mobilizing Members

Case Story: Hanoi, Vietnam

The Problem

In the 2000s, the local churches in northern Vietnam mainly focused on "spiritual missions" (meaning evangelism and teaching of the word) among their church members and therefore missed the opportunities to reach out to the communities outside of the church. Meanwhile, the Vietnamese government restricted NGOs to relief and development (social action) only and they were not allowed to share the truth.

The Action

Four different International Christian NGOs (INGOs) decided to support the formation of a group of local Christian leaders who could impart the vision of holistic and sustainable ministry within the church. These INGOs supported the group by allowing employees who wanted to join the group to use office time to participate in the activities of the group. This is their mission statement: We are a group of Christian development workers who are committed to support Northern churches through training and modelling so that the church can reach out by sharing their own resources to transform the community.

The Result

After more than 12 years, this group of active and engaged Christian leaders continues carrying out their mission. They are regularly involved in mobilizing the church in northern Vietnam so that the church can carry out transformational development. They are passionate about supporting and equipping the church as the impact centre for expanding the kingdom of God in communities through spiritual, physical, mental, and social transformation.

Section 2: Engaging Powers

When we speak of engaging powers we are talking about something that is multifaceted. We recognize that on this earth there are powers of darkness that are at work. The word of God describes Satan and the prince of the power of the air (Eph 2:2). As the body of Christ, we recognize that the enemy is at work in our cities. We as the body of Christ must stand firm against the principalities and powers if we want to see our cities transformed for the glory of God. We must live and stand for justice as the church who is brining light into the dark city.

Additionally, when we speak of powers we understand that there are influencers within the city who need to catch the vision of urban renewal and transformation if we are going to see God work in the city. This can be divided into three groups. First, we think of the corporate sector or the business community, or ".com" Secondly, we need to engage the non-profit or non-governmental sector, or ".org". Thirdly, the government, or ".gov", has strong power with great influence in the city. The church should consider engaging people in all three of these sectors, .com, .gov, and .org. These are the powers that we must engage as the local body of Christ to see transformation.

1. The Congregation Engaging Powers

Engaging the Powers that Stand against Urban Transformation through Prayer

When we speak about engaging the principalities and powers, we understand that this is spiritual warfare. There is a darkness that we know is taking place in the world today. This darkness has blinded the minds of the unbelievers (2 Cor 4:4). They don't know the truth of God and don't desire to live according to the truths of God. Those living in darkness don't want to come into the light. So, we know that without the supernatural intervention of God we will not see spiritual transformation within the city. There is something greater at work than us. There is a spiritual battle. When Dr Jayakumar Christian talks about urban transformation he says, "confronting poverty and establishing the rule and reign of God are uprooting and upsetting the god-complexes — this is spiritual warfare".

Therefore, if we are going to see our cities changed we know that it is going to require us as the body of Christ standing together in prayer. Pastors and spiritual leaders within the city must gather in prayer, specifically pray that the kingdom of God would be established on earth, and pray specifically for the powers of darkness to be exposed and brought down.

Engaging and Understanding the Power within Our Congregation

God has granted great power to his church. We are his body and he has called us to bring his kingdom here on earth. The body of Christ has many members and each of us is uniquely gifted. We must help those in our congregation to know and understand what their gifts are in the congregation and how each person uniquely fits into this plan of urban transformation. We must understand this idea of giftedness in a much broader sense. It is essential to help our members understand that God has gifted them in their secular jobs and skills. If someone in the church is a businessperson or an educator, God has given them these skills to be used for his glory. They can transform their workplace for the glory of Christ. God has given each church member assets to walk out our calling as agents of healing, justice, and transformation in the job or skills that he has called us to.

The church has often engaged in gifts assessments, but has limited those assessments to spiritual gifts to be used for individual purposes or for service in the church. When we think about urban transformation, we have an opportunity to think of gifts in the church more broadly. The work of the ministry exists both inside and outside our church. No longer should we operate in a false dichotomy of sacred and secular but we should be the church wherever we are. We don't go to church, we are the church. Being present and aware as God's people increases our readiness and availability to be a part of God's work of transformation wherever we are and whatever we are doing.

Engaging the Power of People and Institutions Who Can Support Urban Transformation

Within our congregations today we have many people who are naturally influencers in the community (e.g., people who are working in .com, .gov., and .org positions). As local congregations recognize members and their influence within different sectors of society, they can begin to engage them with a vision to be a part of transforming our cities, speaking for justice, and ushering in the kingdom of God.

At the same time, congregations don't need to limit themselves to members only when it comes to urban transformation. God has placed people strategically in different positions in our cities who are willing to collaborate with the church in urban transformation. In some cases, there may even be government funding available to help us bring about the urban transformation we are seeking. Rene August, in her address at the Summit, noted that the biggest threat to the machinery of oppression in South Africa came from poets and musicians. Perhaps part of "finding and releasing the beauty in our cities" will be congregations creating, or collaborating with existing, art co-ops to give space for the articulation of the hopes and dreams of people. Congregations can also support local efforts such as community gardens and neighbourhood clean-up days in partnership with local councils, businesses, and community groups. Cultivating openness toward secular organizations and governments in seeking the welfare of our cities increases both our influence and our witness.

A Vision for the Congregation Engaging Powers

Case Story: Johannesburg, South Africa

The Opportunity

At a conference in South Africa, Ian McKellar preached a message on "Kingdom Strategy and the Marketplace". Taking the example of Priscilla and Aquila in the book of Acts, he asserted that marketplace people were vital to the kingdom strategy of going into all nations and "making disciples" as Jesus commanded.

Priscilla and Aquila were not apostles or pastors but businesspersons. They helped the apostle Paul plant new churches in the cities of Corinth, Ephesus, and Rome. (See

Acts 18:1–3 and 19; 1 Corinthians 16:8 and 19; Romans 16:3–5 and 2 Timothy 4:19). As well they hosted church meetings in their own home.

Paul also had Erastus, the city *oikonomos* (director of public works, or steward, or treasurer)in his team (See Acts 19:22 and Romans 16:23). He had Zenas the lawyer (Titus 3:13) and Luke the doctor (Colossians 4:14) as fellow-workers on his team. In this way, they had an informal team made up of influential people from the marketplace, government, and social organizations.

Someone has said that if you want to rule the world you need to bring together influential people from dot-com, dot-gov and dot-org. Indeed, these three groups have the combined power, authority, and motivation to solve the big problems facing our cities and nations.

The Action

Craig Elliot, the pastor of Junction Church, then called for a morning breakfast with people of influence from the marketplace, government, and NGOs and schools.

They met in a round-table forum much like the Clapham Sect (who were a great inspiration to us all). The Clapham Sect was the group of Christians who were behind William Wilberforce while he was campaigning for the abolition of slavery. And interestingly enough they had businesspeople, members of Parliament, and church leaders and philanthropists in their informal team.

Craig asked each of the twelve or so present to share their vision for the kingdom to come through their life and sphere of influence. He then facilitated connections between individuals to make these godly dreams come true.

The Result

The people in Junction Church have had God's grace to help bless the nation in many amazing ways. They have worked behind the scenes to influence law making, education, and social problems. They have amazing plans to help solve the housing problems and to reduce unemployment and poverty. They have networked entrepreneurs and reformers to create new business that can solve social problems.

The saints in the marketplace are making a difference because they have been mobilized and connected. They have been given a vision and a theology for the kingdom of God that enables them to believe that the kingdom can come through the church (i.e., the individual believers) in a greater measure in their city today.

2. The Body of Christ in the City Engaging Powers

Engaging the Power to Dream Bigger Together

A big problem in many of our cities around the world is that Christian leaders have too small a vision. Many of them are thinking about how to grow their own church and their own ministries. When we start engaging a vision for urban transformation, however, we find the invitation and the call to dream bigger — to dream for our city, for our nation, for the world! From this posture, believers can begin asking this question: "What could we do together that we couldn't possibly do on our own?"

Coming together with other church leaders and members in the city is essential to achieving transformation. We must come together with the purpose of dreaming together for how we can change our cities and our nations. Together we must attempt things that we cannot do on our own and through this cooperation, we can see God move in mighty ways throughout our cities.

Engaging the Powers that Keep Us Apart

We know that from the inception of the church that Jesus prayed that we would be one as the Father and he are one (John 17:21). Jesus understood that if the body of Christ is one and unified there will be great power in our midst. Jesus is sitting at the right hand of the Father making intercession for us and this is still what he is praying for us. He is praying that we would be unified.

The church must acknowledge that we are all on the same team. We have one head and his name is Jesus Christ (Col 1:18). We have one shared calling and that is to be the hands and feet of Jesus. Therefore, we must act in way to decrease competition and increase collaboration. It may be that we need to set aside some of the non-essential differences that we have and come together for the shared task of seeing our cities transformed.

What often happens when churches and organizations work together is the more prominent or larger organization will try to take control of the project. We must not play the power game. We must see each of our individual congregations as fitting into the larger body of Christ within the city. This will happen only when together we learn how to adopt a shared vision and act upon this vision together.

The denominational structures which exist between churches are a huge challenge to collaboration. There are often histories between different denominations which are unhealthy. As a result of old wounds there can be disunity and mistrust of other churches. There may also be some personal differences and challenges between key leaders in the city and as a result, they aren't willing to come together. We must recognize that not everyone is going to be willing to come together. As a result, we engage those who are willing to work together for God's kingdom and bring those people together. What often happens is that those who were hesitant in the beginning will get on board because they see the strength and results of collaboration. Leaders seem to be drawn to visions which are greater than them as well. If we can cast a large vision to them that they can see as having impact and benefit to their individual contexts then they will be more likely to adopt the vision.

Engaging the Power and Influence We Have within the Body of Christ

When we start to see the church as the body of Christ in a place, we start to see the many resources we have. As mentioned earlier, many people in our churches are in positions of influence within the community. In one church, there might be people in two or three sectors of society, but as the body of Christ, we are likely present already in all the sectors of society (political, economic, technological, legal, environmental). As we coordinate our efforts and capacities, we can make significant movements toward urban transformation together. Suddenly our dreams seem more possible to realize.

On the flip side, when we fail to collaborate, we run the risk of duplicating efforts. When we do things in isolation we may take on activities that others are already engaged in as opposed to multiplying our efforts by working together. There is a tendency for us to want to "own" our work, get "territorial" about our efforts, and protect the acknowledgement we feel we are owed for a job well done. Laying these temptations aside is key to partnership and truly moving toward shalom for our cities. As Jayakumar Christian noted, "shared power is multiplied power".

Engaging the Powers that Stand against Urban Transformation Together

Another way the body of Christ can function in moving our cities toward the shalom God has for them is through advocacy and taking moral stands on issues. One congregation crying out is a small voice compared to the diversity and numbers of many congregations crying out on a particular issue together. A unified, yet diverse, voice is able to get the attention of city leaders and inspire action at a policy level. A coordinated stand on an issue can also generate more support at a grass-roots level, leading to long-term, sustainable change within the community. Together, the body of Christ can have a powerful and active voice in the public sphere.

A Vision for the Body of Christ Engaging Powers

Case Story: Hanoi, Vietnam

The Challenge

Some years ago, I read the story of a citywide effort by pastors in Boulder, Colorado. After much prayer, the Lord gave them two simple words: "Love Boulder".[4] This radical idea to unconditionally love the city and its people without any hidden agendas was revolutionary. The pastors went to see the mayor and asked, "How can we help you?" and, when presented with the mayor's long list of needs, they went ahead and did it!

Reading this in faraway Hanoi, the capital city of Vietnam, I thought to myself: "There is no way we can do this here!"

The Action

Yet, what seemed impossible from my perspective has been made possible through Christ. Soon after reading this story, I had the opportunity to meet with the security police department that oversees religious affairs. Our international church had decided to launch a campaign called "Love Hanoi" inspired by the Boulder story. So as I met with the General and Colonels, I was able to ask the question, "How can we love Hanoi better as expatriate Christians?" This question came as a surprise, as usually people would ask for favours instead. Yet, we came there to offer our favour.

The Result

Since then, I have been able to meet with several levels of government offices up to the Chief of Hanoi City Police, always offering our love and help. What this has done for our church and me is to change our posture towards the city and government. We are not just a group of foreign Christian who came "to" the city, or a church that happens to be "in" the city doing things "for" the city. We are becoming a church that works "with" the city to seek its peace and prosperity and to pray for it.[5]

---

4   Eric Swanson and Sam Williams, *To Transform a City: Whole Church, Whole Gospel, Whole City* (Grand Rapids, MI: Zondervan, 2010).

5   By Jacob Bloemberg, Lead Pastor, Hanoi International Fellowship.

Case Story: Buenavista, Marinduque

Background

Marinduque is an island composed of six municipalities, in which Buenavista is one of the largest. The municipality is composed of 15 *barangays*, with each *barangay* having an evangelical church presence. There is an association of pastors and Christian leaders in Buenavista known as BCLEF (Buenavista Christian Leaders Ecumenical Fellowship). Following a seminar by the Institute for Studies in Asian Church and Culture (ISACC) on Integral Mission, these pastors were inspired and challenged to do something about the problems facing their community.

The Problem

The group assessed that the main problem of their province was the massive corruption and lack of good leaders in the local government.

The Action

The BCLEF requested ISACC conduct Voter's Education and Good Governance Seminars in preparation for the 2010 Presidential elections. Working together, the churches responded with a massive anti-corruption and anti-vote buying campaign throughout the province.

Pastors and leaders produced creative materials like fans, comics, tarpaulin ads, t-shirts, and caravans encouraging people to stop vote buying and to know candidates before they voted. They held a series of Candidates' Forums in key strategic places in the municipality so that the people could wisely assess the candidate's platform of governance and know them better personally. They also held Voter's Education that featured information and recent developments on the automated election system, which would be used for the first time during that election.

The Result

The body of Christ working together in Marinduque became a powerful voice. The community noticed a significant drop in vote buying and bribery. The church's strong advocacy also inspired a number of people to run for office, especially those politicians who were truly competent but discouraged to run because of a lack of funding.

After the elections, BCLEF gained the respect of the community. The local government now sought their help about moral values formation in the local government and being corruption "watchdogs".

People around them saw a strong united voice and a unified body moving together rather than as separate religious groups working independently. The BCLEF experience showed that a united Christian community is possible and that the possibilities for it to create an impact in the community are tremendous. It also affirmed that the church could be a political force without necessarily joining the political race for power.

Conclusion

The local church, that is each congregation as well as the wider body of Christ, is an integral part of moving toward God's shalom for our cities. Being a part of God's holistic restoration and transformation in our cities is not optional, side-work for the people of God, rather, it is our identity. This is and has always been the calling of the people of God. So, what do we do now?

A Call to Action:

- Continue engaging in discussions about urban transformation, and holistic and integrated theology;

- Take on a new perspective for what "gifts" you have within your congregation and how to mobilize those "gifts" for God's glory;

- Be willing to share your power, both within the congregation by mobilizing and facilitating members and beyond your congregation through partnership with other parts of the body of Christ in your city;

- Start seeing local authorities and non-Christians who want to bless the city as assets, rather than roadblocks. How can you cooperate and accomplish more through partnership?

- Reflect on your worship services. What words are you using? Do they build up an identity of a community called to bring hope and transformation to our city?

- Work with others to organize round-table meetings with compassionate people who share the same vision for your city. Gather the body of Christ around the task of urban transformation.

- And, of course, we pray.

Father, be glorified, HERE in this city. Father, your kingdom come, HERE in this city. Father, provide for us, all of us, HERE in this city. Father, empower us to be reconcilers, all of us, HERE in this city. Father, protect us, all of us, HERE in this city...

Let us, as the people of God, continue to pray this prayer for our cities, not only with our words, but also with our actions.

References

Spees, H. "Christ Centered Civic Renewal: A 21st Century Movement for Spiritual and Social Renewal of Cities." In *Conference Paper Presented at 2014 ISUM Conference, Signs of Hope in the City*. Kuala Lumpur: International Society for Urban Mission, 2014.

Swanson, Eric, and Sam Williams. *To Transform a City: Whole Church, Whole Gospel, Whole City*. Grand Rapids, MI: Zondervan, 2010.

Trafficking and Exploitation in the Urban Context

Glenn Miles and Jarrett Davis

Trafficking and exploitation are currently taking centre stage as a social concern amongst many churches in the West, but many churches do not feel prepared or able to do something about it. This chapter will explore some of the issues of trafficking and exploitation occurring in the urban context and will look at some research and some case studies of organizations that have tried to do something about it within their communities.

Children Rather Than Adults Seen As Victims

The focus of intervention has primarily been on helping children who are seen as vulnerable and different from adults, who are seen as having choice in their involvement. Children are seen to be less able to navigate risks and threats, they have less negotiating power with pimps, traffickers, and society, and they have less control or influence over their lives. However, the reality is that in the context of poverty adults as well as children have very few actual choices available to them and, even if they say they chose to be involved in sex work, there will be a number of push-pull factors that are leading to this decision, including the strong cultural obligations they may feel to support their families.

Child Trafficking for Sexual Purposes

Different countries have different definitions of whether prostitution is legal or not depending on the age of the person involved. This cut-off age can be related to the age of consent or the UN Convention on the Rights of the Child, which defines a child as under 18 years. Whenever a child is involved in sexual exploitation and/or trafficking, whether they "chose" to be involved or not, it is still considered to be illegal, but it becomes harder to prosecute someone for having sex with a minor when they are over the age of consent, because they are then often said to have consented.

A child is treated as a sexual object and for commercial gains and can be used for prostitution and/or the making of pornography. There is a demand for sexual services from children or there would not be the supply. Sometimes labour exploitation can turn into sexual exploitation as well, e.g., a child working as a domestic helper can be raped by the men in the household.

Trafficking vs. Migration

Although trafficking does not necessarily involve movement, trafficking is different from smuggling of migrants and migration because the victim is intended to be exploited by the persons involved in managing the movement from one location to another. People can be trafficked from rural to urban areas and across border areas, usually from poorer to more wealthy countries. Countries can be receiving, transiting, *or* sending countries but some countries are receiving, transit, *and* sending countries.

Places Where Children Are Sexually Exploited

With the increasing use of the Internet and mobile phones, and with the positive pressure from the international community and media, it is becoming less common now for children to be found in "brothels", especially in main cities. However, the more mobile way of pimping remains, where children are brought to the customer. The children are still owned by adults who control the children — and they keep most or all of the money paid by customers for sex with children. Contacts with customers in cities are made in bars, hotels, massage parlours, Internet cafes, and clubs. Sometimes children sell sex on the street, where adult "pimps" may control them, and these areas become known to paedophiles. The pimps may move the children around if they sense any threat. Sometimes the sex takes place in the customer's home or where the child or the pimp lives. Some children are exploited in schools by their teachers in exchange for good grades.[1] Children who do not live with their own families in residential care centres and orphanages are vulnerable to be exploited by staff or others who know they can access children this way.

1   Plan West Africa, "Break the Silence: Prevent Sexual Exploitation and Abuse in and around Schools in Africa," (2014), <http://www.keepingchildrensafe.org.uk/sites/default/files/break_the_silence_en.pdf>.

Factors Leading to Increased Child Trafficking

Women's unequal status can lead to child trafficking, including the development policies which aggravate the marginalization of women. Globalization of the sex industry also contributes to this, including sex tourism. Countries which depend on tourism for their economy may intentionally or unintentionally promote sex tourism in their country as a development policy. Although tourists from the North who are using prostitutes may only be a small percentage of the overall number of sex buyers, they are still significant because of the money they bring into a country.

There is currently mass/global marketing of sex through pornography, including children as objects, in new information technologies that are accessible and affordable, especially to young men (e.g., smart phones). There is also aggressive recruitment of labour and trafficking syndicates in rural and urban areas.

A Feminist and Human Rights Analysis of Trafficking

The sex industry and its growth are commonly predicated on male-centred ideological assumptions that sex is a male right and entitlement, as well as a commodity that should be readily accessible to men. Women are seen to be sexualized commodities functional to that male right. Trafficking is rooted in this stereotypical construction of the social roles of women and men. It constitutes one of the most serious violations of human rights of women, men, transgender people, and children.

Men Usually the Perpetrators

Although there are some men who want to pay for sex with children, adult and adolescent prostitutes often work together in the same places, so some customers do not know that the prostitute they pay for is still legally a child. They may not be interested in children, but be looking for beauty and freshness. Research in Cambodia found that local sex buyers were really only interested in young women 16 to 22 years who were still "young and fresh".[2] Other men may look for a younger prostitute because this makes them feel more powerful or younger, or more masculine. They do not necessarily look for a child, but for a woman who looks and acts like a child.

There are also increasing numbers of younger men — around the age of 15 years — who are initiated to prove they are men by older family members or by peers who may choose for them an older (and therefore experienced) prostitute. In Cambodia, prostitutes are known to be gang raped ("*bauk*") by young men in hotels. Previously

2   Annuska Derks, "Trafficking of Vietnamese Women and Children to Cambodia," (1998), <http://no-trafficking.org/content/pdf/annuska%20derks%20trafficking%20of%20vietnamese%20women%20to%20cambodia%201998.pdf>.

this was done by university students but now is also known to include high school students.[3]

Male Vulnerability

Trafficking is often seen as gendered:

- *The Supply:* Young, poor, and vulnerable women/girls who are escaping poverty, conflict, and the displacement caused by natural disasters are the targets of syndicates, traffickers, illegal recruiters, and brothel owners.

- *The Demand:* Businessmen, professionals, transport workers, seafarers, military forces, transient and migrant workers, and ordinary men create the market for sex.

But what about boys?

Men and boys are also sexually exploited. Although most information and services about children in prostitution focus on girls, gradually information is increasing about boys who are exploited in prostitution. Some of the earlier research of boys being sexually exploited was in South Asia.

Three ECPAT studies showed different ways in which boys were used:

1. A small study of the exploitation of boys in prostitution in Hyderabad (India) reported few pimps and largely female customers.[4]

2. In Lahore and Peshawar (Pakistan) researchers described boys having sex with older men in long-term relationships that were not always based on money.[5]

3. The exploitation of boys in prostitution in Bangladesh was found to be a traditional practice, based in hotels, in homes, and on the street. Pimps controlled the boys through fear and violence.[6]

3   Tong Soprach, "Gang Rape: The Perspectives of Moto-Taxi Drivers across Cambodia: A Rapid Country Wide Assessment," (2005), <http://iussp2005.princeton.edu/papers/51190>.

4   Sree Lakshmi Akula and Anil Raghuvanshi, "Situational Analysis Report on Prostitution of Boys in India (Hyderabad)," (2006), <http://www.childtrafficking.com/Docs/ecpat_06_sarop_of_boys_in_india_250806.pdf>.

5   Tufail Muhammad and Naeem Zafar, "Situational Analysis Report on Prostitution of Boys in Pakistan (Lahore & Peshawar)," (2006), <http://www.humantrafficking.org/publications/443>.

6   A.K.M. Masud Ali and Ratan Sarkar, "The Boys and the Bullies: A Situational Analysis Report on Prostitution of Boys in Bangladesh," (2006), <http://www.humantrafficking.org/publications/445>.

What About Transgender People?

In many cities in Asia transgender people have a high profile. For example, in India, the *hijira* (transgender communities) take in boys who are more feminine in behaviour. They are generally a despised and "invisible" group. How much they are coerced is unknown. Boys very often have to work in prostitution and may later be castrated in an unsafe religious ceremony. The *hijira* communities are very challenging to access but there have been some faith-based organizations and churches that have started to work with them, e.g., IMCARES in Mumbai, India. In discussion with transgender people in Asia, they often say that they have absolutely no alternative employment apart from begging and occasional dancing at weddings. Very few individuals or NGOs have been looking at the situation of transgender people from a child rights perspective or simply seeing them as human beings. Instead, the focus has overwhelmingly been on sexuality rights and HIV/AIDS risk.

What About Women Seeking Boys?

There is little evidence so far that female customers seek pre-pubertal boys but this doesn't mean that it doesn't happen. However, female tourists looking for temporary, exotic, young male partners have been known to have done so for decades. This is a well established phenomenon in certain areas (e.g., in Thailand and Bali in Indonesia). Clients often see it as a "holiday romance" rather than prostitution. The idea that women can be sex tourists in the same way as men has been disputed but the similarities may outweigh the differences.

Where Do We See Signs of Hope?

In our meetings with individuals working with different ministries we see some clear signs of hope.

Redeeming Roses, Kuala Lumpur, Malaysia[7]

- RR is building relationships of trust between the church and community.

- They were seen to be passionate people who are actually going out and *doing* it.

- Around 10 percent of the church is involved in volunteering with social projects.

7   http://redeemingrosesministry.blogspot.com

- They base what they are doing on a foundation of prayer.
- They have faithful funders, but also see the need to be creative in seeking resources.
- They emphasize how they are not constrained by time — working one person at a time, one church at a time. As long as it takes.

Good Shepherd Sisters, Kuala Lumpur, Malaysia[8]

- We were impressed with their wide and comprehensive understanding of trafficking/exploitation issues and surrounding context.
- Unlike many organizations they have a comprehensive strategy from the time the survivor comes into care until reintegration.
- They are not afraid to challenge the Government and have a reputation for their persistence with the Government.
- They are involved in diverse networking with embassies, UN, INGOs, local authorities, and churches, etc.
- They are not afraid to share their faith within government shelters.

Message Parlour, Phnom Penh, Cambodia[9]

- They have excellent collaboration with a variety of organizations/bodies from secular to faith, police to church.
- They were innovative and creative to the context that evolved, as they were in the context longer: e.g., they added a program for children in the area as the need for a safe space for children became apparent.
- They see their role as empowering the local NGO/church communities to tackle these issues.
- They are involved in doing research that shed light on vulnerable groups, providing evidence for advocacy, access, and improving programs.
- They have a reputation for listening to people, listening to victims, listening to NGOs, and then allowing for an appropriate response.

8   http://goodshepherd.my

9   http://www.themessageparlour.org

Where Do We See Challenges to Hope?

The challenges in these contexts were also extensive.

Redeeming Roses

- A big challenge was overcoming the church's fear of gangs/pimps.

- Alternatively — the apathetic and often unwelcoming environment of the church to marginal groups (sex workers/transgender).

- They described a lack of males involved at every level.

- They said that there was an overwhelming challenge in keeping forward motion when it takes so long to see tangible change. No instant results.

- It was often challenging for survivors to be reintegrated into society.

- They were frustrated by the government complacency about such a significant issue.

Good Shepherd Sisters

- Their role was often fighting corruption at a variety of levels.

- Sometimes difficult not to be overwhelmed by the scope of the problem, yet little engagement from many quarters to address it.

- They described the poor functionality of existing networks.

- They described a distinct lack of space to care for survivors and lack of funding for the same.

- They mentioned a dissonance between government policies and practice where there is a gap in which many survivors are unable to be provided with shelter.

- They were frustrated by the lack of implementation of the law.

The Message Parlour

- They described a lack of human resources — volunteers willing to be involved.

- They were frustrated by a lack of funding — particularly for "gap" groups such as sexually exploited males/transgender people.

- They said that sometimes they were overwhelmed by the magnitude of the problem — that they could only help a few at a time.

- They described how often the supporter community has little understanding of the real needs and scope of trafficking and exploitation, and this led to a very simplistic, stereotyped understanding of what trafficking/exploitation really looks like (i.e., "little girls behind bars"). This needed constant challenging.

- They noticed that there was little being done to challenge clients/address demand apart from prosecution of paedophiles. However, they collaborated with GLUE Ministries in reaching out to men frequenting the red light areas. There is a need to address demand because that's where it starts.

- There was little public understanding of the importance of consent in sex especially among male clients of prostitutes.

- There was seen to be an inability to affirm the humanity and brokenness on both sides: victim/survivor and buyer/perpetrator.

Responses of the Church and Faith Based Organisations So Far

The emphasis has tended to be on practice rather than advocacy or research. There has been some rescue but those doing this have not always considered adequate follow-up e.g., shelters and re-integration. There have been some attempts at vocational training although this is nearly always for girls rather than boys or *hijira* and it hasn't always been useful in the long term.

However, now there is a move to explore re-integration and sustainable livelihoods. Many people are learning what to do "on the job" but there is a move to do more thorough training, e.g., DPTA/CPTA, Celebrating Children, Hands that Heal. There are some attempts to appeal for legal reform/implementation. There is some attempt to develop or improve child protection policies.

How Have We Addressed the Issue?

- Rescue efforts have not always matched aftercare facilities.
- Practice is often not evidence-based.

- There has been criticism by secular groups of spiritual abuse — which may be justified in some cases? For example, children are sometimes required to repeatedly give testimonies about painful experiences, which is in itself exploitive.

- Counselling is often not carefully constructed and may be given by non-professionals. All staff need to be trained in listening effectively to children.

- Sometimes organizations have been afraid of reintegrating children into their "wicked" communities so hold on to them longer than should be necessary, sometimes to the point where re-integration is much harder.

- We need to address our own prejudices in the church against prostitutes, boys, and *hijira* so that they can feel welcome in the church.

- We need to learn how to reach out to men where they are at, addictions and all. We need to be good role models.

- We must inform children about sex and pornography before they learn elsewhere, including through harmful pornography.

Advocacy Challenges

- How can we effectively advocate for children?

- We need to engage with the UNCRC even if we don't agree with everything.

- We need to know our facts and we can only do this through systematic research. We need to be truthful and accurate in informing others — exaggerating or fabricating is lying.

- We need to get a balance between seeing children as vulnerable but also resilient.

- We need to see young people over 18 years as not much less vulnerable than under 18 years.

- We need to find out who the stakeholders are and be prepared to work with them, even if they have different standpoints, e.g., media, gay rights activists, teachers, secular NGOs.

Recommendations to the Church

Engaging Men

- We need to be better at engaging men. Presently, the response to this issue seems to be largely female. There is a need to engage more males to tackle this issue.

- Men need to be better role models in treating people with dignity at every level, especially the most vulnerable.

- We need to mentor and encourage young men and old to be men of integrity and to treat women with dignity and hope. We need to challenge the common mind-set of men in their hesitancy about engaging with marginal groups in society (e.g., transgender).

- Fathers, husbands, and brothers should be encouraged to uphold the sacredness of sexuality, helping to build a strong family.

Engaging Women

- We need to encourage women to be more involved in reaching out to women in red light areas and welcoming prostitutes into the church.

- We need to encourage women to treat men with dignity and hope.

- Mothers, wives, and sisters need to uphold the sacredness of sexuality (including role models for children), helping build a strong family.

- There needs to be mentoring of younger women by older experienced women in the church.

Engaging Youth

- We need to encourage youth towards a greater involvement with vulnerable children.

- We need to engage older youth to function as transformative agents within marginal groups within red light areas / bars / clubs.

- We need youth to receive teaching about vulnerability and resilience.

Engaging Sexuality

- There is a need for open, safe spaces where we can talk about sex and sexuality within the church.

- We need to deal with taboos (including cultural taboos within an Asian context) about sex/sexuality within the church.

- We need to be welcoming people from within the LGBT community, ensuring that the church is a safe place that can be called "home" by everyone.

- We need to deal with fears among Christian leadership and challenge them about why we are not comfortable to talk about these issues.

- We need to enquire about the expectations for Christian leadership in regards to their own sexuality? Are they able to be fellow humans with sexualities, as well?

- We need to promote the development of sexuality without repression, fostering honesty and accountability when it comes to porn, lust, and sex outside of marriage.

- We must engage the church in addressing the "demand" for prostituted people, first by talking about sexual abuse/sexual exploitation of members of the church and the surrounding community.

- We must address porn as a driving factor for abuse/exploitation.

Conclusion

Trafficking and exploitation are widespread today. They are pressing problems for societies and churches. While we see signs of hope, many churches do not feel prepared or able to do something about it. Organisations and churches must work together to engage issues surrounding the trafficking and exploitation of men, women, and youth. We need fresh approaches to advocacy, sexuality, and justice.

References

Africa, Plan West. "Break the Silence: Prevent Sexual Exploitation and Abuse in and around Schools in Africa." (2014). http://www.keepingchildrensafe.org.uk/sites/default/files/break_the_silence_en.pdf%3E.

Akula, Sree Lakshmi, and Anil Raghuvanshi. "Situational Analysis Report on Prostitution of Boys in India (Hyderabad)." (2006). http://www.childtrafficking.com/Docs/ecpat_06_sarop_of_boys_in_india_250806.pdf%3E.

Ali, A.K.M. Masud, and Ratan Sarkar. "The Boys and the Bullies: A Situational Analysis Report on Prostitution of Boys in Bangladesh." (2006). http://www.humantrafficking.org/publications/445%3E.

Derks, Annuska. "Trafficking of Vietnamese Women and Children to Cambodia." (1998). http://no-trafficking.org/content/pdf annuska%derks%trafficking%of%vietnamese%women%to%cambodia%1998.pdf%3E.

Muhammad, Tufail, and Naeem Zafar. "Situational Analysis Report on Prostitution of Boys in Pakistan (Lahore & Peshawar)." (2006). http://www.humantrafficking.org/publications/443%3E.

Soprach, Tong. "Gang Rape: The Perspectives of Moto-Taxi Drivers across Cambodia: A Rapid Country Wide Assessment." (2005). http://iussp2005.princeton.edu/papers/51190%3E.

Global Nomads: Expats on Mission in a New Urban World

Jacob Bloemberg

International churches are uniquely positioned to be strategically engaged in urban mission in any given context. With a wealth of resources, know-how, and well connected people, they can have a huge impact within their cities. Sadly, international churches are often perceived as Christian clubs for expatriates with little relevancy to the community in which they are located. It is true, many do start that way, but that is not the ideal nor should they stay that way.

In this chapter, I will start off by showing how the first missional movement led by the Apostle Paul was birthed in an international church and continued to plant such churches through the Western world. In addition, research has proven that, though much history has been lost, the church thrived in urban centres throughout the Eastern and Southern hemispheres. The global diaspora of people during those early centuries paved the way.

Such a diaspora movement is happening in our century as well. Several networks are envisioning this trend to be an opportunity for ministry to, through, and beyond the diaspora. This is where and how international churches today can be most effective, by mobilizing today's global nomads for urban mission. I will briefly talk about the role of international churches, affluent churches, and pastors in citywide movements.

It is important for international churches to understand their own urban context in order to contextualize urban ministry. A short discussion of contextualization is presented and illustrated by my own context, the city of Hanoi, Vietnam. Moving forward, I will describe how partnerships and networking are vital for international churches to launch citywide movements to love their cities. Using the Love Hanoi campaign as an example, I will explain the first stages of starting a movement. Because, if we can do it in Hanoi, other international churches around the world certainly can too!

1. Biblical and Historical Precedence

The involvement of the international church in citywide movements and global urban mission is not a new endeavour. In fact, there are both biblical and historical precedents from the first century and the first millennium that are repeating it today. To begin with, let me take you back to the sending church of the Apostle Paul. I will then take you across the Asian continent and back to Africa to show how the early church thrived in urban centres of ancient Christian, Muslim, and Buddhist nations.

Antioch: The First Missional International Church

"Now those who had been scattered by the persecution that broke out when Stephen was killed," it says in Acts chapter eleven, "travelled as far as Phoenicia, Cyprus, and Antioch, spreading the word only among Jews. Some of them, however, men from Cyprus and Cyrene, went to Antioch and began to speak to Greeks also, telling them the good news about the Lord Jesus".[1] Although churches had been planted in Jerusalem, Judea, and Samaria, this was the first time disciples of Jesus were venturing outside their national borders towards the ends of the earth. Not by choice, mind you, but some shared the gospel with non-Jews and soon enough the first congregation outside Israel was born. It became so successful that Luke writes, "The Lord's hand was with them, and a great number of people believed and turned to the Lord".[2] For a whole year, "Barnabas and Saul met with the church and taught great numbers of people".[3] The Antioch church was a large, non-Jewish, urban church.

When a visiting prophet came from Jerusalem and foretold about the upcoming famine in Israel, the Christians (for they were first called Christians in Antioch) started sending money down to help the poor. The Antioch church was a missional church. Two chapters later, Luke records the leadership team of the Antioch church gathering for a conference. He relays those who were present: "Barnabas, Simeon called Niger, Lucius of Cyrene, Manaen (who had been brought up with Herod

1   Acts 11:19-20 NIV.

2   Acts 11:21 NIV.

3   Acts 11:26 NIV.

the tetrarch) and Saul".[4] Each of these men came from a different nationality. The Antioch church was an international church. In response to the word from the Holy Spirit, the leadership team set aside Barnabas and Paul and sent them off on the first international mission journey. The Antioch church was a sending church.

The First-Century Diaspora: Global Urban Missional Movement

The church in Antioch was truly remarkable: it was a large, non-Jewish, urban, missional, international, and sending church with great sensitivity to the move of the Holy Spirit. As a result, the Antioch church became a launching pad for a global urban missional movement that is still going on today. It became a model church for all the churches Paul, Barnabas, and their teammates planted throughout the Roman empire. The Antioch church is still a model church for us today.

Within a time span of 25 years, this missional movement had spread from Antioch throughout Asia Minor across to the European continent and as far as Rome, the empire's capital city. This was made possible because of the first-century diaspora of the Jewish people. Since the days of the exile, Jews had settled in cities throughout the Assyrian empire and established synagogues wherever they lived. Only ten men were needed to start a synagogue, though some newer cities like Philippi did not even have that many. Paul and his international church-planting team traversed from city to city — it was an urban missional strategy. The Roman empire had paved the way, literally. In part due to the transportation infrastructure, a common language, and the diaspora network, Paul's mission was a success.

From Antioch to the Far East and Back

Not only was Antioch the launching pad for the Western (Roman) church, but also for the Eastern (Asian) church. It is a popular, though erroneous, belief that after Paul's mission, the gospel kept moving west into Europe, then the USA, then to Asia, and is now making its way back to Jerusalem. However, during the first thousand-year history of the church, it was predominantly an Asian church.

In *The Lost History of Christianity: The Thousand-Year Golden Age of the Church in the Middle East, Africa, and Asia — and How It Died*, Philip Jenkins uncovers the forgotten roots of the Asian church. Long before the Roman Catholics travelled The Silk Road to China, the Nestorian and Jacobite missionaries set out from Syria to the Far East, reaching as far as Mongolia, Shanghai, India, and perhaps as far as Vietnam,

4   Act 13:1 NIV.

the Philippines, and Korea.[5] It is estimated that by the year 1000AD, "Asia had 17 to 20 million Christians" who "stemmed from Christian traditions dating back twenty-five or thirty generations".[6]

Nestorians in the seventh century had contextualized the gospel in such a way that they were able to communicate it in Buddhist and Taoist terms. Here is a sample text from a Nestorian monument dating back to 780AD:

> "The illustrious and honourable Messiah, veiling his true dignity, appeared in the world as a man; ... he fixed the extent of the eight boundaries, thus completing the truth and freeing it from dross; he opened the gate of the three constant principles, introducing life and destroying death; he suspended the bright sun to invade the chambers of darkness, and the falsehoods of the devil were thereupon defeated; he set in motion the vessel of mercy by which to ascend to the bright mansions, whereupon rational beings were then released; having thus completed the manifestation of his power, in clear day he ascended to his true station."[7]

Another example is the design used by the Nestorians to identify themselves, namely a cross on top of a lotus, the "symbol of Buddhist enlightenment".[8] This symbol can be found even today on tombstones throughout China and India. The image below depicts the icon found on a tombstone in China (see Figure 1: Headstone with Lotus and Cross, Yuan Dynasty (1272–1368), Quanzhou Maritime Museum). This symbol is an inspiring example for Asian Christian designers today. For the past two thousand years, Christian artists have been designing church logos or symbols. Designers today are continuing an ancient trade of applying contextualization to their art. What would a contextualized church logo in Asia look like today?

---

5   Philip Jenkins, The Lost History of Christianity: The Thousand-Year Golden Age of the Church in the Middle East, Africa, and Asia — and How It Died, 1st ed. (New York: HarperOne, 2008), 70.

6   Ibid., 70.

7   Jenkins, 15.

8   Ibid.

Figure 1: Headstone with Lotus and Cross, Yuan Dynasty (1272–1368), Quanzhou Maritime Museum[9]

As the title of Jenkins' book suggests, much of the church's history in Asia, the Middle East, and Africa has been lost. Yet, what is known is that at the start of the third century several kingdoms were Christian in religion. The king of Osthoene, with Edessa as its capital city, accepted Christianity around 200AD.[10] Armenia followed around 300AD, of which the capital city Ani became known as "the city of 1,001 churches".[11] Next in line were Georgia, Adiabene, Nubida, and Ethiopia (Abyssinia). Aksum, Ethiopia's capital, became "the kingdom's main Christian see" by 340AD.[12] Ethiopia was so full of churches that it was said one could not "sing in one church without being heard by another, and perhaps by several". Furthermore, the Christians had "a natural disposition to goodness, they [were] very liberal of their alms".[13]

Much of the non-Western church history might have been lost, but Jenkins has proven that Christianity thrived in urban centres and numerous nations during the first millennium. The church, to begin with, was urban and Asian.

9   USF Ricci Institute, "The Lotus and the Cross: East-West Cultural Exchange along the Silk Road," University of San Francisco (accessed 4 June 2014).

10   Jenkins, 54.

11   Ibid.

12   Ibid., 55.

13   Ibid., 56.

2. The Missional International Church Movement of Today

Having established that the church of Acts was a missional movement of international churches which continued to thrive in urban centres of the East, South, and West, we will now jump ahead to the third millennium in which we find ourselves. First, we will briefly highlight current trends of the global diaspora and the Global Diaspora Network. Then, the Missional International Church Network and, as an example, the Hanoi International Fellowship, will be introduced to show how international churches today can play an effective role in urban mission. Considering the wealth of resources in such churches, attention is given to the role of international churches, the affluent, and the pastor.

The Twenty-First-Century Global Diaspora

Akin to the first-century diaspora, the global dispersion of people today is an unprecedented flow of people migrating predominantly from East to West, South to North, and rural to urban environments. According to the Global Diaspora Network (GDN), "there are now over 200 million international migrants, and over 700 million internally displaced people or close to 1 billion scattered peoples".[14] To visualize this global movement, the Wittgenstein Centre for Demography and Global Human Capital has done a beautiful job creating an information graph as show at http://www.global-migration.info/. I had these printed on banners and posted them at our church to raise awareness of this global trend.

Migration flows within and between ten world regions, in 100,000s. This circular plot shows all global bilateral migration flows for the five-year period mid-2005 to mid-2010, classified into a manageable set of ten world regions. Key features of the global migration system include the high concentration of African migration within the continent (with the exception of Northern Africa), the "closed" migration system of the former Soviet Union, and the high spatial focus of Asian emigration to North America and the Gulf states.

Cities are the places where these streams of global migration merge. In these urban centres of globalization, migration, and urbanization is where international churches (ICs) thrive. In every major city around the world there are ICs which serve the dynamic expatriate community. Generally, expatriates roam the world like global nomads from city to city, job to job, posting to posting, and calling to calling. It is

---

14   Sadiri Joy Tira, ed. *The Human Tidal Wave* (Pasig City, Philippines: Lifechange Publishing, Inc., 2013), xxi.

like a rushing river streaming around the globe. Among them are Christians from all kinds of nationalities, vocations, and denominations. The Missional International Church Network (MICN)[15] is focused on mobilizing ICs to empower this global stream of Christian expats to be missional wherever they go.

One of these ICs is the Hanoi International Fellowship (HIF), which I have the privilege to serve as Lead Pastor. HIF started as a fellowship of about a dozen Christian expats in the capital city of Vietnam some 20 years ago. For the first decade, the fellowship was internally focused, primarily meeting the needs of Christian foreigners living and working in Hanoi. In 2005, just before my appointment as the pastor, I attended the MICN conference, which was held in Dubai that year. As a church we had come to realize that God was calling us to become externally focused, but how could we do this as an IC in our context? MICN provided us with a vision, language, and peer group which helped HIF to transform into a missional community.

The Role of the International Church

Joy Tira, director of Global Diaspora Network (GDN), calls upon the church to respond to the global diaspora phenomenon. Tira outlines three ways for Christians and churches to get involved, by ministering *to, through,* and *beyond* the diaspora.[16] This provides a helpful framework to categorize the types of ministries the IC can be involved with. For example, by reaching out to the expatriate community in Hanoi, HIF is ministering directly *to* the diaspora in our city. Mobilizing and equipping HIF members to be missional is ministering *through* the diaspora. When HIFers become acquainted with the culture and context, we are able to minister *beyond* the diaspora and build bridges with local communities and society. International churches are uniquely positioned to become bridge builders between the global diaspora and the local population, between the global church and the local congregations, and between global organizations and corporations to meet local needs.

One of the challenges that I continued to struggle with is this: how can an international church transition from being a church that has come "to" the city, to being a church that is "in" the city, to being a church that is "for" the city, to becoming a church that collaborates "with" the city? Hanoi International Fellowship transitioned some years ago from being a fellowship of Christian foreigners to becoming a missional international church. We have come to realize that we are called to be a

15   Visit www.micn.org for more information.

16   Tira, ed., 163.

city church, a church that is "in" and "for" the city. Today, the challenge before us is the next transition: to become a church that is *with* the city. How can HIF collaborate across sectors and with city institutions to be a blessing to the city of Hanoi? Or, in the words of Swanson and Williams, how can the *whole* church bring the *whole* gospel to the *whole* city?[17]

The Role of the Affluent Church

Equipping expatriate Christians to serve the poor in the city immediately raises the issue: how can the affluent expats help without hurting? Lowell Bakke, professor at the Bakke Graduate University (BGU), stated during a lecture on urban transformation: "The boulevard churches speak to power; the off-street churches speak to people".[18] This means that there is room for both the upscale downtown church as well as the neighbourhood community churches.

During my study in Manila for a BGU course, I had a chance to visit two boulevard churches (Union Church Manila, a one-hundred-year old international church, and Christ Commission Fellowship, a local wealthy church with a brand-new, debt-free, 10,000-seat facility) and two off-street churches (Botocan Christian Community Fellowship in a squatter area and the small church in the Wawa slum community). I know that most members of the international church cannot do what the people in the squatter community churches are doing. However, the opposite is also true: the small house churches cannot influence those in positions of power in the city and nation. What is important is that both the affluent and the community churches work on behalf of the poor.

While reading and researching about urban ministry, I fell into the trap of believing that, unless you move into the poor neighbourhood and live like the poor, you cannot effectively help the poor. Incarnational ministry, as it is often labelled, can be easily misunderstood as being at the pinnacle of the ministry pyramid (see Figure 2).

17   Eric Swanson and Sam Williams, *To Transform a City: Whole Church, Whole Gospel, Whole City* (Grand Rapids, MI: Zondervan, 2010).

18   Lowell Bakke, "Introduction," in *Overture 1: Manila* (Manila, Philippines: Bakke Graduate University, 2014).

Figure 2: The Ministry Pyramid

In the evangelical church exists a mind-set that it is more holy to serve God as an evangelist, pastor, or missionary than it is to have any other job. This view is very much prevalent among Asian churches. The saying is, "If you really want to serve God, quit your job and work for him full-time". This is a false mind-set, since every Christian is called to serve God in their homes, offices, classrooms, neighbourhoods, and wherever else they work, live, and go. The danger is that incarnational ministry is viewed as the most sacred and effective way — perhaps the only way — to serve the poor in the city.

It is true that incarnational ministry can be very effective if done well. Viv Grigg, who helped catalyze Servant Partners, has mobilized many incarnational workers and missionaries who have laid down their riches to live and serve among the poor in slums around the world. Aaron Smith, whom I met in the Botocan squatter community, is one of them. However, it is apparent that only few are called to such extremes and often for a relatively short time. What about the rest of the church? Can they serve the poor besides supporting the incarnational missionaries? If incarnational ministry is seen as the pinnacle of mission, everyone else will always feel like their service is of lesser value — that they will never measure up or can help effectively.

> Thankfully, Grigg offers a much broader picture. He writes, "Typical Christian responses of aid and community development, even when done brilliantly, affect only the micro-environment of the squatter area".[19] Grigg goes on to explain that there is a distinct role for the affluent Christian:

19   Viv Grigg, *Cry of the Urban Poor* (Monrovia, Calif.: MARC, 1992), 262.

"The primary response of middle-class Christians (while not neglecting other issues) will probably be in the transformation of economic life, political life, government bureaucracy, and other structures of the city that perpetuate slum poverty. It will probably also be necessary to deal with international factors that increasingly loom as dominant forces in worldwide urban poverty."[20]

In chapters 20 and 21 of his book, *Cry of the Urban Poor*, Grigg offers his recommendations for middle-class and international elite Christians and churches. "Middle-class professionals ... may effect change in the implementation and governing of the cities at an urban planning level," while "Christians in the international elite may change the macro-economic systems".[21] Table 1 below outlines potential responses of the middle-class to poverty.

In speaking of the role of the affluent church, Grigg states, "Far more important [than giving financial help] is giving personnel who can impart spiritual life and technical skills".[22] Still, it is valid to provide financial support for widows, orphans, refugees, seed capital, expansion capital, scholarships, and community leadership programs.[23] Figure 3 charts out what the upper and middle classes can do in the fight against poverty.

Figure 4 displays how a simplified lifestyle of Westerners (or the affluent) can lift the labouring poor of developing nations out of poverty, which in turn lifts the destitute poor up to becoming the labouring poor.

20   Viv Grigg, *Cry of the Urban Poor* (Monrovia, Calif.: MARC, 1992), 263.

21   Ibid.

22   Grigg, 283.

23   Grigg, 283-284.

Table 1: Middle-Class Responses to Poverty

LEVELS OF POVERTY	POTENTIAL RESPONSES
Street sleepers	Social work relating to existing agencies Direct aid — food, clothing Food for work, housing
Relocation area	Upgrade work operations Food for work for housing Social work relating to existing agencies
Bustees/Slums (Where housing available, no work)	Co-op loans draw local industires into area Co-op into job placement, feasibility studies of jobs Direct grants to establish small-scale businesses: Food line Clothing line Manufacturing line: Electronics Welding Woodworking Chemicals, soaps Avoid handicrafts unless there are existing skills A skills-training institution nearby Food for work Overseas job placement agency
Slum-housed (Majority working)	Co-op housing program Credit co-op
Drug addicts, alcoholics	Specialized long-term pastoral communities and rehabilitation

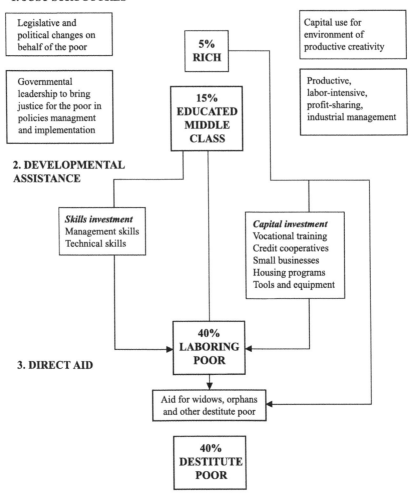

1. JUST STRUCTURES

Legislative and political changes on behalf of the poor

Governmental leadership to bring justice for the poor in policies managment and implementation

5%
RICH

15%
EDUCATED MIDDLE CLASS

Capital use for environment of productive creativity

Productive, labor-intensive, profit-sharing, industrial management

2. DEVELOPMENTAL ASSISTANCE

Skills investment
Management skills
Technical skills

Capital investment
Vocational training
Credit cooperatives
Small businesses
Housing programs
Tools and equipment

3. DIRECT AID

40%
LABORING POOR

Aid for widows, orphans and other destitute poor

40%
DESTITUTE POOR

Aim: To transfer skills, technology, tools, and control of capital to the productive poor.

Figure 3: The Fight against Poverty: What the upper and middle class can do[24]

24   Grigg, 285.

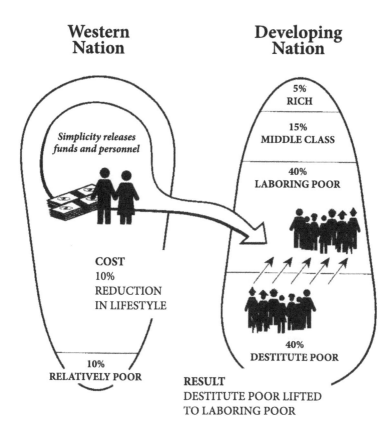

Figure 4: Sacrificial, Simple Lifestyles: Interchurch international economic justice (2 Corinthians 8–9)[25]

At HIF, we are moving in the direction Grigg is pointing through our City Partnerships ministry. It is our aim to connect resources in HIF with opportunities in the city. We recruit volunteers to share their time and expertise, and to raise funds to support initiatives such as orphanages, vocational projects, and start-up ministries. The vision, guidelines, and implementation of City Partnerships need clarification and refinement. It would help our middle-class and international, elite church members to clearly see their individual role in fighting poverty as well as our corporate role in the city.

The challenge of reducing our lifestyle by 10% in order to uplift the productive poor could be turned into a campaign for financial stewardship. The campaign could challenge HIF members to live on 80% of their income, while giving 10% to ministries and 10% to the church.

The Role of the Pastor

To overcome these challenges, one change that needs to take place is in the pastor's posture towards the city. Is he or she the "pastor in a church which *happens to be in* a community or which is *for* a community?" questions Lowell Bakke. The answer to this question unveils what the pastor thinks about their role in the city. During my tenure as pastor of HIF, I also needed to make this paradigm shift. When we decided to be a church *for* the expatriate community and *for* the city, it changed my role and posture as well. The city had become my parish.

During one of our lectures in Manila, Raineer Chu, attorney with Mission Ministries Philippines (MMP), challenged us to consider the posture of the Catholic priest. "Learn to journey with the poor, all other things become secondary," said Chu. In coming to a community, the comparison between a Catholic priest and an evangelical pastor provides quite a contrast in posture. Chu explained:

> "When entering the slum, a priest has a very graphic image of Jesus (as a statue) whereas a pastor has the image of Jesus' presence (ethereal). A priest has a theology of God's presence everywhere. A priest comes to the community to find God there whereas the pastor goes to bring God. The priest in his order goes there to grow old there, die there, and be buried there. Francis Schaeffer, in his books, says evangelicals have already "found" Jesus whereas the orthodox have a great sense of journey. Pastors divide between members and non-members; the priest is called to the parish."[26]

---

26   Raineer Chu, "Exegeting the City," in *Overture 1: Manila* (Manila, Philippines: Bakke Graduate University, 2014).

The table below lists the differing postures between priest and pastor (see Table 2). Obviously, this is exaggerated and stereotyping, but it worked on me. Looking at the pastor column, I can identify more with the pastor than the priest: bringing God to the city, focused on accomplishing a project, moving fast, and a focus on preaching and communication. Now I have a dilemma: I want to see the city as my parish, but I have to fight against my default approach to the city as a typical pastor.[27]

Table 2: Contrast between the Priest and Pastor[28]

PRIEST	PASTOR
• Theology of finding God	• Bringing God
• Journey	• Project accomplished
• Walk slowly	• Walks fast
• Called to entire parish	• Divide members/non-members
• Focus on sick, poor, dying	• Focus on Scripture

One excellent example of such a priest is Father Ben Beltran of the Smokey Mountain community in Manila. When Fr. Beltran moved to what was the largest garbage slum, he made it his parish and saw every person as a member of that parish. He started by asking everyone, "Who do you think Jesus is?" Through this exercise he discovered that Jesus was already present in the community. This became the thesis of Beltran's doctoral degree and was later published as *The Christology of the Inarticulate: An Inquiry into the Filipino Understanding of Jesus the Christ.*[29]

Beltran said, "No one will follow you unless you spend time with them, it is about relationships".[30] So he spent time with the members of his parish and asked a simple question. As a result, Smokey Mountain is no longer a garbage dump. Through collaborative efforts, Beltran and partners were able to transform the city's garbage collection and processing, launching their own businesses and recycling programs. Veritas Social Empowerment, Inc. runs an IT school and other educational programs, and takes an entrepreneurial approach to working with the poor. The company's slogan, "Imagine. Innovate. Impact." states clearly the vision and intent.[31]

27   Ibid.

28   Ibid.

29   Benigno P. Beltran, *The Christology of the Inarticulate: An Inquiry into the Filipino Understanding of Jesus the Christ* (Manila: Divine Word Publications, 1987).

30   Benigno Beltran, "Social Empowerment," in *Overture 1: Manila* (Manila, Philippines: Bakke Graduate University, 2014).

31   Ibid.

3. From Contextualization to City-wide Movements

The Nestorians knew how to communicate the gospel in the Asian context. Today, the same strategy and skill are needed when talking about the involvement of the international church in urban mission. By definition, the church members and leaders are foreigners and outsiders in the host city. First, I will give a short introduction to the concept of contextualization. Then I will paint a picture of the urban context of Hanoi City, Vietnam's capital. It will become apparent that only through networking and partnerships can the international church be effective. In conclusion, I will introduce several formats of consultations to gather like-minded people for learning from and serving with the city.

The Need for Contextualization

Simply put, "contextualization means doing theology ourselves," explained Dr Tim Gener, President of the Asia Theological Seminary, during our class on Filipino theology in Manila.[32] Doing theology is thinking biblically about something. Thus, Asian contextualization is "thinking biblically in the Asian context". As Gener stated, Christians have "the right to articulate the evangelical traditions in their own terms in light of their own issues".[33]

It was a pleasant surprise to discover a number of theological books in Manila published by the seminaries there. The Asian Theological Seminary (ATS) holds an annual forum and publishes the presenters' papers in book form each year. The publisher, OMF Literature Inc., is working on making these resources available in eBook format. However, the following titles are currently available in print at ATS:

1. *Doing Theology in the Philippines* (2005)

2. *Naming the Unknown God* (2006)

3. *The Church and Poverty in Asia* (2008)

4. *The Earth is the Lord's* (2009)

5. *Walking with God* (2012)[34]

---

32   Tim Gener, "Filipino Theology," in *Overture 1: Manila* (Manila, Philippines: Bakke Graduate University, 2014).

33   Ibid.

34   Asia Theological Forum, "New Books," ed. Jacob Bloemberg (Hanoi: Asia Theological Forum, 2014). Books may be ordered from ATS by sending an email to: theoforum@mail.ats.ph.

For example, the book *The Church and Poverty in Asia* is a compilation of thirteen papers presented at the fourth Theological Forum in 2008. It represents a broad range of evangelical thought and practice in the Philippines. Based on Mary's song from Luke 1:53, the conference's theme was, "He has filled the hungry with good things". In response, presenters were asked to answer the question, "What is to be our theology of poverty and how are we to make our theology actionable in a fallen world filled with need?"[35] The book is divided in two parts, the first wrestling with the theological and theoretical challenge, and the latter discussing best practices of working among the poor. The forum was hosted at the Union Church of Manila (UCM), the oldest international church in the city.

Another similar book is *Asian Church and God's Mission*, edited by Wonsuk and Julie Ma, former Korean missionaries to the Philippines. This is a collection of papers presented at the *Asian Mission* symposium held in Manila, the Philippines, in 2012. The theme of the conference, "Empowering the Asian Church for God's Mission,"[36] was expounded upon by a selection of sixteen experts in the field. The presenters came from various nations: Honduras, Finland, Burma, Korea, the Philippines, Canada, the USA, Nepal, Japan, and India. The collection is divided into three parts: Reflections, Context, and Strategies. The Asia Pacific Theological Seminary supported the event.

Having lived in Asia for seventeen years, it is the first time that I have come across such rich resources in contextualization. I have collected the books available from ATS and am looking forward to receiving this year's book on the theme, Globalization, Migration, and Diaspora. It is an inspiring idea to think of writing, presenting, collecting, and publishing such papers in my context of Hanoi, Vietnam.

Example: The Urban Context of Hanoi

Hanoi is a unique city. Unlike Manila or Bangkok, it does not have significant slum areas and only few squatter houses. City government has a tight control of the expansion of the city, which is a good thing in many ways. Hanoi is also unlike Western cities, which are the focus of so many urban mission textbooks, and unlike African cities, another textbook's favourite context. To start thinking about loving Hanoi, first a clearer picture must be painted of the local context.

When trying to understand who the urban poor are in Hanoi, it is useful to use Viv Grigg's list of eight specialized groups. Segmenting the population helps in creating

35   Lee Wanak, ed. *The Church and Poverty in Asia* (Manila, Philippines: OMF Literature Inc., 2008).

36   Wonsuk Ma and Julie C. Ma, *Asian Church and God's Mission: Studies Presented in the International Symposium on Asian Mission in Manila, January 2002* (Manila, Philippines: OMF Literature, 2003).

specialized ministries. Questions to ask are: do these groups have a communal identity, meet one another, have some kind of influence on each other, and is there a church ministry already working among these groups?[37] Below is a listing of these groups with a description of the people for each segment.

- **Street vendors:** These are the people trying to make a living on and off the streets. Although the city government as restricted street hawkers from the main boulevards and roads, they can be found on many street corners, along sidewalks and in front of shops and homes. From the women selling flowers, bread, kitchen ware, clothes, and pottery off their bicycles to the men and women serving tea and cigarettes, noodle soup, and lunches, or doner kebabs and egg sandwiches, vendors are found everywhere throughout the city. Repairmen ride bicycles through the neighbourhoods calling out for any needed jobs.

- **Marketplaces:** Long before daybreak, suppliers of produce and meats are riding their motorbikes into the city or deliveries in the multitudes of marketplaces. Mostly run by women, the sellers work from morning to night, living hard lives day in and day out.

- **Street children:** Because of government efforts to keep children off the streets, these have now gone into hiding. Blue Dragon, an international NGO working to rescue street children, has found one of the hiding places to be on top of a train bridge pillar 25 meters off the ground. Because sales of postcards or shining shoes are banned, the young boys and girls run a much higher risk of getting involved in the sex trade and being trafficked.[38]

- **Drug addicts:** With drugs available cheaply, students especially are susceptible to drug addiction. An epidemic problem throughout the city with low success rates at government rehabilitation centres has provided churches in Hanoi with a unique opportunity to be of help. At least five house-based Christian rehab centres are in the city with another ten in surrounding provinces. At least eight to ten churches, including HIF, are collaborating together upon invitation by the government rehab centres to minister there several days per week. Graduates from their three-year program now have the option to join Christian halfway houses in the city.

---

37   Grigg, 46–50.

38   For more information about the work of Blue Dragon, visit www.bluedragon.org.

- **Alcoholics:** An unrecognized social issue in Vietnamese culture, beer halls and hard drinking are a deeply ingrained problem. Men will spend food money on cheap beer, feeling obliged to drink all hours of the day during business-related meetings, and will drink until they are hospitalized or die of alcohol poisoning. This happened to a friend of mine, who explained that he had to drink in order to win clients for his travel business. Alcoholism is not admitted to be an addiction, but it is everywhere, greatly impacting health, families, and society.

- **Prostitutes:** Although illegal, prostitutes can be found in most karaoke bars, discos, massage parlours, and hostels. Prostitution is hidden, yet it is always there and available everywhere. Men are almost expected to have extramarital relationships. Prostitutes who are drug addicts will sell their service for as little as $2.50 to get their next dose of heroin. Recently, Christians were given access to a government rehab centre for prostitutes to evangelize among them in hope of transformed lives. When prostitutes leave the centre, government staff tell them to "find a church in the city because they have the answer".[39]

- **Deaf, blind, and amputees:** Lacking equal opportunities in education and the job market, the handicapped are often kept inside the house or sent to centres. Slow progress is made to integrate them into mainstream society. Several NGOs and social businesses have been successful in providing vocational training and setting up handicraft shops and a bakery café.

- **Prisoners:** Jail ministry is not yet allowed in Vietnam, except for those who minister at the rehab and prostitution centres, which function much like prison camps. It will not be surprising if recovered addicts, prostitutes, and criminals will soon be allowed to start prison ministries because of the testimonies of their transformed lives. It is also unknown to me if there are international prisoners who could possibly be visited by members of our international church. This is a typical ministry provided by fellowships like ours in other nations.

These eight groups can easily be identified in Hanoi. Several others may be added, such as garbage collectors and street sweepers, migrant construction workers, day labourers, students from poor and ethnic families in the provinces, and those with serious health problems awaiting treatment they cannot afford at government hospitals. Clarifying

39 Anonymous source.

and improving this list with further details and statistics will be most helpful in developing ministries among the urban poor.

The Need for Networks and Partnerships

During my six months of study focused on urban transformation in Manila, the red ribbon running through all the educational experiences is that of partnerships and networking. All the success stories, whether from Veritas or Servant Partners or the Centre for Community Transformation or Grameen Bank, are the results of networking and strategic partnerships between for-profits, non-profits, and government institutions.

Speaking of the success of National Coalition of Urban Transformation (NCUT), founder Corrie DeBoer writes:

> "Networking is the key to the success of this project. Networking helped to reduce the competition in the Christian arena, both among Protestants and between Protestants and Catholics. This study has shown the wisdom and strength of pulling leaders from different churches and religious organizations together to advise each other and seek enlightenment about relations between organizations and the lessons that can be learned in dialogue. The result has been successfully completed plans because of this pooling of resources and cooperation. Networking has brought about this ecumenical cooperation."[40]

Referencing Marvin Weisbord of Future Search, Corrie explains that for collaborative relationships to succeed, partners must first develop and commit themselves to a set of common goals and objectives. Secondly, they must be willing to contribute their organization's resources to these common goals.[41] DeBoer experienced that, when using the term "collaborate", Catholic and Evangelical seminaries were cautious as it felt too close for them. Instead, the seminaries preferred the term "networking" and organized themselves as a loose alliance under the banner of "Network for Theological Education". As a result, the seminaries "decided to work together in sharing library facilities, faculty, and other resources".[42]

On the other hand, DeBoer experienced "that the urban practitioners were more open to the concept of 'partnership' than the theological educators". She explains:

40   Lorisa DeBoer, "Developing a Plan for Collaboration in Urban Leadership Development" (Eastern Baptist Theological Seminary, 2000), 90.

41   Lorisa DeBoer, "Developing a Plan for Collaboration in Urban Leadership Development" (Eastern Baptist Theological Seminary, 2000), 96.

42   DeBoer, 97.

"Other reasons for interest in partnership were found to be the common ground and interest they held with the other members, the enjoyment of being in partnership in working among the poor, the trust that being in partnership elicited, the ownership to the expected outcomes this partnership provided, and sharing of resources with each other. These characteristics went beyond the descriptions normally ascribed to groups working together."[43]

Looking at the establishment and impact of NCUT as a role model for Love Hanoi, it is clear that we need to gain more understanding of what is meant by networks and partnerships; how these are different from a movement; and how they can be best utilized in our context to serve the goals of Love Hanoi.

Networks and Partnerships Defined

Phil Butler, author of *Well Connected,* believes the brokenness and divisions within the body of Christ to be a great sin. Jesus, right before his betrayal and death, prayed for the unity of the church. "I pray also for those who will believe in me through their message, that all of them may be one, Father, just as you are in me and I am in you. May they also be in us so that the world may believe that you have sent me."[44] It is the Lord's desire for all Christians to be united for the purpose that the world may know that the Father has sent his Son because of his great love for them. Working in collaboration through networking and partnerships is an outward demonstration of God's love.

Butler lists seven primary motivations for and benefits of partnerships and networking: greater efficiency, building on each other's strengths, increased effectiveness, greater flexibility, expanded resources, reduction of risk, and expansion of options for action.[45] Not to confuse networks and partnerships, Butler defines each of them distinctively:

- **Networks:** "Any group of individuals or organizations sharing a common interest, who regularly communicate with each other to enhance *their individual purposes.*"

- **Partnerships:** "Any group of individuals or organizations, sharing a common interest, who regularly communicate, plan, and work together *to achieve a*

---

43   Ibid.

44   John 17:20-21 NIV.

45   Phil Butler, *Well Connected: Releasing the Power and Restoring Hope through Kingdom Partnerships* (Waynesboro, GA: Authentic Media, 2005), 25–26.

common vision beyond the capacity of any one of the individual partners."[46]

The key difference between networks and partnerships is the purpose for collaboration, either for their own purposes or for their common goals. "While networks may bring people or organizations together through a common interest," explains Butler, "partnerships galvanize linkages around a common vision or outcome. By working together on that common vision or outcome, they can achieve ends far beyond the capacity of any of the individual members of the partnerships".[47] The book has been made available as a free download at www.connectedbook.net.

From Networks to City-wide Movements

In his book, *The Good City*, Glenn Barth outlines the six "stages of development for organizations serving city movements". [48] These six stages are as follows: exploration, formation, operation, breakthrough, transformation, and replication.[49] Each stage requires different functions and skills by the movement leader. The table below shows how movements develop and what kind of leadership is needed from stage to stage.

STAGE	FUNCTION	SKILL
Exploration	Catalyst Visionary	Relational Communication Convening
Formation	Visionary	Communication Facilitating Management Creative Thinking
Operation	Management	Decison Making People Building Motivational
Breakthrough	Prayer	Doing the right things at the right times
Tranformation	Discipling	Presence-based Prayer
Replication	Teaching	Training and Coaching Skills

Table 3: Stages of Development[50]

46   Phil Butler, *Well Connected: Releasing the Power and Restoring Hope through Kingdom Partnerships* (Waynesboro, GA: Authentic Media, 2005), 34–35.

47   Butler, 35.

48   Glenn Barth, *The Good City* (Tallmadge, OH: S.D. Myers Publishing Services, 2010), 41.

49   Ibid.

50   Barth.

In 2012, inspired by Swanson and William's book, *To Transform a City*,[51] HIF launched the "Love Hanoi" campaign. To get the movement off the ground, we first had to go through the exploration stage. Barth states, "Exploration is a foundational stage and must be given adequate time for relational equity to develop".[52] For stage one, the leader needs to be a catalyst and visionary with the skill set of being relational, a good communicator, and able to convene mixed groups of people.

Referencing Butler's Process of Partnership Exploration from *Well Connected*, Barth lists six parts to stage one: gathering initial information; doing initial interviews; reviewing and expanding information; doing further interviews; drawing initial conclusions; and deciding whether or not to move to the formation stage.[53] Currently, I am the champion of the Love Hanoi movement, which at some point will need to transfer to another leader.

Now, Love Hanoi needs to transition to the next phase. "Formation is a critical stage that can only be entered into when there is evidence of significant buy-in from, and relational equity built, with key leaders around the vision for the development of a coalition to lead a city movement," writes Barth.[54] Formation is needed for the organization of the movement to go operational. It is critical that Love Hanoi passes through this stage in the coming year to avoid either getting stuck in exploration indefinitely or remaining solely an HIF campaign. Often I am asked, what is Love Hanoi? It is therefore helpful to clarify the differences between a campaign, movement, network, and partnership and how they all relate.

Campaign: As the initiator of Love Hanoi, HIF is the owner of what would be best defined as a campaign to promote loving the city. It is not a program or project (although in Vietnamese the word "dự án" is broader in meaning). It is more like an idea or initiative. It is not a committee and does not have a structure or budget, which would likely kill it. It is a promotional campaign in the way the word is used in advertising, to promote the idea of loving the city. In translation to Vietnamese, it is important to use appropriate language to avoid making it sound like a military campaign or like the Christian crusades of the middle ages.

Movement: The vision is for Love Hanoi to become a movement, to inspire collaboration among churches and across the three sectors of society (public, profit,

---

51   Swanson and Williams.

52   Barth, 43.

53   Ibid.

54   Barth, 47.

and non-profit). Love Hanoi will likely not become an organization, but remain as a vision and inspirational idea. A good example is the "I'm a City Changer" campaign, which is described as "a global movement to share and spread individual, corporate, and public initiatives that improve our cities". As the website states, "I'm a City Changer campaign is convened by UN-Habitat, the United Nations Human Settlements Programme, with support from partners from the private and public sector".[55] This vocabulary is very helpful and has been adapted to describe the Love Hanoi campaign in our brochure and website as follows: "Love Hanoi is a campaign to inspire and mobilize individual, corporate, and public initiatives for the benefit of the city. It is promoted by City Partnerships, the charity arm of Hanoi International Fellowship".[56] This wording works well in our expatriate context.

On the other hand, Love Hanoi could become organized and have various working groups and discussion forums working on specific issues. Taking the Lausanne Movement as an example, it defines itself as "a global movement that mobilizes evangelical leaders to collaborate for world evangelization. Together we seek to bear witness to Jesus Christ and all his teaching, in every part of the world — not only geographically, but in every sphere of society and in the realm of ideas". Lausanne's purpose statement is, "Calling the Whole Church to take the Whole Gospel to the Whole World". [57] If Love Hanoi were to become solely an evangelical movement, the Lausanne statement could be adapted as Bakke and Swanson use it: Calling the Whole Church to take the Whole Gospel to the Whole City. This, however, may be too evangelistic for our expatriate and political contexts, hindering us in building relationships with government and non-Christian organizations. At this time, it would be better to use the language from UN-Habitat and integrate it with biblical references and perspectives such as Jeremiah 29:7, to "seek the peace and prosperity of the city" and to "pray for it".

Networks: Although Love Hanoi is already creating an informal network through relationship building, consultations, and joint projects, the question is, should Love Hanoi organize itself as a network. As a movement, Love Hanoi can give birth to networks, such as a network for non-profit organizations, an association of Christian drug rehabs, or a coalition for promoting integration of the handicapped

---

55   UN-Habitat, "I'm a City Changer", UN-Habitat http://imacitychanger.org/ (accessed 19 June 2014).

56   For more information, visit www.lovehanoi.org.

57   The Lausanne Movement, "Faqs", The Lausanne Movement http://www.lausanne.org/en/about/faqs.html (accessed 19 June 2014).

in mainstream education. If Love Hanoi were to become a network, it may limit the freedom to start other networks.

Yet, the need for a network is there and was clearly identified during our informal workgroup meeting. Like NCUT in the Philippines, a network is needed to unite and strengthen the various efforts for urban transformation. NCUT became the mother of other networks, groups, and organizations. The idea of a national coalition also increases the scope from focusing on one city to expanding nationwide, learning from and strengthening urban transformation initiatives throughout Vietnam. This might be a good reason not to call it the Love Hanoi Network, but perhaps the Hanoi Network for Urban Transformation and later change it to a national network.

Partnerships: It is only through relationships that God's love can be expressed more fully and completely. Love Hanoi as a movement can become an incubator for networks and partnerships. As DeBoer learned in Manila, some organizations and individuals may be more comfortable staying at the network level, while others are more eager to collaborate closely on shared projects. Partnerships not only strengthen each partner and provide synergy to accomplish the goal, they also are a witness of the unity among Christians to outsiders. During the previous Tet Holiday visit by ECVN, HIF, and a Korean Baptist church with the National Religious Affairs office, the Vice Director encouraged increased partnerships among the churches, specifically to do social work. The Easter concert was a display of partnership and collaboration, praised by city government. These partnerships can now be extended into other realms of ministry to express God's love for the city.

City Consultations: Big and Small

In order to connect more people, build networks, and create partnerships, the Love Hanoi Movement can implement more and varied consultations. Bakke and Sharpe give a number of ideas for one-day consultations and provide an outline for a three-day, city-wide consultation. Examples of one-day models are as follows:[58]

- City Ministry Summit: celebrate signs of hope, address most pressing issues

- New Pastors Orientation: introduce to civic leaders, ministries, congregations

- City Tour: expose church members, leaders, pastors to the city

- Think Tank: one issue, sharing, present papers, action steps

58   The models listed and quotations are quoted from Raymond J. Bakke and Jon Sharpe, *Street Signs : A New Direction in Urban Ministry* (Birmingham, Ala.: New Hope Publishers, 2006), 246-256.

- Denominational Consultation: assess urban ministry nationally and internationally

- Academic Seminars: one week, lectures and immersion, academic credit

- Three-day consultation: city-wide catalyst for creating partnerships and initiatives

A possible course of action for the Love Hanoi Movement to move forward is to establish what Bakke and Sharpe call the Envisioning Team which will organize on-going consultations, leading up to a three-day, city-wide event. Sharpe explains,

> "A team capable of networking widely in the city and providing the necessary resources to do good research is vital. This team should represent diverse ministries, churches, mission organizations, educational institutions, and ethnic groups and should have whole church connections. The team should include Roman Catholic, orthodox, mainline, evangelical, and Pentecostal representatives, as well as people from ministries working with homelessness, poverty, refugees, youth at risk, and other social issues."[59]

To find such team members, we need to ask the question, "Who knows everybody, and who can we trust?"[60] For example, Corrie DeBoer is mentioned as being the person in Manila with relational capital. Who are the Vietnamese and expatriate "Corries" in Hanoi? Who is a networker, has the influence to gather people across denominational and organizational lines, and has the relational capital needed to make this team successful? From what denominations and organizations do we want to pick these members? In addition to networkers, the team will need people with analytical skills and experience in the socio-economic and political realm as well as people with administrative skills.

Conclusion

The book of Acts tells the story of the first-century, missional, international church movement. Originating in Antioch of Syria, this movement spread not only westwards, but also to the Eastern and Southern hemispheres. The church thrived in urban centres, some known for their many chapels and cathedrals. The diaspora of the early centuries made it possible for the gospel to spread through word and deed.

59   Raymond J. Bakke and Jon Sharpe, *Street Signs: A New Direction in Urban Ministry* (Birmingham, Ala.: New Hope Publishers, 2006), 220.

60   Bakke and Sharpe, 221.

Today, the global diaspora is at a high point with almost one billion displaced around the world. Almost a quarter of those are intentionally and predominantly moving from rural to urban areas, from East to West, and from South to North. These are expatriates who, if they are Christian, find themselves attending international churches. The Global Diaspora Network and the Missional International Church Network see this as an opportunity to minister to, through, and beyond the diaspora. International churches are uniquely positioned to make an impact.

To do so, a number of things must be taken into consideration: What is the role of the international church and of the affluent church? What is the role of the pastor of such churches? Viv Grigg has helped to understand these roles and Catholic priests have shown us how to make the city our parish.

Finally, I have outlined how international churches can move within their given context to become missionally engaged through partnerships, networking, and starting a city-wide movement to love their cities. Using HIF and the Love Hanoi movement as an example, I have illustrated how international churches can be effective in urban mission around the globe. If it is possible in Hanoi, it surely can be done elsewhere.

Appendix: Three-Day Urban Consultation Agenda[61]

Concept: Bring together key people in the city to discover the signs of hope in the city, in a sense to cooperate with the Lord in the city. The consultation is designed to bring people together, through a broad spectrum, to get a greater grasp.

"Whole church, whole gospel to transform the whole city."

Anticipates: 100–200 people in attendance

FIRST DAY

Evening: 7:00 pm – 9:45 pm

1. Start off with case studies/ video (1 hour)

2. Singing (30 minutes)

2. Divide people in small groups (15 minutes)

   - What did they come looking for? (30 minutes)

   - What do they want to go home with?

4. Write responses on post-it board paper and maybe have three or four teams share (30 minutes). Their answers to these questions will serve as a "contract" for them.

SECOND DAY

Morning: 9:00 am – 12:30 pm

Refreshments

1. Signs of hope for the city (60 to 90 minutes: 6 individuals, 10–15 minutes each); Government leaders, non-profit leaders, business leaders: maybe three leaders share with everyone.

2. Divide into small groups:

   - Share the signs of hope for the city

   - Needs: what are the needs for the city

3. Lunch.

---

61   Bakke and Sharpe, 279–280.

Afternoon: 2:30 pm – 5:30 pm

1. Visit sites: See ministry in action — homeless, orphans, street kids, government people, education, tutoring. Have about fifteen available sites, each group will visit approximately three (duration: about five hours). Notice powerful vs. powerless.

2. Social event?

THIRD DAY

1. Visit a few more sites

2. Talk about what we have seen, what we have heard

3. Ray Bakke speaks

4. In groups: what should be done about it? New network/new relationships.

References

Asia Theological Forum. "New Books." edited by Jacob Bloemberg. Hanoi: Asia Theological Forum, 2014.

Bakke, Lowell. "Introduction." In *Overture 1: Manila*. Manila, Philippines: Bakke Graduate University, 2014.

Bakke, Raymond J. and Jon Sharpe. *Street Signs: A New Direction in Urban Ministry*. Birmingham, Ala.: New Hope Publishers, 2006.

Barth, Glenn. *The Good City*. Tallmadge, OH: S.D. Myers Publishing Services, 2010.

Beltran, Benigno. "Social Empowerment." In *Overture 1: Manila*. Manila, Philippines: Bakke Graduate University, 2014.

Beltran, Benigno P. *The Christology of the Inarticulate: An Inquiry into the Filipino Understanding of Jesus the Christ*. Manila: Divine Word Publications, 1987.

Brosowski, Michael, "Kids in Danger", Blue Dragon Children's Foundation http://www.bluedragon.org/meet-the-kids/street-kids/kids-in-danger/ (accessed 21 June 2014).

Butler, Phil. *Well Connected: Releasing the Power and Restoring Hope through Kingdom Partnerships*. Waynesboro, GA: Authentic Media, 2005.

Chu, Raineer. "Exegeting the City." In *Overture 1: Manila*. Manila, Philippines: Bakke Graduate University, 2014.

DeBoer, Lorisa. "Developing a Plan for Collaboration in Urban Leadership Development." Eastern Baptist Theological Seminary, 2000.

Gener, Tim. "Filipino Theology." In *Overture 1: Manila*. Manila, Philippines: Bakke Graduate University, 2014.

Grigg, Viv. *Cry of the Urban Poor*. Monrovia, Calif.: MARC, 1992.

Jenkins, Philip. *The Lost History of Christianity: The Thousand-Year Golden Age of the Church in the Middle East, Africa, and Asia- and How It Died*. 1st ed. New York: HarperOne, 2008.

Ma, Wonsuk and Julie C. Ma. *Asian Church and God's Mission: Studies Presented in the International Symposium on Asian Mission in Manila, January 2002*. Manila, Philippines: OMF Literature, 2003.

Sander, Nikola, Guy Abel and Ramon Bauer, "The Global Flow of People", Wittgenstein Centre for Demography and Global Human Capital http://www.global-migration.info/ (accessed 29 March 2014).

Swanson, Eric and Sam Williams. *To Transform a City: Whole Church, Whole Gospel, Whole City*. Grand Rapids, MI: Zondervan, 2010.

The Lausanne Movement, "Faqs", The Lausanne Movement http://www.lausanne.org/en/about/faqs.html (accessed 19 June 2014).

Tira, Sadiri Joy, ed. *The Human Tidal Wave*. Pasig City, Philippines: Lifechange Publishing, Inc., 2013.

UN-Habitat, "I'm a City Changer", UN-Habitat http://imacitychanger.org/ (accessed 19 June 2014).

USF Ricci Institute, "The Lotus and the Cross: East-West Cultural Exchange Along the Silk Road", University of San Francisco (accessed 4 June 2014).

Wanak, Lee, ed. *The Church and Poverty in Asia*. Manila, Philippines: OMF Literature Inc., 2008.

The Church's Call to Action, Advocacy, and Public Engagement

Written by Trish and Nigel Branken, with contributions from Rod Sheard, Paul Lau, and Pebbles Parkes

What is advocacy? What does public engagement include? What does it mean for the church's involvement in current affairs? Can the church be involved in politics and political decision-making? What is the current state of the church worldwide with regard to implementing strategies around action, advocacy, and public engagement? What does the Bible have to say about justice on behalf of the poor? Where has the church deviated from these texts? What are some solutions to this? How can we address the church worldwide, calling it to action on behalf of all people everywhere, regardless of income, race, class, religion, gender, or age? And will the church in our generation rise up to this challenge of getting involved in the messy issues of our world, or will it continue to abdicate its responsibility towards the "least of these"?

This report on the working group discussions, held at the 2014 International Summit for Urban Mission and which explored the subjects of action, advocacy, and public engagement, will attempt to partially answer these questions, while examining leading examples of advocacy in Malaysia. This report also includes looking at some Old and New Testament accounts of advocacy, as well as some current day examples of Christian advocacy in local communities.

Introduction

Jayakumar Christian, in his keynote address at ISUM 2014, concerning perspectives on poverty and transformation, said, "Poverty exists because the world did not give its best. We, the church, need therefore to give the poor our best. The church does not have the excuse to be mediocre". He preceded this by saying that "those who live among the poor live between hope and grief daily" and also encouraged all present to create their own moments of what he termed "intentional conflict" as part of a prophetic lifestyle, drawing on the examples set by Jesus where he healed people on the Sabbath (Mark 3:1–6 and Luke 13:10–17).

These were foundational thoughts for the working group examining the subjects of action, advocacy, and public engagement. The group wrestled with these challenging issues which frequently form part of the daily life of those involved in community transformation and those living amongst the marginalized. The group soon realized that this was mostly uncharted territory for many of the group's church contexts and that many questions would need to be asked and answered before any groundbreaking conclusions could be drawn.

Expectations

Initially, an expectations exercise was conducted amongst the team of twenty, who set out the following objectives:

- To learn about successful advocacy initiatives that have been tested and have become sustainable, firstly in the Malaysian church, and

- To hear stories of hope around the world in this area

- To exchange ideas for the building of awareness about advocacy and the empowering towards advocacy itself

- To develop effective strategies around issues of advocacy which result in lasting change in society and also which influence government policy towards marginalized groups

- To learn how to influence the public to care enough about injustice to act on it and to live differently

- To get a biblical perspective on advocacy including studying examples thereof

- To discuss how to move the local church to engage with justice issues, especially at a time when many churches do not model this

- To explore ways of bridging differing church viewpoints about engaging in issues of injustice

- To find successful methods of advocacy which avoid feeding into "god-complexes" which create unhealthy patterns of helping people

- To learn ways of leveraging the unique voice of university students and young people

- To discuss ways of developing a social movement.

Over the four days of discussion, the working group was invited to three different "immersion experiences", each of which had a measure of involvement in and success with advocacy issues.

Immersion Experience 1: Citizens' Network for a Better Malaysia (CNBM)

First on the program was a visit to the Citizens' Network for a Better Malaysia (CNBM), also called the dream centre, just outside of Kuala Lumpur. The CNBM was founded by Damansara Utama Methodist Church (DUMC), to create an awareness of national concerns based on biblical and sociological principles, and to defend the rights of people, including Christians, in need. CNBM has a keen interest in advocacy, generating public interest in policy, and working towards bringing about its change. Some key strategies with which they carry out their work are organising group discussions and events based on current issues, and networking with other NGOs. One of the organization's advocacy focus areas has been corruption and bribery.

Based on an analysis of the existence of bribery in both public and private sectors in Malaysia, some of CNBM's key points in forming a basis for their advocacy against corruption have been:

- The existence of a deeply entrenched patron/client mentality, even in the educational systems

- The inaction of Malaysian governments on critical issues and reports

- Highly biased politicians using their religion as a political tool, and

- A lack of sufficient external pressure on government to make changes in policy.

Some of the activities CNBM have launched as a result among their members in the area of bribery and corruption have been:

- Organizing forums

- Anti-corruption walks

- Car bumper stickers

- Voicing their opinions in publications, and

- Having display booths at various events.

They have also succeeded, in collaboration with the Centre for Public Policy Studies and the Institute for Democracy and Economic Affairs, in highlighting the fight against corruption to the Performance Management and Delivery Unit of the Prime Minister's office (PEMANDU). The key message of CNBM to their members is to actively try to stop corruption together, and not just to report on it.

Another specific area of work that CNBM has engaged in is that of election reform, and specifically fairer demarcation of electoral boundaries. The organization has also found it crucial for Christians to be vocal about political issues in their predominantly Islamic country, and especially to ensure that all marginalized groups have a voice in political decision-making. As a result they have set up electoral education groups, public opinion groups, and a "Christians in politics" support group. They have also trained polling agents and have conducted research into politics and the electoral landscape, as well as regularly meeting with politicians in government. There is a special focus on the poorest regions in Malaysia, Sabah and Sarawak, to increase their knowledge of their rights and democratic processes. People living in these communities suffer many injustices, including being pressurized to convert to Islam as well as the loss of their land to government without compensation.

Some other opportunities for exposure to advocacy that CNBM has initiated are:

- Special interest groups

- Weekend experiences

- Panel discussions

- Special events

- A newsletter which creates more discussion and awareness around this subject.

All of these initiatives are aimed towards mobilizing the church and increasing their involvement in justice issues.

The last presentation to the working group by CNBM was specifically on the rights of indigenous people groups in Malaysia to self-determination. There are two indigenous groups of Malaysians, the *orang asli* and the *anak negerit*, who make up only a small percentage of the population. These two groups of people are in fact the original inhabitants of the land but are often discriminated against and marginalized. The key issues raised in this final presentation by CNBM about indigenous people groups were:

- Their land rights

- Health

- Freedom of religion

- Education

- Birth certificates and

- Deforestation.

CNBM draws its inspiration for this work from Proverbs 31:8–9:

> "Speak up for those who cannot speak for themselves, for the rights of all who are destitute. Speak up and judge fairly; defend the rights of the poor and needy."

Working Group Reaction

Our working group was amazed at the coverage of this organization and how through its local church it was mobilizing its members and the church congregation to actively participate in advocating for the rights of different groups in Malaysia. This highly creative and organised group of people seemed so far ahead of many other local churches in their practice and understanding of their own church's involvement in this subject.

After this presentation we concluded the following about advocacy:

- Collaboration is very useful for work in advocacy.

- Many have found utilizing social media and other publications useful in creating awareness and mobilizing the church.

- The church, through its sheer volume of numbers and diversity of experience and influence, has the potential to be a powerful network to mobilize people for change.

- Evangelism and social justice should go together and need not be two separate arms of the church. This supports the holistic nature of the gospel. This idea was strongly upheld by Jayakumar Christian in his opening statements at the ISUM conference.

- Christians are sometimes reluctant to be associated with political activities and view these as challenging the authority that God has placed over them.

- The group agreed, however, that advocacy on behalf of the poor and marginalized is integral to the Christian faith and needs to be normalized within the church

Signs of Hope

There were so many encouraging lessons to learn from this unique immersion experience, one of which was succinctly captured by one of the presenters in this closing statement: "Getting involved in community work has changed the animosity against the church. People's perceptions of Christians have changed as they see them helping the community with different issues."

We saw each area of action and public engagement initiated by CNBM as a sign of hope in itself, as this well organised group committed itself fully to carry out the mandate of the Proverbs 31: 8–9 text.

Challenges to Hope

- The enormity of what this church was trying to take on in terms of the entire political and religious system was courageous and at times overwhelming.

- For many in the group this church was so far ahead of our own experiences that it would be very difficult to replicate their programs in other churches.

- It was evident that CNBM's involvement in electoral reform sometimes placed them at risk of religious and political persecution, as exemplified by a recent ban on public protests imposed by the government.

- CNBM is clearly a remarkable light on a hill. A major challenge to hope, however, is that their example is unique and not widely seen in the church.

Calls to Action

We recognized that this was an amazing model to the broader church of what advocacy, action, and public engagement could and should look like, and so left the dream centre feeling envisioned and encouraged, and determined to make a difference in our own communities back home, as challenging as that might be.

We realized that, in order to see these kinds of programs replicated, this would require deeper theological convictions about calls to justice as being central to integral mission.

Immersion Experience 2: Christian Advocacy Network On Poverty Issues (CANOPI)

Our second immersion experience was with a representative from CANOPI (Christian Advocacy Network On Poverty Issues) — Joyce Thong, its coordinator. CANOPI is a network of Christian organizations reaching across all denominations that aims to be the voice of people in need in Malaysia. It is a loose network for the sharing of stories which inspire and challenge actions, as well as a platform for acting together on different issues of advocacy. CANOPI aims to position Christians as advocates of justice and transformation in the nations that they are called to serve in. Malaysian Care was the first organization to be included in this network, followed by Micah Network and Micah Challenge.

The first campaign run by CANOPI was 10/10/10, a campaign to remember the poor and pray for them. It was a gathering of those working in the field of advocacy for the poor. A key recent campaign, "Exposed: Shining a Light on Corruption", was a global call for action against corruption, which dream centre/CNBM also took part in. In this campaign the church first started with the corruption they found in themselves, taking the speck out of their own eye, before attempting to remove the log found elsewhere (Matthew 7:5). They aimed therefore to create awareness in the church first, before confronting corruption in their society.

During this immersion experience the group discovered how widespread corruption proves a significant hurdle in eradicating poverty in Malaysia.

CANOPI works together with the Christian federation of Malaysia and is in partnership with the government's transformation program ministry, PEMANDU, and Transparency International.

Signs of Hope

Signs of hope that the group noted during this presentation included:

- The power and encouragement of working together as Christians from different organizations and churches

- Hearing a united voice from the church on different issues

- Seeing the church actively engaging in issues challenging to society

- As the church first dealt with its own issues of corruption, before taking on that of society around them, Ghandi's words rang true: "We must become the change we want to see in the world". As we take action in our own lives, we create hope that a new world is not only possible, but has already come.

Challenges to Hope

In this area the group felt that:

- The judgmental and often hypocritical attitudes and approaches of the church are a hindrance to change;

- It is easy to become discouraged in the absence of wide-scale societal change and thus true Christian hope is essential;

- There is an immense burden on the individuals who are part of CANOPI who are truly passionate;

- Fear often prevents people from taking on issues of advocacy.

- Calls to Action from the Church

In spite of the limited resources within the church for action, advocacy, and public engagement, there are often opportunities presented to the church in which small interventions can be significant and powerful. Being ready to seize these moments — which are often in times of national suffering following tragic or prominent historical events or in the face of obvious injustice — can amplify our voice and efforts. The church should be ready to embrace these opportunities.

It is important in our advocacy efforts to ensure that the voice and the participation of the poor and marginalized are valued and given prominence.

The local church should create networks with other church groups and/or Christian organizations in order to collaborate.

In the church's advocacy efforts, "god-complexes" should be avoided by working in equal relationships with the poor and not only on behalf of the poor.

Much work needs to be done to equip and empower marginalized groups, not only with a knowledge of their rights but with tools, resources, and methods to fight for their own liberation.

Immersion Experience 3: The Malaysian Bar Council

Our third immersion experience was a presentation by Andrew Khoo from the Malaysian Bar Council. He began by giving a thorough historical and political background to the current situation in Malaysia that gave a very helpful perspective on current human rights concerns and advocacy issues. He emphasized the fact that many of the current challenges of the disadvantaged have deep historical roots. This highlighted the need for a thorough understanding of these roots before embarking on any advocacy work, a principle the group felt could be applied to any community or issue requiring advocacy.

The Malaysian Bar Council is a professional body and an independent bar made up of over 10,000 advocates and solicitors, who together continually protect the cause of justice and the interest of the public and legal profession in Malaysia. The Council also supports and assists economically disadvantaged persons to be represented by advocates and solicitors, and uphold justice without the influence of fear or favour.

One area of work that the Malaysian Bar Council advocates in is cases around refugee status and rights — there are currently about 145,000 people registered as refugees in Malaysia. Other work includes assisting people on death row (of which there are 700 such people), cases of human trafficking, and immigrant labour conditions, to name a few.

The Bar Council continues to advocate for human rights in Malaysia despite many government restrictions on such civil society organizations.

Working Group Reaction

This presentation highlighted the need to engage in policy and legal reform through utilizing the courts. There are many lawyers in churches who should be encouraged to use their gifts to work towards a more just society. We were impressed by the volume and variety of legal aid that the Bar Council was providing to disadvantaged people.

Signs of Hope

Lawyers working together for justice are an example to other professions to seek ways of using their knowledge, skills, experience, and gifts to stand for a more just world.

Challenges to Hope

It was concerning to hear of governments exercising further "god-complexes", resulting in excluding the most marginalized.

Civil authorities often utilize their power to favour one religion to the exclusion of others.

In addition to this, those advocating for justice often face the challenge of religious persecution and professional exclusion.

Calls to Action

Work of this kind by a professional body of skilled lawyers and advocates should also be translated into similar advocacy work in different fields as represented by members of churches. In many of our local church contexts this kind of advocacy using networks of similarly skilled people does not seem to function on any level. We felt that the church worldwide should be urged to form groups of different skills or livelihoods which could together fight for justice in its various forms on behalf of marginalized groups.

Biblical Reflections

The Bible needs to inform church practice. With this in mind, the group discussed some of the many examples found in the Bible of action, advocacy, and public engagement.

Together, the Old and New Testaments contain over 2,000 texts about the poor and marginalized. American activist, pastor, and author, Jim Wallace, demonstrated the Bible's emphasis on the poor in his experiment a few decades ago, when he cut out with scissors all the texts referring to the poor, widows, orphans, refugees, and other marginalized peoples. What he found was that his Bible no longer held itself together when ignoring these texts.

There are many individuals throughout the Bible whose actions of advocacy were remarkable in carrying with them the heart of God towards marginalized groups.

In Genesis 18: 16–33, Abraham pleaded with God to save the people of Sodom and not bring upon them the judgement they deserved for their sins. (In fact, their sin is laid out in Ezekiel 16: 49–50: they "were arrogant, overfed and unconcerned; they did not help the poor and needy. They were haughty and did detestable things".)

Then in Genesis chapters 41—47, Joseph advocated on behalf of his whole family to be looked after in a severe time of famine, using his position of power and influence as second in command of Egypt. He thus secured the future of the Israelite nation, which was in desperate need at the time.

The book of Exodus reveals the character of Moses who appealed to the new pharaoh of Egypt many times to "let my people go", and with God's help performed many signs and wonders in the attaining of this freedom from a cruel slavery. He continued to advocate before God for the continuance of the Israelite nation during frequent times of subsequent sinful behaviour: the most life-threatening example of this perhaps being in Genesis 32: 9–14, during Moses' meeting with God on the top of Mount Sinai, where Moses pleaded for mercy for all the Israelites whom God was threatening to annihilate; while below his brother was encouraging everyone to make their own gods out of their golden ornaments.

Even the tent of meeting where Moses regularly met with God in a pillar of cloud "face to face, as a man speaks with his friend" (Exodus 33:11) represents a level of advocacy on behalf of a large group of refugees, the Israelites, who needed help to find their way towards their promised land.

This is starting to look familiar in many of our current day contexts and nations, where many displaced groups of refugees are being further discriminated against and victimized, held in captivity, often without access to legal review of their detention. Many are abused and even tortured. Challenging questions are raised:

- To what extent is the church willing to take up any of these causes before God and before new "pharaohs" who subject minority, marginalized groups to cruel, often inhumane, treatment?

- Do we, as twenty-first-century Christians, continue to read the laws found in the books of Exodus and Leviticus in terms of this never-ending theme of justice and dignity for all mankind, which comes from the heart of the triune God?

- And do we still strive to apply those laws that refer to the poor, the servant, and the alien in our midst, to our current day situations?

- For example, have we as the church recently considered the implications of our "manservant or maidservant" and "the alien within (our) gates" being included in the rest God commands from each of us on the Sabbath in the fourth commandment as laid out in Exodus 20: 8–11?

- And when last in our churches was there a message from one of the many texts found in the book of Proverbs exhorting us to treat the poor with fairness and dignity?

- When last did we hear spoken the words found in the first part of Proverbs 31, "speak up for those who cannot speak for themselves, for the rights of all who are destitute. Speak up and judge fairly; defend the rights of the poor and needy"?

And these examples are only a taste of the justice and social action that God is requiring of us as followers of Christ, as found in the first two books of the Old Testament. There are also the lives and actions of Joshua, Deborah, Gideon, Samson, and Daniel to further examine, and of course Esther, who was willing to risk her own life for the sake of the Jews whose lives were about to be sacrificed. And then there are the prophets, all of whom spoke out against Israel and surrounding nations, carrying a message from God against their evil practices.

In the New Testament, the incarnation, life, and teachings of Jesus (and even his death, where he identifies with a group of criminals on a cross) invite us into a lifestyle of living and working with the poor and marginalized:

- We have the Sermon on the Mount to consider with its ideas of practising love of our enemy.

- We can study the stories of how Jesus embraced:

  - Lepers shunned by the rest of his society (Matthew 8:1–4)

  - Samaritans (John 4:4–38).

- We can watch as Jesus stood on the side of:

  - Adulterers (John 8:1–11)

  - The demon-possessed (Mark 5:1–20)

  - Children (Matthew 19:13–15)

  - Poor widows (Mark 12:41–44),

  - Tax collectors (Luke 5:27–32 and Luke 19:1–10)

  - Prostitutes (Luke 7:36–50).

- We can also decide on the implications of how Jesus engaged with the rich young ruler in Matthew 19: 16–30, a topic of fierce current debate, and lastly
- We can consider what Jesus meant by his teaching about the sheep and the goats in Matthew 25: 31–46, whether these are really the criteria by which all people everywhere will be judged on the last day.

The Bible calls all Christians to embrace integral mission. There is no dichotomy in the Bible between social justice and evangelism. Both are critical to loving this broken world.

Examples of Advocacy in Our World

As part of our examination of this subject, we drew inspiration from some of the lives and teachings of those who are or have been living examples of advocacy on behalf of marginalized groups:

History is full of examples of individuals who have risen up to speak on behalf of the poor and marginalized: St Francis of Assisi, Dorothy Day, Martin Luther King Junior, Dietrich Bonheoffer, Nelson Mandela, Mahatmas Gandhi, Steve Biko, Desmond Tutu, Dom Helder Camara, Mother Teresa, William Wilberforce, and countless others. These people have all influenced history and shaped our cultures as they have lived lives committed to acting justly, loving mercy, and walking humbly before their God (Micah 6:8b).

Drawing on their inspiration, and continuing in their footsteps, across the planet, across denominational boundaries, signs of hope are emerging in the church. We see this in the lives of many Christians worldwide relocating, returning, or remaining in marginalized communities, living out their Christianity incarnationally.

Examples of this new movement are numerous and include:

- The new friars movement, which includes organizations such as Word Made Flesh, Servant Partners, and UNOH (Urban Neighbours of Hope) among others. Each of these organizations has stories of standing in solidarity with the oppressed and testimonies of lives devoted to justice. Ash Barker, founder of UNOH, shares many of these stories in some of his books, such as *"Finding New Life"*, *"Making Poverty Personal"*, *"Slum Life Rising"*, and *"Risky Compassion"*.

- Some, who were formerly part of these organizations, have gone on to start their own organizations, where they too continue the fight for justice from

198 SIGNS OF HOPE IN THE CITY

within marginalized communities. Craig Greenfield, from Alongsiders, and Kevin and Leakhena Knight, from Mannah for Life, are two outstanding examples in this regard. The Knight family live in the slums of Phnom Penh, Cambodia, and are constantly advocating for the land rights of the slum dwellers around them.

- In South Africa, again many examples can be found of families moving into marginalized communities to stand with the oppressed in a counter-cultural and subversive manner, against the values of consumerism, materialism, greed, individualism, and racism:

    - Eighteen years ago, after the fall of the apartheid government, Jan Viviers (a prominent South African lawyer), Karin Viviers, a social worker, and their three children, moved from the luxurious town of Stellenbosch to a small, previously "blacks-only" township nearby called Kyamandi to practise reconciliation.

    - Organizations such as Fusion, Oasis, Servants, Transform, and others have also pioneered with families moving into marginalized communities. There are many other families demonstrating hope in this way in South Africa.

In addition to this, many Christians around the world are beginning to take up specific causes of injustice, fighting issues like:

- Human trafficking: e.g., Annie Dieselberg of Night Lights International in Bangkok, Thailand;

- Female genital mutilation (fgm): e.g., Ann-Marie Wilson of 28toomany;

- Domestic violence and rape: e.g., Wangu Kanja of the Wangu Kanja Foundation in Nairobi, Kenya;

- Refugees and indefinite detention: e.g., Brad Coath of UNOH;

- The Palestinian/Israeli conflict: e.g., Sami Awad of the Holy Land Trust.

There are, of course, many other examples of action, advocacy, and public engagement which have been embarked upon by church groups and individuals, which, together with those above, should be an inspiration to the church as a whole to lead lives of love and compassion towards others, especially those on the margins.

General Signs of Hope

The following signs that the church is beginning to embrace advocacy encouraged us:

- Churches in many areas all over the world are starting to work together with other organizations to advocate for justice.

- The church is starting to see advocacy as part of their calling to the world and is seeing this as urgent.

- There is a growing deeper recognition in certain church groups that Christians are advocates with and for the poor. In some areas advocacy has become infectious between church groups.

- Many are beginning to live in solidarity with marginalized groups and talk with, rather than on behalf of them, thereby adopting a position of powerlessness when confronting those in power.

- The wider church has the skills and resources in people and finances to bring about change in the world around them.

- Advocacy is good for us. We become like Jesus; we understand Jesus better.

General Challenges to Hope

Our working group also noted the following challenges to hope in advocacy work implemented by the church generally:

- While there seems to be an initial response among Christians who affirm the ministry of advocacy in various forms, this response is often not sustainable and does not create movements of positive change around it, leading to a lack of consistent commitment to the on-going needs of marginalized groups.

- Many Christians do not have a holistic view of mission, instead seeing the primary purpose of mission as getting people "admission tickets" to heaven. Changing these mind-sets is difficult.

- Wealthier local churches that are inward-looking with a "clubhouse" mentality are not particularly concerned with issues of justice and this often leads to:

    - Lack of cooperation, unity, and reconciliation with other churches, Christian organizations and the community in the area of advocacy

- A privatized perspective of the gospel in its proclamation which does not concern itself with the wellbeing of the broader community and its struggles and inequalities
- Hand-outs towards marginalized groups to ease their own consciences, without any changes towards more just and sustainable lifestyles.

- Often the church seems more interested in protecting the status quo than in fighting for issues of justice — issues like capitalism, exploitative wages and working conditions, imperialism, patriarchy, etc., are often defended, sometimes even interpreting biblical texts to support its actions.

- The church is often unwilling to associate itself with subjects of a so-called "political" nature, which may challenge the corrupt ideals and practices of the government itself. These subjects include:

  - Inadequate, undignified, sometimes illegal housing
  - Exploitative minimum wages
  - Unequal provision of education for children from different economic backgrounds
  - Poor health care
  - Inadequate and undignified provision of water and sanitation, etc.

Many if not all of these issues are seen to be irrelevant to the church's gospel proclamation, which is often restricted to a narrow view of salvation, rather than upholding practices that give dignity to all of God's creation.

- Advocacy initiatives in the church sometimes arise from guilt complexes rather than genuine, transformative love, which can lead to practices that damage those whom the church is attempting to help.

- The church is often passive in the face of real trauma and suffering around them while maintaining active involvement in oppressive patterns of life. For example, there has been little church debate or protest about the continuing oppressive minimum wage imposed by the South African government, while most Christians who employ workers in their homes or companies continue to exploit their workers with the adoption of this wage. Most Christian employers are ignorant of the Bible's requirements to treat their workers justly.

- Lastly, advocacy is difficult to measure in its impact. Sustainable movements of change across the world are easier to quantify compared to the changed lives of individuals who are helped through many processes over differing time periods.

General Call to Action to the Church Worldwide

"Advocacy is not safe or risk free. We need to be prepared to give our lives" — Jayakumar Christian.

With these words as a foundation, based on biblical teachings and examples in the area of action, advocacy, and public engagement, our call to action to the broader church is:

- To urgently embark on sustained training programs to train its members in advocacy issues and to encourage their involvement, using its own resources, as has wonderfully been demonstrated by the dream centre/CNBM.

- To normalize integral mission including incarnational living within the church.

- To start with what each local church already has in resources and people, without waiting until it seems to have enough to engage with issues of advocacy.

- To give its best and not a token gesture, just to ease its conscience, to advocacy issues.

- To find common ground between churches, allowing and enabling people to work together and pooling their resources and people skills for advocacy work.

- To concern itself with holistic, integral mission which includes confronting the powers with enemy love, and creative, humanizing, and humble actions, and finally

- To adopt sustainable changes in individual and corporate lifestyles which seek to narrow the gap between rich and poor, advantaged and disadvantaged, in all of our communities across the planet.

Conclusion

We believe in a church that, motivated by the sacrificial and unconditional love of Christ, can bring about the change required to bring dignity and self-worth to every human being on planet earth.

We believe that the church can make the changes towards this end.

We invite the church worldwide to engage more fully with the issues their communities, their regions, and their countries face.

We implore the church to relinquish its comfort-seeking, apolitical, and judgmental exclusivity in order to embrace a suffering world and to work towards greater equality and dignity between all people, regardless of gender, race, religion, class, or sexual orientation.

We invite the church to re-examine their lives and the life and teachings of Christ their leader, in order to arrive at a fairer and more loving representation of the heart of God towards all of his created image-bearers.

Engaging the Powers in Transforming Community

Emil Jonathan Soriano and Rey Lemuel Crizaldo

Should the people of God join the squabble for securing positions of power in this world? Can a Christian be partisan and plunge into the political arena, fight tooth and nail, to wield the authority to run the affairs of the government? Such questions of whether the church should meddle with politics have always been contentious. Opinions and theological positions range from separation and seclusion at one end, and models of religious political "domination" at the opposite end. But if T.S. Elliot is right when he argues, "The church's message to the world must be expanded to mean 'the church's business to interfere with the world,'"[1] then how exactly should the people of God do it in the realm of politics?

This story features how churches, united and conscious of their distinct role in the community, could be a potent force in transforming the political atmosphere of a community within the political configuration of Philippine society.

It narrates an experience of "Christian" political engagement during the national elections of 2010 in one of the largest municipalities of Marinduque, Philippines. Through training towards the promotion of doing "Integral Mission", particularly expressed in good governance, churches were able to sharpen their understanding of the political process and deepen their understanding of how a Christian framework can enrich their political activities and its impact on the people in the community.

---

1   Eustace Lovatt Hebden Taylor, *The Christian Philosophy of Law, Politics, and the State: A Study of the Political and Legal Thought of Herman Dooyeweerd of the Free University of Amsterdam, Holland as the Basis for Christian Action in the English-Speaking World* (Nutley, NJ: Craig, 1967).

Background: The Lure of Partisan Politics

In 2004, the Philippines witnessed for the first time evangelical Christians coming together and becoming intensely involved in the political scene. This was brought about by a popular evangelist and founder of one of the largest evangelical churches declaring his intention to run for the highest office in the land on the platform of restoring righteousness in the government. Many local churches all over the country participated in launching an unprecedented, massive grassroots election campaign. The evangelical community suddenly found itself engrossed and as well divided over the issue of "partisan" politics.

During the campaign period of the 2004 Presidential elections, the churches in Marinduque were quickly mobilized by influential evangelical leaders from Manila to support the candidacy of the popular evangelist. Within the local association of pastors in the province, campaign organizers were formed into the Marinduque Christian Movement (MCM) as a platform for the campaign machinery and the motorcades that circulated all over the province.

At that time, the pastors had no clear-cut framework for Christian political involvement. But most of them felt a strong sense of solidarity with other Christians desiring a godly and righteous government. It was this resonance with the rest of the Christian community that made it easy for them to be convinced to jump on the campaign bandwagon. Said one of the local pastors, "*Because of our desire for change... we were easily persuaded to join in the campaign*".

Amidst the overwhelming support, some of the pastors admitted a degree of hesitation: "*It is not clear to us the very reason why a minister or a servant of God would want to govern the nation. We are not that confident to explain to our people a biblical basis for our involvement in the issues of politics.*" Others pointed to the constitutional provision of the separation of church and state in the Philippines, but confessed the lack of proper understanding on its specific application. "*What we know of the separation of church and state is that church should not meddle in the affairs of politics.*"

Nonetheless, the desire to see change in the political system and the need to install a righteous government prevailed. Among the loud sentiments at that time were the following:

- "We need to have a taste of a righteous government."

- "We need a leader who loves the country and God."

- "We can have a leader that truly fears God and one who is a true worshipper of God."

- "This is the opportunity and the way towards change."

The unstated assumption in all these sentiments was that an unflinching Christian who hates corruption so much, holding the seat of Presidency, would be the answer to the corruption that has ravaged the country like a plague. This political "partisanship" pretty much describes the churches' attitude towards the election campaign of 2004. Unfortunately, the "evangelical" candidate miserably lagged in the polls and eventually lost the heroic bid for political position. Coming with the loss was a severe fragmentation among the body of Christ in the Philippines over the issue of whether the path of political partisanship had been injurious to the church's witness or not.

Shift in Political Engagement

Six years later, in the national elections of 2010, a remarkable change in the political orientation occurred among the pastors and church leaders of the municipality of Buenavista in Marinduque. There was still a heightened sense of vigilance and a desire to move in fresh ways that would help shape good governance in their province and the country. A pastor remained resolute, *"The Church should not remain silent in the issues of politics"*.

But from being driven by the simplistic notion that having a Christian president sitting in the halls of power would yield a favourable leverage for the spread of the gospel and the fight against corruption, a more nuanced political understanding emerged. They started to look at their political engagement as a form of Christian witness and also developed the notion that churches are a catalyst for change and therefore instrumental in God's desire to transform politics. As a local pastor put it, *"The church is called to function not just as priest, but also as prophet, bringing the Word of God to the world"*.

Noticeable also was the change of outlook on partisan politics.

Unlike in 2004, where they openly campaigned for a certain candidate, the pastors and church leaders instead focused in a "non-partisan" electoral advocacy. Upon ascertaining that vote buying remained the perennial root of corruption in their province, the pastoral association invited Bishop Jonel Milan, founder of the ASIN advocacy ("Ang Suhol Iwaksi Natin — Let's put a stop to bribery and vote buying"). He issued a challenge for the group to counter bribery and vote buying in the coming elections. This made a huge impact among the pastors. One leader reported, *"Our involvement in this election went deep to the root cause of our problems which is bribery/vote-buying"*.

With much prayer and discernment, the church leaders unanimously shifted to a massive "voter education" program in the community.

1. Two months before the election day, they launched the ASIN Caravan, saturating every *barangay* and spreading the message of their advocacy on anti-vote buying. The caravan was comprised of motorcades going around the municipality encouraging citizens to resist selling their votes and to carefully study their choice of candidates. A jingle was played on loud speakers as the caravan rolled through the streets. They produced and distributed creative campaign materials like fans, comics, tarpaulin ads, and t-shirts. Huge, colourful and creative tarpaulin ads were posted on every church building warning people never again to sell their vote.

2. Back in 2004, there had been direct persuasion for church members to vote for a certain candidate. Discernment and selection were in the hands of pastors and church leaders, and endorsed to the congregation. Some used to believe that, *"As leaders, it is our responsibility to persuade our members to vote for the Christian brother who truly fears God"*. But in 2010, while some pastors and leaders still opted to vote for the popular evangelist (who chose to run again for the second time), the church leaders in the Buenavista pastoral association agreed to educate their members and allow them to weigh candidates on their own. The pastors and church leaders opted to empower their members by providing the necessary data and criteria for making an informed choice. They distributed clear biblical criteria for selecting candidates: the 5 K criteria that includes "Karakter" (character), "Kakayanan" (competence), "Karanasan" (experience and track record), "Kongkretong Plataporma" (concrete platform), and "Koneksiyon" (political connections).

A series of local candidates' forums was organized in key strategic places in the municipality to allow their members and other people in the municipality to hear from politicians themselves about their respective platforms. Moreover, the forums allowed the audience to interact with and challenge the candidates with several essential issues needing attention in the community: opportunities for abundance, health care, provision of education, and environmental care. The candidates' forums proved to be a key strategy. They provided a venue for the people to have the chance to meet the candidates in person, ask questions, and air their concerns. The face-to-face process helped the people to better discern the characters of the candidates. A powerful feature of the forum was the participation of young people through a forceful rendition of theatre exposing the various schemes of vote-buying and showing the audience its dire consequences.

3. Another critical component of their voter education initiatives was the effort to provide information and recent developments on the new Automated Election System (AES) implemented by the national government for the 2004 elections. This activity helped people, in particular the technologically challenged in the far-flung areas of the municipality, to become familiar with the PCOS machine, the new ballot form, and the flow of voting in the precinct. They observed, *"Many people are discouraged from voting because they are quite intimidated with using computers"*. Unfortunately, the Government's Commission on Elections (COMELEC) was unable to provide awareness raising and capacity building with regards to the use of AES in Buenavista. This motivated the leaders all the more to provide education on AES.

They also promoted a positive stand on the automated election system. While national media and many groups tended to focus on the negative scenario and conspiracy theories about the possible technological glitches, the pastors embraced a more positive attitude, but at the same time a vigilant stance, on the AES. Against the huge amount of doubt and loss of confidence that people can absorb from media reports, the pastors built hope and confidence in the credibility of the electoral process among their constituents.

The above shift in the strategic involvement of the pastors and church leaders from their 2004 stance to their 2010 engagement emanates from a development of a clearer biblical framework. They went through a careful process that allowed them to understand the biblical implications of viewing and handling power, and engaging "the-powers-that-be" in a particular way. Their understanding of this framework manifested, for example, in their view of their own exercise of power and authority in their respective churches. They shifted from endorsement to empowerment, recognizing that the more significant ministry they could provide for their members was to allow each voter to choose and to live a life with dignity, purpose, passion and risk. As one pastor puts it, *"It is important that people have the freedom of choice"*.

With popular local actors and media personalities so often endorsing candidates with much effectiveness, this education drive enabled the church to wield influence in Philippine society. People gained a better appreciation of the role of the church as an alternative and prophetic voice in society on national concerns.

These realizations led pastors and leaders to seek tools that will provide information and education for their members. Instead of focusing on political personalities, they opted to focus on issues. They sought to provide people with clear Bible-based criteria for choosing a candidate. A pastor reported, *"The people's consciousness was opened... people were made aware of how to become more responsible voters... voting not on the basis of kin relations and ties... but knowing their true vision and purpose"*.

While the pastors and leaders recognized that such an endeavour would be a daunting task, they were nevertheless determined to go head on with the issue. Some leaders commented that, *"People in Marinduque grew up in this culture of bribery. This will be very hard to eradicate... they can sell their votes for a kilo of rice"*. They knew that at the core of it was an economic issue of poverty as well: *"People here have this thinking that they can make money during election time. There is a free market of money"*. But this did not weaken conviction. On the contrary it drove them to consolidate all the more their efforts, pool their resources together, and draw strength from their united stand for clean elections.

Also, the pastors and leaders chose to extend understanding on matters where they knew they may differ. It proved inevitable that some church leaders chose to carry a particular candidate and engaged in partisan campaigns, but this did not affect their unity. They handled it with a great deal of maturity. Remarked one of the pastors, *"We have high respect for one another and we honour one another's perspective. Even if other pastors are vocal about supporting one particular candidate, this was a non-issue. What unites us all is our focus on the anti-vote buying campaign."*

The Story behind the Change

This inspiring story of collaboration among church leaders for ushering transformation in the community was a product of another layer of partnership.

Four years after the 2004 elections, the pastors and church leaders of Buenavista received help from the community organizers of Norwegian Mission Alliance Philippines (NMAP).[2] NMAP is a Christian development agency which at that time had decided to expand their work in the island of Marinduque. Through NMAP's facilitation and mediation, the pastors reorganized themselves and formed a new

2   http://nma.org.ph/

ministerial fellowship called Buenavista Christian Leaders Ecumenical Fellowship (BCLEF). Compared to their previous attempts to form an association, the new coalition had a wider composition of membership cutting across denominational and religious affiliations to include the Roman Catholics, Aglipayan (Philippine Independent Church), and some more evangelical groups previously not in their circle. United in one fellowship, churches that were once hostile towards one another are now sitting and doing things together for the common good. They resolved that they needed some capacity-building in the area of political engagement and social transformation.

As a response, in 2009, NMAP partnered with the Institute of Studies for Asian Church and Culture (ISACC) to journey with the pastors in articulating a theological framework for community transformation. ISACC conducted a series of training on doing "Integral Mission" and popular political education in support of the thrust of Micah Challenge Philippines campaign for deepening Christian engagement with poverty and corruption. The "Integral Mission" training helped the pastors to develop a sense of transformational mission, consciousness of social responsibility, and pro-active community involvement. The popular political education provided the pastors with an overview of Philippine political culture, particularly the recent involvement of the evangelical church in the political life of the country. It also provided the option of actively engaging in non-partisan electoral engagement.

The training series helped the pastors to crystallize their framework for political engagement. It helped solidify their biblical convictions and foundations regarding the relationship of faith and politics. The changes from political endorsement to voters' education, the shift from partisan campaigning to non-partisan advocacy, and the aggressive awareness-raising regarding the Automated Election System are but manifestations of the development of a more mature and coherent framework for the role of churches in the political life of the community.

Legacy and Impact for the Community

BCLEF's united thrust against vote buying and provision of strategies for voter education grew into a powerful voice in Buenavista. A woman pastor commented, "*The politicians were surprised; they thought we would be carrying a particular candidate*". For the alarmed local politicians, BCLEF's collective voice proved to be too strong to be disregarded. Their attendance in the candidates' forum organized by the pastors attested to this.

Moreover, the municipality of Buenavista noticed a significant drop in vote buying and bribery. Since the people were becoming more aware of the ills of vote buying, some candidates tried to raise the price of the bribe per vote. One pastor reported, *"Although there was still vote buying, the numbers have dropped significantly. We cannot eradicate vote buying in just one election. Some candidates who had a reputation for buying votes ceased to buy votes; as a result they lost."* BCLEF was able to serve as a true conscience in the community. One pastor observed that, *"Those who bribe and buy votes cannot look us straight in the eye, and likewise those who sold their votes truly felt ashamed"*.

Others said that BCLEF's strong advocacy inspired a number of people, especially those politicians who are truly competent but discouraged from running due to lack of funds. A woman pastor told us that, *"Some of the aspiring politicians who are competent but poor gained hope. They saw that it is possible to run for public office without much money."*

After the elections, BCLEF gained the respect of the community, and the local government started to seek the help of the pastors. Their collective effort was truly a testimony to the unity of Christians. People around them saw a strong united voice and a unified body moving together rather than as separate religious groups working independently, and at times, against each other.

Some Concluding Reflections

As a general note, the BCLEF experience highlights the significance of a clear biblical framework for political engagement. The united stance of the pastors was largely due to their solid understanding of what the Bible says about the role of the church in the political affairs of the nation. Without such a consensus, it would have been hard for the once fragmented group to unite under one advocacy banner.

Also, the BCLEF experience showed that a united Christian community is possible and that the possibilities for it to create an impact on the community are tremendous. It also affirmed that the church could be a political force without necessarily joining the political race for power. Its non-partisan stance has helped to build its credibility and integrity among the non-Christian community and even among the politicians themselves. Beholden to no one but to the sole interest of promoting good governance, the BCLEF experience is a testament to the power of the church's prophetic voice to create an impact within the community and effect transformation.

This is a vivid picture of what Melba Maggay, President of the Micah Network, articulated as the role of the church in the political life of a nation. *"The church has no need to play politics in order to wield influence. Simply by being itself, by being true to the power of its convictions and the purity of its purpose, it has power. Its authority lies in its own capacity to persuade others to believe in the integrity of its propaganda, not in the acquisition of political clout descending to the level of a power bloc."*[3] Elsewhere, she differentiated how the use of this "power" could take form. She said, *"From your faith tradition, and your world values, you stand up for it in public space... This 'prophetic tradition' is different from politicking...Politicking is when you use your institutional influence to put people into office. Now, the Church is not supposed to be in that business. The Church is supposed to be in the business of upholding moral values in secular space. That's prophetic."*[4]

The political engagement of the church leaders of Buenavista in Marinduque is a glimpse of this "prophetic" dimension of the church's ministry.

References

Maggay, Melba Padilla. *Transforming Society*. Oxford: Regnum, 1994.

Taylor, Eustace Lovatt Hebden. *The Christian Philosophy of Law, Politics, and the State: A Study of the Political and Legal Thought of Herman Dooyeweerd of the Free University of Amsterdam, Holland as the Basis for Christian Action in the English-Speaking World*. Nutley, NJ: Craig, 1967.

---

3 Melba Padilla Maggay, *Transforming Society* (Oxford: Regnum, 1994), 61–62.

4 http://www.rappler.com/specials/pope-francis-ph/stories/75815-catholic-church-role-politics

The Whole Church on a Whole Mission to the Whole World

By John Perkins

Transcribed by Sarah Strip

I am really excited to be speaking here today. I have spent my last 57 years becoming a Christian. I grew up with a non-Christian background in Mississippi and dropped out of school somewhere between the third and fifth grades and never went back. I did not see much Christianity and knew little about it because my family did not participate often in church. I was 27 years old when I came to Christ. Then I began to understand Christianity more. The reality was that in my community Christianity had become a therapeutic religious system that had very little to do with the social and economic conditions of the people. African Americans adjusted themselves to the ever-present racial oppression and responded with a religion that focused on things like healing people so that they could function within the system.

So I came to faith in that context. I began to read the Bible and study it. I was trying to learn about Christianity and how it works through the New Testament, and what the early church was like. I found that I had to learn all over what I had been taught about Christianity growing up. During this time of learning, I went back to Mississippi from California where I had moved. While I was trying to express to our people this newfound faith, all kinds of opportunities opened up for me to share the gospel. I had an area that circles about one hundred miles, and I got to go into the public schools. I ended up with 15 high schools and elementary schools, and two junior colleges that I visited on a monthly basis. In that process, I became a teacher, teaching the Word of God. Then I worked to establish the Christian Community Development Association (CCDA) and have become a big part of that movement in America and the rest of the world.

The CCDA has put together what we have come to call holistic Christian community development. We define that as the whole church taking on the whole gospel. We think in terms of the universality of the church to understand all of the vision within it. We are taking the whole church on a whole mission to the whole world. It seems to me that this mission fits what Jesus did when he was incarnated God here on earth. We believe that is what he did after his death and resurrection. Jesus sent the disciples out into the world by saying something very unique to them. He said, "Go into all the world and very carefully disciple the nations and teach them to observe the life of Christ and how he lived".[1] As he was, so we are to be in the world. We see this in all four Gospels, and Luke continued to tell this story in Acts by looking at the church as it began to emerge.

While I'm excited about all the new church planting, particularly in my country, but also around the world, the big excitement is that these church plants are confronting the great evil, the evil of enslavement and oppression. Confronting the great evil is what I call justice. I see justice as a management and stewardship issue. It is really about us understanding who owns the earth. In the biblical account, the earth is the Lord's and the fullness thereof and all that dwells therein. You cannot understand justice apart from being a good steward. It seems like that is really what it is about. If you come at justice as just a social issue, you miss the full understanding. Another social issue is not radical enough in our society, so justice must include stewardship. If you follow Jesus' teaching here on earth, he talked of God as the creator and that we have responsibility over that creation. The poor are those who do not have open access to the land and the management of it. Jesus challenges this system in his parables in terms of stewardship when he said, "I have come that you might have life, and life more abundantly".[2]

We should not over-embrace the world's political, social, and economic structures and deify them in life. In our society we have deified capitalism instead of using a prophetic voice within it or calling it to be accountable. But the church is to be God's prophetic people. They are to be the children of God and the continuation of the incarnated Christ on earth. The idea is that God, through the Spirit, is living out that

1   Matthew 28:19.

2   John 10:10.

life in us, and we are to be that prophetic people. We are to be a witness to society and a witness of peace within the church. We are to accept that suffering and pain will come, but not stop our mission. Rather we are to go forth in it. Since the church was established on the rock so that the gates of hell cannot overcome it, the church is to be this witness and force in the world and follow Christ's teachings.

The Call to Discipleship

What I now see as the weakness of the church is the life of discipleship. We are making people Christians before we disciple them. The church at Ephesus is the exemplary church in terms of discipleship, based on the teachings of Paul. I think we all accept that our teachings on discipleship come from Paul (and a little also from Peter and John), but what we have to worry about in the church is the apostasy and the turning away because of false teachers in the church. For example, I think we have a very serious problem in the church with personality cults. Instead of praising God for his redemptive work and what he can work out through us, we have twisted Christianity into a financial prosperity church, which is not being challenged. The issue is how do we put Jesus back into the centre of the church as the real Shepherd of the flock and the sheep? — where Jesus is the leader and the pastors are the under-shepherds, who are careful not to make the church just their own. I see that as a real weakness, and I see that weakness spreading throughout the world.

As I get information from the field about these growing churches in Africa and other parts of the world, it grieves me that we are not challenging the prosperity gospel with discipleship and teachings in the Word of God. We need to choose Paul's teachings in Ephesus, including his warning to the church when he was on his way to Jerusalem. This is a big warning, and it is applied to all the teachings of the church as they relate to false teachers and personality cults that would like to replace Christ and become heads of churches. I think this is very, very serious because we have a lot of churches not demonstrating the power of discipleship as they should be.

This is the reason why I am so committed to the multiracial church because racism, bigotry, and tribalism are really just economic exploitation at the heart of them. Now every time we turn around the church is exploiting the poor people, and they are not being taught. I am in some ways an example of that. I think it is great to know a lot about theology, I believe that. People all over are establishing centres at colleges and universities in my name and giving scholarships and things like that. But within the church I think that the Spirit of God can use the feeblest people, and I see that in life too. I go to jails and mental institutions and many times I can find people there who have a greater understanding of the biblical texts than the theologians in the schools. I believe that the Holy Spirit is the main teacher of the Word of God. Jesus taught that "when the Holy Spirit comes, he will lead us and guide us into church and will guide us to the things to come".[3] Therefore, churches have the responsibility to disciple people and teach them the Word of God. I believe that we are falling down on making that discipleship happen.

The principles that undergird this approach to discipleship have come out of our struggle as we have read the Word of God and tried to put together a philosophy of development that included a holistic approach to humanity's problems. The Word of God is central because it is when people are obedient to the Word of God that the power of God is released in people's lives. Somewhere between hearing God's voice and believing it, faith is born. Faith comes by hearing the Word of God with the idea of obeying it. As we try to share in this holistic, social, economic work of the church, the principle is that we are actively doing social projects for the public good, such as providing healthcare and meeting the needs of the people and the church. We are at the very least reflecting the kingdom of God that is coming.

We believe that the church has to be a community of alternatives, that is, an alternative to the world's systems which are fallen, and an alternative people here on earth. Of course, the greatest miracle of all that we should be part of is breaking down the racial and cultural barriers in society instead of going around them. God's radical love must fuel us, and we must find ways to express that love in action. I hear this call to love when Paul says, "I am not ashamed of the gospel for it is the power of God to bring salvation".[4] I think at times the church has minimized the power of the gospel and has accommodated heresy within the church. This destroys the power of the gospel. We need to nurture people in this holistic truth that Jesus Christ is absolutely our Shepherd. I am afraid of these personality cults because I am afraid they are not getting at the deep issues, but are looking at success based on materialism.

Today many Christians do not know how to read the Bible with enough depth. As a result, we have created a long history of disobeying the central truth of the Word of God, and we are not seeing its power as present in our society. As the church we are losing our first love. Yes, there was good fellowship last night, and I felt joy being a part of the Malaysian people. I know in most places people enjoy us Americans

3   Acts 1:8.

4   Romans 1:16.

singing and our dancing, and those are wonderful things. But all cultures are fallen, and all cultures need to be redeemed. We too easily forget to depend on each other even as we bring people together. We leave them in their little cultural villages and behaviour without challenging them, and if we are not careful, we start to deify a culture instead of challenging a fallen society. The key of love is that it is stronger than racism and bigotry, for the world will know we are Christians by our love.

Discipleship is a journey. In this holistic approach we find three roads of a well discipled life: the Damascus Road, the Emmaus Road, and the Jericho Road. These are images to show us what it would look like to be an effective, New Testament-like disciple. These three roads are a journey, the pilgrim's progress. We are on our way somewhere, and all of the tribes are there, but we are keeping our eyes on Jesus, the author and perfecter of our faith.

The Damascus Road

The first road is the Damascus Road. It gives us a picture of an evil person made good. You all know the story of the apostle Paul. He was an intellectual, a genius. The Christians were witnessing in Jerusalem; they were living in community and turning the city upside down. At Pentecost there were people from every language under heaven. That is important for challenging our thinking when we accommodate racism or tribalism because at Pentecost we see a miracle that is the radical love that can burn through the racial and cultural barriers. Jesus demonstrated that in his own life and ministry in the villages. In a word, the church has become too easy because we have benefited from the exploitation of others. Life becomes very cheap.

But the first road is the road of conversion, of becoming a Christian, being born again. You can see this in the story where Esau and Jacob were fighting over the birthright. Eventually there came a time when Jacob was reborn from above. You can see this in Jesus' talk with Nicodemus. Nicodemus was a great leader of Israel and an educator and historian. But when he was confronted with Jesus, Jesus told him, "You must be born again".[5] Nicodemus was confused, but Jesus told him that even though he was a great teacher, he did not recognize that Jacob had to become Israel, and when he became Israel he was born again, born into the kingdom of God. Jacob came to the end of his own trickery and at the end of his own trickery he was born again, and then out of that came that relationship with his brother.

Conversion is not a human effort. People are not born again because we make

5   John 3:3.

it happen for them. No one comes to God unless God himself draws that person. Salvation is absolutely by grace. Grace is all of the attributes of God towards humankind in redemption. All of those great principles are put together, and they are called grace. God uses grace to bring us to himself as people obey and teach the Word of God. The Word of God is God's creative power released in the world. The world is created by him, and by faith we understand the world is held together by the Word of God. So the ability to teach and disciple people is what we equip people with when we send them into the world. I can't overemphasize that.

We see this first road lived out in this mean apostle. He persecuted the church. He participated in killing Stephen, and it filled him with such anger (and joy really) because of the message Stephen preached. Stephen's message was one of the most intelligent, historical messages in the New Testament. You see, Stephen's message confronted Paul's arrogance. Paul believed that he had learned from the best teachers, and so he killed Stephen. Then Paul went to the high priest and got letters to arrest even more followers of Christ. Paul knew about the Christians because he heard they were turning the world upside down with their love for each other and their teachings about Jesus Christ and the Word of God.

After the stoning of Stephen, Paul ended up on the Damascus Road where he met the Saviour. God spoke to Paul. Paul heard the voice, yes; but more importantly, he believed and came to know with certainty that the voice was the voice of God. On the Damascus Road the apostle was handcuffed, or we could say, embraced by God's love. When he was struck down, he heard Jesus say, "Saul, Saul, why are you so mean? Why are you persecuting me?"[6] In an angry outburst, Saul said, "Who are you?" The voice said, "I am Jesus". In this encounter the apostle was apprehended by God's love, and he wanted to be apprehended again and feel the squeeze of love that he first felt on the Damascus Road. Then he cried out and heard the voice and believed. He asked, "Lord, what is it you would have me do?"[7] The voice spoke through Ananias, "I have called you to send you far away to the Gentiles to have you appear before kings, and judges, and governors of the world to turn people from darkness to light and from the power of Satan to the power of God".[8] At the end of his ministry, Paul testified, "I was not disobedient to that heavenly vision".[9]

6   Acts 9:4

7   Acts 9:6

8   Acts 9:15

9   Acts 26:19

So the first road is conversion where you come to know Jesus Christ. You confess your sins, and turn from your sins. For three days after encountering God's voice, Paul confessed his sin. Ananias was involved in this process so that Paul would not be a cult leader. All disciples of Jesus Christ need others involved in their lives. You need people to disciple you so that you can live a life of discipleship. We really cannot do it alone; we need the small groups in our churches; we need the personal relationships we have with each other. That helps us with some sense of humility. The church should be a place that together equips the saints for the work of the ministry.

When we deeply, radically love each other and care for each other, we can confess our sins to one another, which is a part of conversion. It is there we discover we are blind like Paul on the Damascus Road. When Paul met up with Ananias, his eyes were opened to a vision from God. It is important to follow that vision: God calls us, he gifts us, and he gives us skill. We need to seek that vision, learn our gift, and serve Christ in unity. The gifts ought to be used in the ministry of the church. People say to me that they are discovering their gifts for their own personal ministry. But I teach them that their gifts are supposed to be used and exercised within the body of Christ. Gifts are for the nurturing of the saints first and foremost, so that we need each other. The body needs to commission us to go out and be an extension of God's grace and love as we ordain people. Then the church needs to send them forth, so that there is a sense of responsibility and you are not on your own.

The Emmaus Road

The second road is the Emmaus Road. The Emmaus Road is living the resurrected life. Christ is living his life through us. The Christian life is the out-living of the in-living Christ. Prayer is listening, so that Jesus the Good Shepherd can lead us and guide us. Oh yes, God tells us to talk to him and to call on him. God already knows everything we tell him, but we need to affirm that with our own lives and words. We have to confess with our mouth to make a promise to God, and make a promise to people around us. It is important to live in that promise and be faithful in light of that promise that God has made to us.

On the Emmaus Road are Christ and the resurrection. As the men were going back home, they discovered that Jesus was walking with them. That is an experience that I love. God needs to walk with us and talk with us, and the big thing is that he needs to tell us that we belong to him. Out of that we have the joy of the Christian life. It should be joyful that God has enlisted us to be involved in his redemptive plan. That should be enough. That should be enough for our pride that this God of heaven, the God who said let there be light, has shined light into our hearts to give us the light of the knowledge of the love of God as we follow the Great Shepherd of the sheep. So the Emmaus Road is the road of discipleship.

The Jericho Road

The last road is the Jericho Road. These roads ought to be lived together at the same time. It is not that we perfect one and then the next. We are perfecting them all as we obey. As soon as we are converted we should be telling someone else the gospel. So the Jericho Road is the road of service. The road of rescuing the perishing, caring for the dying, snatching them from bondage to sin. It is the Jericho Road that goes across racial barriers. That is the great truth, the great miracle. I cannot get over it, and I am not ashamed of the gospel because it is the power to bring Jews and Gentiles together in one body, for in Christ there is no Jew or Gentile, slave or free, but we are one in Jesus Christ. That is the beauty and the miracle of miracles when God brings humanity into relationship with himself and in relationship with others.

There is great joy when we are able to experience the overcoming of these barriers. The Jericho Road is what happens when there is radical love that is turned into compassion. Our God had so much compassion that he put himself in the condition of human beings. In the story of the Good Samaritan, which took place on the Jericho Road, the religious teachers were in a hurry as they had some other things they thought were more important than compassion, more important than life. A man was dying and in pain, groaning, and they pretended that they did not hear him because they had other issues. So they left him in the ditch. But the Jericho Road, the holistic gospel, is caring for the whole needs of broken people, as the Good Samaritan did. If you are compassionate, then you are compelled to reach out in love. Love is giving; it is the greatest gift we have.

A Warning and an Encouragement

I think that God has brought us together. I think we are now at a crucial place in the world. We face this discipleship challenge to be God's people and expect a miracle. We expect the sign, and, yes, the problem may be too big for us, but that is when God provides miracles; miracles that his gospel might go forth in the world and that people might know that he is alive. The gospel is that power if it is shared without compromising it in a way that makes it lose its power. We must not become the church of Laodicea, so compromised because the Christians thought they were rich and in need of nothing. They were doing religion, but they did not know their own misery and poverty. That is my warning and also my encouragement. I think we are at a unique time. I know in my country I am seeing a new generation of people who are beginning to see diversity and difference as a value, as enrichments to their lives. I felt the same about the Malaysian people last night in the experience we had together, and I will leave with that experience as a true enrichment to my life.

Let us pray:

Father, thank you for this time. Thank you for what you are doing, Lord. Thank you for these church planters who are going into these countries and finding ways to express your love and finding ways to love the policemen and officials. They are finding ways to express that love, that radical love that burns through these racial and cultural barriers, and that reconciles your people to each other. Oh Lord, bless us and guide us. We ask this in your name. Amen.

Perspectives on Poverty and Transformation (Part 1)

By Jayakumar Christian

Transcribed by Cassi Easthorpe, Donna Easthorpe, and Graham Hill

I want to thank you all for giving me this opportunity to be here and share a few thoughts. I come to this summit with a lot of respect for you, for what you have done through the investment of your life. Some of us have admired the way you have lived and ministered, so I come to this event with a lot of respect for your ministries. So please accept my simple way of saying, I'm learning from you, I read a lot of your materials. I've been in the prior meeting listening to a lot of your stories and I have been blessed.

This morning I will start with two stories, talking about hope: one more recently, and another a few years ago. This was in Imphal in Manipur. Those of us who know the map of India, this is somewhere in North East India. I was travelling with a community there, and as soon as I reached the community — we work among HIV positives in this community — a little girl named Sonya came running to me and said, "Uncle! This is Sonya, do you know me?" And I said, "I don't know you", because honestly that was my first time meeting her. So Sonya said, "Uncle, you don't know me? I'm the peer educator in this place". We have young adolescent girls who serve as peer educators in the HIV positive program. When I asked my colleagues about Sonya, they had glowing tributes for the role that she plays — such a bubbly little girl.

Sonya said, "Uncle, you must come and see my mother. My mother's not well. So you must come see my mother". I agreed that I would come and see her before we went off. So I walked around to those communities and came back to see where Sonya was. Sonya's mother was in the program office; she was getting a drip. She was very much in pain. She was crying from the pain. Then, Sonya told me her story. She said a few years ago her father passed away because of his fever, later becoming known that he was HIV positive. Then they also knew her mother was HIV positive, and then they said that her younger sister was HIV positive. She said, "Uncle, I'm taking care of all of them. My father passed away and now I'm taking care of my mother and sister". She was in tenth standard at that time — tenth grade. And she said, "Today my mother's not well". As I listened to her mother, she had a lot of stomach pain, but the hospital was hesitant to accept her because she was HIV positive. Staff would give blood to her every now and then to keep her going. Sonya said, "Uncle, she is crying because when my father died he also had a severe headache and pain like this. So, she is worried that she also might die and leave my sister and me alone". I asked Sonya if I could pray with them and Sonya said, "Yes, Uncle". And we prayed. My colleagues and I went and stood next to the bed and prayed. By the time we finished our prayer, all of us were in tears, except Sonya. Sonya said, "Uncle, don't cry. Jesus will heal. Don't cry".

Those of us who work among the poor live between hope and grief. We do not have the luxury of staying with hope or grief: we live in this space between hope and grief, on a daily basis. We need to discover what this means. I want to, this morning, look at perspectives of poverty and find ways to describe that space between hope and grief.

Many years ago I was in Makare slum in Kenya, Nairobi. There's a huge church there, and they'd asked me to speak. Right in the centre was a cross. And the whole church sang together the song, "The Old Rugged Cross". The bodies were swaying. We South Asians have bodies that don't swing or sway very easily. The Africans have song in their blood. They were singing "The Old Rugged Cross" with such gusto. And I thought of it as very meaningful. The cross was really rugged, and fitted so well in that slum church, as compared to my church. In our church the cross is so polished and neatly kept, not at all "Old Rugged". It looks too neat to be "Old Rugged", and I thought to myself how real this old rugged cross is and it fits so well in this context. And then as I walked out I met this very old lady. She could not look up. She was bent down very badly. She said to me, "I pray for World Vision on a daily basis". And I thought to myself, World Vision exists because of her prayer. Not because of our smartness or strategy or connections or size or whatever it is. Our work among the poor is really a product of the world praying for us. They pray on a daily basis prayer like, "Your kingdom come, your will be done" and God answers it by sending us. It's really God's answer to the cry of the poor. We are there because they are praying, "Your kingdom come, your will be done, on earth as it is in heaven". God says, "Jayakumar, can you be my answer to their prayer?" And we discover this place between hope and grief.

This morning I want to offer you six perspectives on poverty. I want to deliberately and intentionally suggest that each of us who works among the poor owe it to the poor to deliver the best. Poverty in many ways exists because the world did not give the poor the best, and we cannot afford to add to that mess. The poor deserve the best, so it is not enough just to be simply present among the poor. We need to ask, "What does our presence mean?" We need to be qualitatively better in our work among the poor. We have really no excuse to deliver the second best to the poor, or even the crumbs off the "competence table". We need to be able to give the best to the poor. That is why I believe God has placed us among the poor — to deliver the best, because the other name for poverty is "giving the poor our second best". That is why the poor are poor. The church — you and I who follow Jesus Christ — do not have that excuse at all. We need to give the best.

It is important to incarnate. But what do you do with incarnation beyond that? I want to offer you a few thoughts this morning.

I want to say right at the beginning, when we tend to use the word "holism" we, unfortunately, confuse it with "comprehensiveness". Holism is an *impact statement*. Comprehensiveness is *your input into a specific situation*. So, what you and I are really looking forward to is a *holistic impact* throughout our work. And I want to suggest that these perspectives will give us clues how our ministries — and the communities we serve among — can arrive at holistic destinations.

More Than Just Development + Evangelism

My first proposal is that we need more than just "development plus evangelism". For generations, the church has tried to bridge two banks that were never there: evangelism and development. We've had conferences. We first divided and then tried bridging them: evangelism and development. The church has wasted huge amounts of energy trying to bridge this gap that was never there in the first place. And then we spent all our time and all our conferences trying to see how much evangelism and how much development — and then we call it balance. Balance is a bad word, I think. We burn out trying to maintain balance, instead of just being ourselves: just simply being ourselves. It is so important. When I read the Gospels I don't see Jesus doing this balancing act. He is just Jesus. He is just simply Jesus. He is not saying "Okay, today I've done 60 percent development and 40 percent evangelism, and maybe tomorrow I should correct it and do 40-60." He doesn't do that — he's just himself. And he's enjoying life. He's in a relationship, and he enjoys that moment. He enjoys the moments as if that is all he came for! He's alone with God and enjoying it as if that was the only purpose that he came for. So I want to suggest that we need an approach that liberates us from the artificial categories of development and evangelism.

Search for Response Marked with Integrity

One other thing, which I think we owe to the poor, is "response with integrity". That is how I would define myself on day one, which would be the same self-definition I would use on the last day. That there are no surprises for the poor.

Somehow we sneak in this agenda of evangelism through the back door, and say, "Wow, I caught you at your weak moment". We cannot afford to do that. The world has surprised the poor too many times. So Christians and kingdom people cannot afford to spring surprises on the poor. Who we are on *day one* should also be who we are on *day last*. This is integrity. We need to be careful that we don't slip in our personal agendas, because that's why there's huge suspicion of Christians in countries like India. "What is your real agenda?" they ask. And I should be able to say, "What I told you on day one, that's my agenda". And I'm hoping that as we move on today that we will discover a few handles on how to do that. I'm not good at giving answers. I'm very good at asking questions. So, I'll just leave you with more questions than answers for your own reflection.

Some Assumptions

Let me lay out some assumptions. The first is: *A comprehensive analysis of poverty is a prerequisite for developing holistic responses.*

I've learnt this from experience, and from people who have been in the front lines of work among the poor. A comprehensive analysis is critical for arriving at a holistic response. We need to be able to understand "poverty" comprehensively. We need to be good students of poverty. We need to be able to understand: What is the pain? What is the grief? What are the joys? What are the celebrations? And many other things that you discover as you go on. But it is so important for us to do due diligence on poverty. We don't want to do the slip-shod work on poverty, and give easy answers, and then wonder why we are not arriving at kingdom destinations. It is so important for us to do due diligence as we seek to understand poverty.

My second assumption is: *Poverty by its very nature demands a response that is marked by spirituality.*

We are not doing spirituality a favour — poverty requires it. For sustainable solutions to poverty, it is so important to engage at a spiritual level. And I shall explain why we should do that. It's not something that we add on. We don't sprinkle Bible verses around and assume that makes our work spiritual. Spirituality has to be in the DNA of our mission and service. Poverty requires it. The nature of poverty requires a spiritual response.

Faith Affirmations

I also want to offer some faith affirmations.

A. God is at work in our communities. God is at work in those communities before you and I get there. That is the beauty about this work. God is already there. Our step will always be the second step: we are never the first step. I learnt this from my son when he was much, much younger. During one particular church service it was difficult to keep him quiet. So I had to walk around the church. We were standing next to the baptism pond, and in the waters of the baptism pond, you could see the reflection of the moon that night. So he walked down, got a long stick and touched the reflection of the moon, and stirred it and *looked up in the sky to see if the moon was shaking*. We do this so often in our work. We do our work here, and say, "God, are you happy up there?" Instead, we should ask, "God, what are you doing, so I can follow you in obedience?" Our business is about obedience. It's not to take God into a place, but to follow him and join with him. Just simply to be obedient. If the people we work with come to the conclusion that these are an obedient people to their God, we have achieved our purpose. They may never come to a conclusion about our God. But they can come to a conclusion that these are a people who are obedient to their God. Then, their next question might be, "Who is this God?" Our business is to simply obey God and be there — believing that God is already at work among the poor. That is why to Moses he says, "I've heard their cry, I've seen their pain". And then says to Moses, "Why don't you join me?" Our invitation is only a second. We are never pioneers. God is already there. And, fortunately, God will continue to be there even after World Vision withdraws. I love that! If we at World Vision believe that we're taking God into places we become gods in the process. Just to know that we are not God is so liberating. And that we are not taking God on our shoulders — it's so liberating. And that God will continue to be there after we leave is even more liberating. God is already working among the poor.

B. *We are dependent on God*. The second faith affirmation is: Our credibility is enhanced when people see that we are dependent on God — simply dependent on God. Clay feet, weak knees, and feeble hands prone to failure — this is our CV. So we will have to be dependent on God. Whoever thought that we could solve India's poverty? It's not at all possible without God. We'd be kidding ourselves and playing games, if it was not for God. And, very often, as I walk with my colleagues in the field, I notice that what is in the *report* and what is in the *plan* are *so different from what God is doing in the community*. And then you think, "I'm so grateful that there's a living God, and that World Vision is not God. I'm so grateful for that". I was in a community recently. And a little girl gets up and gives a speech. She calls me Dr Jayakumar: "Dr Jayakumar, we want to welcome you". And she rattles on in Hindi, a pure gold speech. Here's her story. She refused the pressure from her parents to get married at thirteen or fourteen years. She takes a stand, and she lives today. I was so proud of her. And I was even more grateful that there is a living God, one that we can depend on.

C. *Spiritual undergirds all (sacred/secular)*. The last faith affirmation I want to offer for consideration is that spirituality undergirds all. Spirituality is not a category on its own. It undergirds all. Spirituality undergirds economics, politics, everything. Walter Wink calls it "spiritual interiority". Unfortunately, urban, educated, young people in the West have this "spiritual" category. And you put it in the same box as economics and politics and wonder why you're not arriving at holism. Because, in the first place, we have fragmented it. I would like to suggest that spirituality undergirds everything. There is a spiritual ideology that seeks to answer life's higher questions in politics, economics, society, you name it. There is a spiritual interiority in society and people and institutions that needs to be addressed. Spirituality is not simply a captive to religion. It is in all areas of life, and that is an area that you and I need to look at.

There are six themes that *redefine poverty*. We need to understand these six themes and shape transformational responses.

1. Captivity of the poor in the god-complexes of the powers, powerful, and the non-poor;

2. Poverty results from broken relationships;

3. Marred identity of the poor;

4. Distorted interpretations of history;

5. Distortions of truth;

6. Manipulations of principalities and powers.

Captivity of the Poor in the God-Complexes of the Powers, Powerful, and the Non-Poor

People often like to be powerful. And the non-poor often like playing "god" in the lives of the poor. You and I are not simply addressing statistics gone wrong. We are really up against people who pretend to play god in the lives of the poor. When people play god in the lives of the poor we should call it for what it is: "poverty and oppression". So when we work among the poor, we are not doing any ordinary welfare or charity work. We are confronting the tendency of the powerful and the non-poor to play god in the lives of the poor. I want to use Walter Wink's material in this a lot. He calls it "god-complexes" — a term suggesting people trying to play god in the lives of others. He doesn't use the word "poor". Wink develops this idea, and describes god-complexes, in a very interesting way. Here's a summary of what Wink says about these "god-complexes":

- Survivors are ones with technological, military, and economic strength;

- Production of wealth is a first priority;

- Property is sacred and ownership is a right;

- Institutions are more important than people;

- God, if there is one, is patron of the powerful.

I just want to share a few things here. Walter Wink says, for example, that there is an assumption that social order is defined by the powerful. These dominate and set the agenda for the poor and powerless. Walter Wink later calls this "abuse of power". It's the tendency to play god in the lives of the poor. It hurts the soul of the poor. This is not simply some external feelings of hurt. It hurts deep within the soul of the poor. That is the language Walter Wink uses. He then goes on to say that in this "god-complex" the poor are mere instruments of economic wealth. They are just tools in the hands of the people who produce wealth.

This is something that you and I need to recognize. When we work around the poor we are up against people who tend to play god in the lives of the poor. George Ladd says that God's kingdom doesn't co-exist comfortably with other kingdoms. He actually says "Every nail space belongs to God". That is the definition of the kingdom of God. That is why when you and I work among the poor, we are involved in establishing the kingdom of God. Poverty is about people playing god in the lives of the poor. That is why the kingdom of God is not an afterthought. It's a fundamental solution to alleviate poverty in a sustainable way. That is why I would like to suggest when you and I work among the poor that we will work on establishing the kingdom of God. Poverty requires that we challenge this tendency to play god in the lives of the poor. And I want to suggest to you that it's important for us to redefine our work among the poor in the terms of the kingdom. This is because we want to be sustainable in the solutions we bring to the poor and poverty. I don't know of any alternate solutions.

Towards Transformational Responses

I want to suggest a few transformational responses.

A. *The purpose of our involvement must be extending the kingdom of God — this is foundational to an adequate response to poverty.* The purpose of our involvement must be the kingdom of God; the rule and reign of God. That should be foundational in our work among the poor. This doesn't make us in any way extra Christian. We are about establishing the rule of God, which will uproot and be a viable alternative to anyone else playing god in the lives of the poor. That is why we are involved in kingdom work. So it is important for us to look at the kingdom of God as our end destination.

B. *We need to communicate that power belongs to God (not power to the people).* We need to be able to give an alternative in terms of power, and communicate like Psalm 62 says, "Power truly belongs to God". Liberation theology sometimes suggests that power belongs to the poor — not so. You and I communicate the message that power truly belongs to God. The problem with this is that it will cause us to naturally ask questions about ourselves. What is my demonstration of understanding of power? That is the danger in this transformation. What you think about power — and what you think is providing solutions for the poor — boomerangs back on you. God says to us, "What do you believe about power?" How do you treat your colleagues? Do you demonstrate the kingdom's understanding of power? That is why we don't touch or see or experience transformation. We pay lip service to transformation and do business as usual. Where will the poor learn otherwise? They will have a look at the way my teams work and think, "this is the way power should be": This is how I should treat my wife in my home; this is how I should bring up my children. Because then they will learn not simply how to take care of home and keep it clean — but how to use and not use power. How will power be used in the kingdom?

C. *Involvement among the poor is a prophetic act.* Our work among the poor is really a prophetic act. The space between hope and grief is a prophetic space. We challenge grief because grief is not the end point — hope is. We need to be able to recognize that our presence among the poor is a prophetic presence. We are not simply taking care of the poor and wiping their tears, or giving them promising behavioural changes. We are really challenging the powers that tend to play god in the lives of the poor. It's a dangerous space, and we have seen this over and over in our line of work among the poor. We work in Orissa, India. And we worked in this community for probably six or seven years. One of the first things we tend to do is mobilize women into self-help groups. They end up saving and lending to each other. So much so, that they stop lending to, and borrowing from, the moneylenders and vendors. These moneylenders and business people came and beat our World Vision staff up. They destroyed our office, burnt our jeep, destroyed everything! And their accusation against us was that we were converting people to Jesus. They were looking for an excuse to shut down our work and assault our staff.

Who are we converting? The real issue was that we upset their business. Because we empowered the women so much, they were not borrowing from the moneylenders anymore. And an easy whip to use is conversion. And they used it so badly that our jeeps were burnt, our offices were completely destroyed. Our office can hardly accommodate 10 to 12 people. But 100 people walked into the office to attack our staff and ruin the building. There was not a piece of furniture left standing. Everything was destroyed because they said we're involved in conversion — but the real reason was because we upset the "god-complexes". Your presence — don't undersell your presence. Your presence is a prophetic presence among the poor.

D. *Creating intentional conflict is an essential part of a strategy addressing poverty.* I like to remember the number of times Jesus upset his audience. And I would like to suggest he deliberately upsets. For example, the man with the withered hand whom he healed. He could have done it on the Monday, or the next day after the Sabbath. The man had lived his whole life with a withered hand. He could have lived another day and it would not have made a big difference. But Jesus was interested in healing the withered life and spirit and soul of the Pharisees. They were the candidates for healing, not the withered hand, which Jesus could have done the next day. The famous parable of the Good Samaritan is wrongly titled. It should really be called, "Upsetting the young Jewish lawyer". That was the intent, not the parable of the Good Samaritan. No, you don't tell stories to a lawyer. Jesus chooses to tell the story. And as Jesus tells the story, he could have chosen the Pharisee to be the hero of the story, but instead he shows the Samaritan to be the hero of the story to the Jewish lawyer. What was Jesus' intent? To upset the Jewish lawyer. But we take this Good Samaritan value and make a big deal out of it. But Jesus was really about upsetting the Jewish lawyer — creating intentional conflict is very important. You and I need to know how to do that by our presence. It's not a bad thing. It's very important.

Let me tell you about a doctor who works among the poor in Maharashtra. He is a doctor at the Christian medical centre in the college hospital. He started his work and he was a good surgeon. One of the things he would do is to set his surgeries on a day the people considered as a "bad" (i.e., "unlucky") day. He would deliberately do that. And he would say, "Oh, that's the only day and time I'm available". Our Hindu calendar has bad days and bad times, and he would deliberately set surgeries on that day. And so the patients would say, "Sorry, bad day, bad time, I'm not free". So, they would not come for surgery. Or, they'd come scared. But, over time they found that surgery that was done on bad days and bad times was actually successful. So it was not just healing of the body that was happening — he was healing their attitudes about bad days and bad times — he was creating intentional conflict.

This doctor also had a midday meal program in that community. He made sure the food was cooked by the lower caste. The higher caste children would never come because the food was cooked by the lower caste. He said: "I will not change — the lower caste will cook the food, and if you don't like it, tough". Over time they saw the lower caste children looking very nourished and healthy. Slowly, the higher caste children started coming to meals — what got changed was not their nutritional status, but their attitude and their relationships. Don't undersell your incarnational presence. You are there as a prophetic presence to create intentional conflict among the poor and among the non-poor.

E. Ultimate dependency on God should be a daily discipline. Because power truly belongs to God, we need to learn the daily discipline of depending on God. In World Vision, it's so easy for us to fall into the temptation of believing that the secret of our successes lies in our strategies, size, connections, and everything else. We just need to remind ourselves — it doesn't work. We need to always depend on God.

Poverty Results from Broken Relationships

The second perspective that I want to offer you this morning, is that poverty is a product of broken relationships. This is how I've seen it happen. Very often the poor are considered as damaged goods, not worth listening to. In India, we have a local government quota system to get women into politics. The government has come up with this way of "empowering" women by saying one third of the committees of local governments should have women as presidents. But, sadly, these women who are presidents of these committees are really proxies for their husbands. So their husbands will also attend the meetings. And what's the woman president doing? She's getting tea for others. Broken gender relationships in India mean that women aren't listened to — they're treated like property or "damaged goods".

One also sees broken relationships when power confronts powerlessness. When the powerful challenge the powerless, these powerless poor have three options. (1) They simply exit. They quit. (2) They raise their voice, and that is almost always crushed. Civil society, civil voices, and dissenting spaces are shrinking fast in the name of globalisation and democracy. (3) Or, they submit in loyalty to the powerful. In all these three ways, community is broken. When they exit or stand up, or simply submit in loyalty, there is no more community. There is no more relationship.

Broken relationships are also seen in different systems used to exclude the poor. We have different systems that are used to keep the poor, poor. The education system is an example. In my country, "A" will always have to be for "apple", even if a child has never seen an apple in their life. Children will know the names of all the major rivers in India, but they do not know the name of the river behind their house. Who designs their education system? It's intended to keep the poor, poor. Law is another system used to exclude the poor. It's said that in the eyes of the law, everybody is equal. But, unfortunately, in the eyes of the interpreters of the law, not everyone is equal. The poor get so interpreted that they are marginalized. Our health system is expensive, and only really available to the wealthy. It keeps the poor, poor. It keeps them excluded from health and from the mainstream.

Power, by nature, is divisive. Power doesn't thrive in situations where there is unity. In one of our communities we have a program which plays a song about "united we are strong, divided we fall". It's a very simple theme. And we didn't think it would do great miracles. Within a few months, we found that a political candidate from a lower caste was elected to be the president of that village. So we went and asked, how did this happen? And this person who was elected said it was because of that song we gave them. But we didn't understand how that song about strength in unity made him president of the village. And he said that when it comes to elections, the higher caste will sponsor *many* candidates from among the lower castes. This way they are divided. This way the higher caste candidate will win. And all these years the higher caste candidates won because the poor were divided. So, after singing the song about unity given to them by World Vision, the lower caste leaders decided not to sponsor many candidates. Instead, they sponsored one candidate who went on to win the election.

Going as a Healed, Covenant People to a Broken Community

Power, by nature, is divisive. Not so with kingdom power. It tends to create covenant communities. I can be different, and still celebrate oneness. I don't need to be standardized or uniform. The richness in the kingdom is the diversity. The poor and the non-poor can work together. Community organizations sometimes divide. They make enemies out of the other. That's how social movements have thrived — by making an enemy of the other. Being issues-based means you need an enemy for a movement to run. Not so with the kingdom. In the kingdom, we need to be able to see how the poor and the non-poor can be in a covenantal relationship. Be different and yet celebrate. Challenge the lines that divide people. God is deeply interested in the lines that divide people. A line that divides people from each other is a lie. We need to be able to create covenantal communities. We need to be careful that we don't reduce the poor to a mere statistic. When Mrs Gandhi was killed in New Delhi, *India Today* had a great article about the statistics of people killed, houses destroyed, buses burned, etc. Then, the journalist finishes with: "All said and done, statistics never bleed. It's people who bleed." Poverty is about people bleeding, it's not about statistics gone wrong. We, as kingdom people, bring this unique perspective about poverty. We recognize that people bleed. We are not dealing with statistics. That's okay for politicians and planners. Not for us. Each one has a name, and that name is special to them. We need to be able to build relationships. We need to be able to celebrate diversity and invest in relationships. That is why your relationship with me is so important — it is an investment in poverty alleviation. We cannot have broken teams that seek to minister to the poor. Not possible! It's a contradiction in terms. The rule of life is to heal others. Hurt people multiply hurt. Our teams, our workspaces, and our organizations should be spaces where the balm of Gilead is available in plenty for healing. So we can go as healed people, to a broken community.

Perspectives on Poverty and Transformation (Part 2)

By Jayakumar Christian

Transcribed by Cassi Easthorpe, Donna Easthorpe, and Graham Hill

I want to thank Ash Barker and the team for this privilege again to be part of this community. As I mentioned yesterday, I come with a deep sense of respect for the work that all of you do in different parts of the world. This evening, in many ways, I would like to continue where I left off yesterday. We looked at perspectives on poverty, suggesting that it's important to incarnate. It's important to have a ministry presence, but it's also important to deliver the best for the poor.

In many ways, the poor are a product of the world not delivering its best. The church should not add to that mess and it's important for us to give the best to the poor. And we said that we would look at six perspectives, to suggest that maybe there are clues in these perspectives for us to develop our model of response to the poor that we work with.

The Captivity of the Poor in the God-Complexes of the Powerful and Non-Poor

We looked at two perspectives yesterday, suggesting, firstly, that *poverty is the captivity of the poor in the god-complexes* — people playing god in the lives of the poor. Humans are designed to yield their spirit only to the Creator. And when anyone tries to play god in the lives of the poor, it's called poverty or oppression. And the church is the only institution that has these sustainable alternatives to people playing god in the lives of the poor. And that alternative is called the kingdom and rule of God. The kingdom of God is not something that you sneak in, but actually a valid response to poverty where people play god in the lives of the poor.

Broken Relationships

The second theme that we explored yesterday is that *poverty is about broken relationships*. Here again, the church is so uniquely placed, where you and I know the power of covenant relationships. This is unlike other institutions that do not know how someone unequal could celebrate that relationship. In a world that tends to standardize and make everything look very alike, and look often very much like the powerful, the church says, "This is not necessary". You can be who you are and celebrate a relationship. The clue is in our covenant theology, and in the church. And only the church has that answer. This is why I wonder why the church is quiet when it comes to the poor and to poverty.

The Marred Identity of the Poor

The third theme I want to address is that *poverty is the result of marred identity of the poor*. If you were talking to the poor in any context and you keep asking the question, "Why are you poor?" they will say initially it's an economic question. It's about the lack of resources. And at a certain point they will say, "I am poor because of who I am. I cannot do anything about the family in which I was born". A friend of mine would say the only mistake the poor made was to select the wrong parents. And my sons selected the right father, who could afford anything. They know if they lose a pen, their father will give them another one. They lose a book and they know their father will give another one. They want to go for an excursion, picnic, or somewhere far away, and they know that their father will ask a few questions but finally give in. But not with the poor. The poor do not have the choice. They have selected the wrong parents.

In many ways, they are saying, "The cause of my poverty is me". What they're saying is that it's not about *dignity* so much as about *identity*. Like we said earlier, Walter Wink asserts that when power is abused and used against the powerless it hurts the soul. Not just simply the externals — it hurts the soul of the person. And the tools and instruments that the powerful have to keep the poor, poor, are many. For example, chronic years of poverty numb the mind in many ways. They just begin to believe what the world says about them: "I am poor possibly because of my past life. Or, I am poor because of certain things that are wrong with me". And they begin to believe that. Poverty is when the poor believe the lie that the world markets to them, or sells to them. Economic systems tend to reduce the poor merely to tools of production. Their "value-add" tends to be their value for the economic system. And the poor are poor when they start believing this worldview, which is distorted and inadequate.

It is important for us to address their marred identity. It's not enough to just simply talk about justice. It's important to heal the person. Because the causes of poverty are found deep in the identity of the person — it's not simply about dignity or socio-structural issues. It is important for us to engage at that level.

A. We are all made in God's image. I want to suggest a few leads for us to construct a response to the poor. The first one I want to suggest is that we must fully grasp the implications of humans being made in the image of God. This is something I don't understand about the church. If there is one faith that knows that humans are made in the image of God, it is the church. And we sit so tight on this great secret. We don't tell anybody about this. There is really no faith in the world that believes that humans are made in the image of God, except for the Christian faith. We don't share that. We don't let anyone know this. And we seem to celebrate within our four walls and go out and behave as if others aren't made in the image of God. The Hindu faith teaches that humans emerged from the various parts of the body of God. And those who did not emerge from the body of God are called outcasts, beyond redemption. They have to work their way over generations to be accepted. In this context, only the church has a response. And this is what I believe the church can bring to the poverty and development conversation.

If you and I want sustainable solutions to poverty, it is within the church. The secret is within the church. You and I believe that humans are made in the image of God. We also know that nothing can separate us from the love of God. Romans 8 talks about it. It shows how a sinner, completely condemned, can be accepted, and then become a person from whom the love of God can never be separated.

Clarification of identity is possible in our faith. And it is important for the church to bring that to the poverty and development debate and conversation. You and I also know that the good news is particularly spoken to the poor, affirming that the poor have a unique ability to respond. That's why the good news is so targeted toward the poor. The world tells the poor, "You're good for nothing, your voice is damaged goods, you cannot be good for anything, and God has forsaken you". The church takes its presence among the poor and says, "No. God has not forsaken you. Evidence? We are present among you. Our presence among you is evidence that God has not forsaken the poor".

B. We must invest life. If identity is our focus, it's important for us to invest life. One of the things that World Vision has learnt is that when we invest, we can't simply reduce our investment among the poor to programs or money. When we do that we make the poor "beneficiaries". When we reduce our investment to simply money, we make them beggars. But if you and I are about transforming lives, it is important to invest life. This is because the rule in life is that "only life reproduces life". Programs and money never reproduce life. Only life can reproduce life. And you and I have seen this in our work among the poor.

We work in a community in Rajasthan in North India, and in this community, as part of our work, we build community-based organizations. And the leader of this community-based organization happened to be also the leader of a Hindu fundamentalist organization. So, when his president in the state capital heard his friend was working with a Christian organization, he was very worried. So he came running to this village, met his leader who was working with Christians, and said, "Is it true that you're working with World Vision?" And he said, "Yes. World Vision does this and that, and all kinds of things". The president said, "Do you know they're a Christian organization?" And the leader said, "Yes, I know they're a Christian organization". The president said, "Did you know that today they'll give you a well and clinic and other things, and tomorrow they'll ask you to accept Jesus Christ and join their faith". Our friend told the state president, "If you look at their lives, you would also want to follow their God". This is a statement that *life invested is worth it*. Life invested is absolutely worth it. You and I are not simply about incarnation. We are about healing an individual whose identity is marred. We are about moving beyond dignity to identity. And moving beyond justice to healing.

Here's a rule in life: only healed people heal others. Hurt people multiply hurt. And only the church can do it, because we are a healing community after all. We come together for fellowship so that we heal each other. We go out and heal others because poverty is about the marred identity of the poor.

Distorted Interpretations of History

The second theme that I want to elaborate on today is that *poverty is a result of distorted interpretations of history*. History is always written from the perspective of the winner. We tend to believe this myth that history is neutral. History is *never* neutral. It is *always* written from the perspective of the victor. And what you and I remember is not a body of facts, but an interpreted version of history. And the interpreted version of history of the poor is handed down to them by the powerful.

I remember walking in a community. I was talking to a group of men who were playing cards that evening. In our village, and especially in communities of poverty, this happens often. Men sit there and whittle away their time. They have no jobs and no hope for the future, so they sit around and play games — often they play cards. So, I went and sat next to them. We started talking. The name of their village means "high respect" or "high dignity". So, I sat and asked them the meaning of the name of their village and I was shocked at their response. They said, "We don't know the meaning. You should go and ask the village priest, he knows". They were giving their right to interpret their history to someone else — very often to the powerful. That is called poverty. When you give up your right to interpret your history — that is called oppression. And, very gladly, the powerful take on that responsibility. But, in that interpretation are the seeds of oppression.

We are up against distorted interpretations of history. That is why you and I are present among the poor. We are not simply tweaking with a few statistics that have gone wrong. We are dealing with the roots of poverty. We cannot afford to simply put a band-aid on poverty and assume that we have healed the cancer called poverty. It's important to go deep and address these distortions. The tools that are in the hands of the shapers of history are plenty. And, very often, it begins with education. It begins with what is called, "social norms"; or, "the right way of doing things" as defined by the powerful.

In our communities, especially among the landless, when they have a baby, or when they want to have a baby, or a wedding for their daughter, they will have to consult the landlord. And if they didn't consult the landlord, all hell is let loose on them. There is no way they will have their wedding in peace. And it is important that they do all that is right, as defined by the landlord. The right to interpret is handed over to the powerful. This is what I call "meta-power". The definition of power itself changes — and that seems to be in the hands of the powerful. Walter Winks says that when people use power this way in the present, they often quote the past, but shape and influence the future. When a landlord can tell the landless person, "Your father and your ancestors always worked for us, so I will decide whom your daughter will marry", they are redefining and abusing power. Using the past, they access power today, in order to influence the future. And the poor will continue to be poor, forever.

We work among commercial sex-workers on the Delhi–Mumbai highway. On the first day we started the program, I went into this community. As I walked into the community, I could *feel* hopelessness in that community. The women were all sleeping — tired because they'd worked all night. The men were playing cards. The children were playing in the dirt. As I walked past, I met a woman who was supposed to be the president of this village of the commercial sex-workers. And I asked her, "What is your dream?" (She is a commercial sex-worker.) She said, "That my younger sisters would never join this profession. That is my dream".

A few months after we started the program, I went looking for her. She was missing. Those with power had sent her to Mumbai for commercial sex-work. The world is waiting to snuff out any little evidence of hope among the poor. And they do it so fast, before you know what happens.

We also sent a girl from this community, as a child representative, to a conference in Toronto. She was so proud, and we were so proud of her. We had a tough time getting a passport for her because she couldn't say who her father was in her application. They said, "Unless you tell us your father's name we will not give you a passport". So, she gave her grandfather's name as the father, and got a passport. She went, came back, and was very proud that she was able to go to Canada and meet other children like herself. She came back with a great dream that she was going to organize the young girls in her community into a strong group that would prevent them from getting into commercial sex-work. The next we knew, she was having a baby. Her family of five or seven men needed some income, and she was the only candidate they had for a job — commercial sex-work. We've lost her completely. It broke our heart, because we loved her.

After many months in this community I attended the first wedding in this community. I attended the wedding and gave a small gift from World Vision. As I was talking to an elderly man with tears in his eyes, he said, "I have never seen a wedding in my community".

Hope is possible, but the ones who define the rules of the game are often more powerful. The church should be careful that we don't play power games as defined by the powerful. Instead, we need to challenge the rules of the game itself. We know that one day you can be abandoned by the world, and the next day you can turn the world upside down. It's possible — and the church knows that. Yet, the church is too often absent when it comes to redefining power. The church is busy doing its own thing. The world is asking, "Tell us another definition of power that will be empowering, liberating, and healing". They're looking to the church for answers, but, unfortunately, the church is busy playing the game of power according to the rules set by the world. We must challenge the rules of power as set by the world.

We have great opportunities to transform nations! We in World Vision India believe that God has called us in India not simply to do a few projects. We are there to transform the 1.2 billion people of India. How? By taking a stand among the poor, exactly the way Jesus did. We want to stand among the most vulnerable. Then, one day, India will see that it is possible to transform the poor, and ask, "Who is your God?" And Indians will one day bow their knees to the Lord Jesus Christ. Because they see transformation is possible among the poor.

How do we shape transformational responses among the poor? Let me offer a few handles. First — and here again the church is uniquely placed — only you and I know *God is active in the history of the poor*. By our presence, we let the poor know that God has not abandoned them. We can show, in the history of the poor, that God was there. God is there. Remember that time of natural disaster? God was there. We must help the poor trace for themselves the hand of God. We help the poor see evidence within their history that God is active among them. Remember, your step and my step are only the second steps. We kid ourselves if we call ourselves "pioneers". God is already there. And he will continue to be there after we leave. This is so liberating. One of the things that takes the guilt off me in World Vision is knowing God will continue even after World Vision leaves. It is so liberating. God will continue to be there among the poor. And just to be able to let the poor know that within their own history there is plenty of evidence of God's presence — showing that God has not abandoned them — this is so redemptive.

One of our roles is empowering the poor to dream dreams, and then helping them reach those dreams. The world tells the poor, "You cannot afford a dream. The size of your purse cannot afford a dream". We tell the poor, "Your right to dream is found in that fact that you are created in the image of God. Your right to dream, and your ability to dream, is in your image — which is made in the image of God. That cannot be robbed by anyone". And we also remind them that history, and historical interpretations, cannot bring salvation — because it is only God who can bring salvation.

Distortions of Truth

The third theme for today: *poverty is about the distortion of truth*. Here's a lie that the world seems to promote in many ways: "Power always belongs to the powerful. Power always comes from the assets I own and the wealth I create". We need to call that bluff. We need to speak truth about people: humans are made in the image of God. They are uniquely tailor-made. God has designed them. And we need to speak truth about power. Power isn't found in resources and privilege. Power belongs to God alone.

Poverty happens when the poor are captives to a web of lies. Unfortunately, the poor come to believe those lies. You and I can name some of the various lies that tend to perpetrate poverty. Some are given in the examples I've provided. But there are others. In a Hindu community, the poor begin to believe that their current poverty is a result of their past life. What do they do with that? They can't change their past. They simply go through poverty. Here's another lie: my identity is defined by the caste in which I'm born. Unfortunately, the poor come to believe these lies. Another lie is that poverty relationships cannot be changed.

Another lie is that the future is merely an extension of the past — that who you are and where you were born define what your future will be. A person who is born in a lower caste cannot aspire to be in a higher office. And, Hindu literature even defines such social progression and improvement as sin. Who would want to commit sin by aspiring? Hindu philosophy says if anyone in the lower caste aspires to anything else other than that which is assigned to his or her caste, they are committing sin. You don't want to commit sin, do you? It's another lie that binds the poor. So when a development worker says to the poor, "Let's aspire — you are a lower caste, why don't you try to become an engineer?" They are probably hearing, "Let's commit a sin". We are dealing with fundamental lies here. We are not simply dealing with behavioural change. We are dealing with worldview issues — very often couched as truth. We need to be able to say, "That is a lie".

There are other lies about power. See Walter Wink's work on god-complexes. These are distortions of truth. Lies include: (1) Force always prevails over ideas. The survivors are those with technological, military, and economic strength. (2) Choice always belongs to the powerful. (3) Power is truth. (In the Scriptures, truth is power, but the world seems to communicate that power is truth.) (4) Assets are an all-important powerbase. Production of wealth is first priority. Property is sacred, and ownership is a right. (5) Power is a zero-sum game. (But, in Scripture, power is a positive sum dynamic. Power multiplies when you share. But the world says there are limited supplies of power. Don't share, because if you share, you will lose it. We need to call this a lie). (6) Powerful institutions are more important than people. (7) God, if there is one, is patron of the powerful.

These are all lies. We need to communicate that power belongs to God (not power to the people).

Prophetic Involvement

I want to suggest that *our work among the poor is a prophetic involvement*. Our presence among the poor is not simply incarnation, in its harmless sense — it's a prophetic presence among the poor, because we are calling attention to truth. We are calling attention to truth that has kept the poor, poor, for generations. These people have been abandoned to poverty. We need to be able to say, "No, that is not necessary. You don't need to live that way. There is a future that is possible". We need to re-order the relationship between truth and power — and model this in Christian institutions. This is the dangerous thing about this model of transformation — invariably it boomerangs on us. So, I ask you some questions: "How is truth outworked in *your* organization? Where is power in your organization and in my organization? Is it ordered by the powerful? Is it defined and designed by the powerful? Is truth more powerful than power. Does truth define power? Or does power define truth?" We must ask serious questions about how we run our organizations.

Truth is foundational in the kingdom of God. John 8:32 says: "You shall know the truth and the truth shall set you free". What a powerful and redemptive message for the poor. The way we conduct ourselves in public life should communicate that truth is essential and foundational. We cannot make short cuts and compromises. When we refuse to do this, the poor know that truth is foundational. And then when we communicate truth, it sends a message like Ephesians 3:10 says, to the powers in heavenly places. This message was kept, over years, as a mystery, made known to the church, so that the church will communicate to the cosmic powers, that Jesus is Lord. The truth is not simply to flesh and blood, but to principalities and powers. And we must start communicating truth to principalities and powers.

Manipulations by Principalities and Powers

I'll close with this: *poverty is about the exploitation and manipulation by principalities and powers*. Many years ago, we worked in a community. And when I used to go to my work, I used to cycle — in those days, motorbikes were not allowed in our organization. And I used to cycle around these communities and there were no Christians — hardly any Christians whom I met on this journey that I used to take. Every morning I would cycle, travel village to village, basically trying to know who these community members were. I did not meet any Christians. But I was not disappointed, because I knew that we were working in a country and a nation that was predominantly Hindu.

I spent time with each community and, after many years, we got greater access into one of the communities. In that community, the president of the village was also the president of the anti-god association. They had an association of atheists, and he was the president of that area. And I would meet him every time that I went into that community. I would sit and talk to him about everything other than God. We would talk about the weather. We would talk about this and about that. And when our evaluation team went into that community, that man told my colleagues: "I have been the president of this village for the last three decades. But I didn't know how to love my people, until I saw how *your* people love my people. Only now do I know what it means to love my people". A few months later he passed away. And his son-in-law came and asked us to organize the first vacation Bible school in that village. We'd never had that opportunity before in that community. His grandson wrote to us from the Indian army, saying, "My grandfather would always talk about your God. Can you send me a Bible?" We sent him a Bible, and a church was born in that village community — simply because we dared to challenge the fundamentals of poverty. We dared to confront the principalities and powers, and proclaim Christ.

I value your prayers for India. We are going through a very challenging time — a great time, I think! So, I value your prayers. Thank you very much.

Contributors

Jacob Bloemberg has been serving in Vietnam since 1997. Jacob is the pastor of the Hanoi International Fellowship, a congregation which serves over 30 nationalities. Jacob also serves in a drug rehabilitation centre.

Trish and Nigel Branken live together with their five children in the notorious inner-city suburb of Hillbrow in Johannesburg, South Africa. As they stand in solidarity with those facing extreme poverty, Nigel says, "What we focus on is primarily becoming friends to our neighbours and then trying to become good neighbours to our friends".

Jayakumar Christian, a development practitioner and author of several books on development in India and the international context, is the National Director of World Vision India, a child-focused, community-based agency seeking fullness of life for all children.

Brad Coath and his wife Colleen, together with their two sons Samuel and Hudson, live and serve in Broadmeadows in Melbourne's northwest. Broadmeadows has some of the highest levels of disadvantage in Melbourne, where many face challenges such as poverty, addiction, unemployment, and settlement issues. They seek to build Christ-centred community on the margins, by being a Christian presence in the neighbourhood, and partnering with local organizations and people to bring empowerment, discipleship, and community growth.

Michael D. Crane teaches urban missions with two different seminaries. He has lived most of his life in multi-religious cities. In addition to teaching, Michael and his family live in an Asian city ministering among refugees. Michael has written articles for a number of publications and is the author of *Sowing Seeds of Change: Cultivating Transformation in the City* (forthcoming in 2015).

Rey Lemuel Crizaldo is advocacy coordinator at the Christian Convergence for Good Governance (CCGG) for the Micah Challenge Philippines campaign. He is a faculty member of the Asian Seminary of Christian Ministries (ASCM) handling courses on the integration of faith and social work. He has authored three books published by OMF Literature on topics of public theology.

Jarrett Davis is a social researcher who has spent the past six years in Southeast Asia. He completed his Master's studies in the Philippines where he studied Identity Development within a socially marginalized people group on the outskirts of Manila. He has worked under Love146 as an independent researcher since May 2012 and is presently leading his fifth baseline study on sexually exploited persons in the Southeast Asian region.

Kimberly Drage is the Adviser for Monitoring and Evaluation of Allianz Mission in Vietnam.

Bruce Edwards is the Director of the Fiji Community Churches of Christ. He has 17 years of ministry and leadership experience at the Nowra and Devonport Churches of Christ. Bruce is involved in leading and growing the ministries and life of the Fiji Churches of Christ with a focus on leadership development, exploring community development project possibilities, additional church planting opportunities, and outreach.

Michael Frost is the Vice Principal (Faculty Development) of Morling College and the founding Director of the Tinsley Institute, a mission study centre located at Morling College in Sydney, Australia. He is the author or editor of fourteen popular Christian books, the most recent of which are the highly successful and award-winning *The Shaping of Things to Come* (2003), *Exiles* (2006), and *The Road to Missional* (2011).

Viv Grigg directs the Urban Leadership Foundation, is an Associate Professor at Azusa Pacific University, and is International Coordinator of the Encarnação Alliance of Urban Poor Movement Leaders, http://www.urbanleaders.org. Their grassroots, city-learning networks of slum pastors in one three year period have established over 1800 new churches. He is author of seven books including the paradigm-shifting *Companion to the Poor*, whose call to radical incarnation among the poor and lifestyles of simplicity has challenged many.

Graham Hill is the Vice Principal (Communications) of Morling College. He is the author of *Salt, Light, and a City: Introducing Missional Ecclesiology* (2012) and the forthcoming book *GlobalChurch: Reshaping Our Conversations, Renewing Our Mission, Revitalizing Our Churches* (2015). He is the Director of the GlobalChurch Project. http://www.grahamhillauthor.com

Pham Thu Huong is the HR and Finance Manager of Allianz Mission in Vietnam.

Glenn Miles has been working on issues around children at risk and vulnerable young adults for the past 25 years. He is a trained child health nurse. He has a PhD that focused on Cambodian children's experiences and understanding of violence and abuse. He currently teaches up to graduate level in child rights and sexual exploitation, and is doing action research in seminaries and colleges in Cambodia, Malaysia, and the Philippines, with a series of child protection workshops in Cambodia as well as the UK and USA.

René Padilla has a PhD in New Testament from the University of Manchester, England. He was a member of the staff of the International Fellowship of Evangelical Students for Latin America from 1959 to 1982, General Secretary of the Latin American Theological Fellowship from 1983 to 1992, and founding member of the Kairos Community of Buenos Aires from 1976 to the present. René is currently Emeritus President of the Kairos Foundation and Director of Kairos Books.

John Perkins is president of the John and Vera Mae Perkins Foundation of Jackson, Mississippi. He is one of the leading evangelical voices to come out of the American civil rights movement. He is also an internationally known author, speaker, and teacher on issues of racial reconciliation and Christian community development. He is the author of nine books, including *A Quiet Revolution, Let Justice Roll Down, With Justice for All, Beyond Charity, He's My Brother, Resurrecting Hope,* and *A Time to Heal.*

Howard A. Snyder has pastored and taught in several cities, including Detroit, Michigan (1966–68); São Paulo, Brazil (1969–74); Chicago, Illinois (1980–88); Dayton, Ohio (1988–96); and Toronto, Ontario (2007–12). He is now retired after teaching positions at Asbury Theological Seminary and Tyndale Seminary, Toronto. He authored several books, including *The Problem of Wineskins* and *Salvation Means Creation Healed.*

Emil Jonathan Soriano is a fellow of the Institute for Studies in Asian Church and Culture (ISACC). He is currently serving as national coordinator of the Peace Assemblies Network in the Philippines and secretary of the "Stargrass Coalition" of the Philippine House Church Movement.

Lightning Source UK Ltd.
Milton Keynes UK
UKOW06f1755070316

269754UK00011B/354/P